THE IRON TRIANGLE

HOOVER INTERNATIONAL STUDIES
Peter Duignan, general editor

Publications in the Hoover International Studies series of the Hoover Institution on War, Revolution and Peace are concerned with U.S. involvement in world and regional politics. These studies are intended to represent a contribution to the discussion and debate of major questions of international affairs.

Conflict in Northwest Africa: The Western Sahara Dispute
John Damis

Oil Supply Disruptions in the 1980s: An Economic Analysis
Karim Pakravan

The Arabian Peninsula: Zone of Ferment
Robert W. Stookey, editor

The Iron Triangle: A U.S. Security Policy for Northeast Asia
A. James Gregor and Maria Hsia Chang

THE IRON TRIANGLE

A U.S. Security Policy for Northeast Asia

A. James Gregor
Maria Hsia Chang

HOOVER INSTITUTION PRESS
Stanford University | Stanford, California

Hoover Press Publication 292

Copyright 1984 by the Board of Trustees of the
    Leland Stanford Junior University

First printing, 1984
Manufactured in the United States of America
88   87   86   85   84   9   8   7   6   5   4   3   2   1

Library of Congress Cataloging in Publication Data
Gregor, A. James.
    The iron triangle.

    (Hoover international studies)
    Bibliography: p.
    Includes index.
    1. United States—Military relations—Japan.   2. United States—Military relations—Taiwan.   3. United States—Military relations—Korea (South)   4. Japan — Military relations—United States.   5. Taiwan—Military relations—United States.   6. Korea (South)—Military relations—United States.   I. Chang, Maria Hsia.   II. Title.   III. Series.
UA23.G79   1984   355'.03305   84-630
ISBN 0-8179-7921-2
ISBN 0-8179-7922-0 (pbk.)

Contents

Map appears on page 2.

Editor's Foreword

In an amazingly short time the Western Pacific Basin has become a zone of industrial and commercial vigor that rivals the North Atlantic as the center of the world economy. By the year 2000, the combined industrial power of Japan, Taiwan, South Korea, Singapore, Hong Kong, and Malaysia is likely to be as great as that of the United States or Western Europe. This economic vigor has been made possible by two things: the free trade and free enterprise policies of the region's governments and the peace that the Pacific region has enjoyed since 1945. The prime agent of free trade and peace has been the U.S. presence.

Professors A. James Gregor of the University of California at Berkeley and Maria Hsia Chang of the University of Puget Sound offer us an acute analysis of the most vital part of the Pacific Basin—Northeast Asia and the security triangle made up of Japan, South Korea, and Taiwan. The authors show that the future of Northeast Asia depends on the United States' and the region's own armed might. The United States obviously wants to continue to contribute to the stability and economic development of the region, to deter revolutionary change, and to halt communist military expansion. To do this, the United States must work with the states of what Gregor and Chang call the "Iron Triangle."

Opposing these states and the United States is the armed camp of Communist Asia, whose economic performance pales in comparison with the states of Northeast Asia. Threats to peace in the region come only from the communist side: the Soviet Union, China, North Korea, and Vietnam. Yet recent U.S.

policies have weakened the alliance system in Northeast Asia. The present U.S. China policy not only threatens the Iron Triangle states but does not reduce the Soviet threat to the region.

Gregor and Chang rightly call for a restoration of U.S. credibility as a secure, reliable defense partner. Going along with the People's Republic of China has undermined the security of all the nations of Northeast Asia, as well as those in the Association of Southeast Asian Nations. The governments of Asia, rightly or wrongly, fear China more than the Soviet Union, and they believe that any deferring to Chinese wishes for hegemony in Asia will be disastrous. It is necessary therefore to support Taiwan, to arm and upgrade its defenses. Taiwan has great potential for basing and servicing facilities for jet aircraft. Jet interceptors from Taiwan could make up for the paucity of aircraft carriers in the region and allow for greater flexibility in protecting the important sea-lanes of the area.

Japan must be persuaded to rearm at least for defensive purposes (such as antiaircraft and antisubmarine weapons, aircraft, frigates). A rearmed Japan, plus continued support for South Korea and Taiwan, should forestall any Soviet military adventures. Communist China is militarily a paper tiger and unreliable; nor does it have enough military power to affect the military balance in Northeast Asia as long as the Iron Triangle remains strong.

Gregor and Chang's excellent study offers clear and coherent policy recommendations for the United States to follow in Northeast Asia.

Peter Duignan

Coordinator, International Studies
Hoover Institution

Preface

In this study we attempt to assess the range of options open to the United States and its allies in the strategic defense of Northeast Asia. It seems reasonably clear that neither Washington nor its allies have, at present, a determinate policy for the defense of the region—current policy being the consequence of ad hoc responses to episodic tensions that have manifested themselves in the area. Since the early 1970s, Washington has been unable to formulate a coherent East Asian policy, and still less a policy designed to protect and further U.S. interests in the northeast quadrant of East Asia. For all that, it seems equally evident that the interests of the United States require a long-term policy. Why that has not been forthcoming is difficult to say.

What appears certain, as of this writing, is that Washington has been reluctant to review its current policy of accommodating the People's Republic of China. The Reagan administration, initially so well-disposed toward both the Republic of Korea and the Republic of China on Taiwan, appears to have mortgaged some of their vital interests in the effort to placate Peking. If that can be said of an "anticommunist" Republican administration, it is difficult to anticipate what one might expect from any succeeding Democratic administration.

In effect, U.S. foreign and security policy in Northeast Asia requires review and reassessment. In the pages that follow, we attempt just such a preliminary reassessment.

In undertaking such an enterprise, we have become indebted to many institutions and individuals. Among the most important are the Institute of

International Relations in Taipei and the Center for Strategic and International Studies in Washington, D.C.; and Drs. Chang King-yuh, Ray Cline, Martin Lasater, Chiu Hungdah, and Wei Yung, all of whom contributed ideas to this exposition—but are not responsible for any errors it may contain.

The Pacific Basin Project of the Institute of International Studies at the University of California, Berkeley, and the Pacific Cultural Foundation provided support for the work; Professor Thomas Metzger of the History Department, University of California, San Diego, and Dr. Ramon H. Myers, curator of the East Asian Collection at the Hoover Institution on War, Revolution and Peace, inspired the enterprise. We hope that what has resulted justifies, at least in part, their respective contributions.

1 | Introduction:
The "Iron Triangle"

*We must bear in mind . . . that we cannot consider Japan, South
Korea, and Taiwan separately from one another, not only because of
geography but also for reasons of collective security.*
    *Therefore, if one of the three nations were to break down, the rest
would be obvious. Northeast Asia would be thrown into a state of
uncontrollable confusion—even with the help of the United States.*

Ichiji Sugita,
"Japanese Perspectives on Security,"
in Foster, Dornan, and Carpenter, eds.,
Strategy and Security in Northeast Asia.

Gradually, since the early 1950s, the countries of East Asia have thrust
themselves more and more insistently into the deliberations of Washington's
policymakers. Immediately after the close of the Second World War, East
Asia appeared to be of little more than secondary importance to the United
States. Japan was disarmed and occupied, China was to be left to its own
devices, and whatever interests the United States had in Korea were marginal
at best.[1]

All that notwithstanding, in the years that followed, the United States found
itself drawn into two major land wars in East Asia—one of which was fought
on the Korean peninsula. For more than a generation Washington remained,
and to this day remains, embroiled in the ongoing conflict between Communist China and Nationalist China. The indifference that characterized U.S.
policy in the immediate postwar years has given way to a kind of frenetic
preoccupation with East Asia, for in the three decades that followed the
surrender of Japan in 1945, Japan transformed itself from a market for U.S.
surplus goods into the "key" to the contemporary global "balance of power."[2]

Beyond that, since 1945 East Asia has achieved the most rapidly increasing
economic growth rate of any region in the world. By the mid-1970s the
volume of foreign trade between the United States and Asia exceeded that

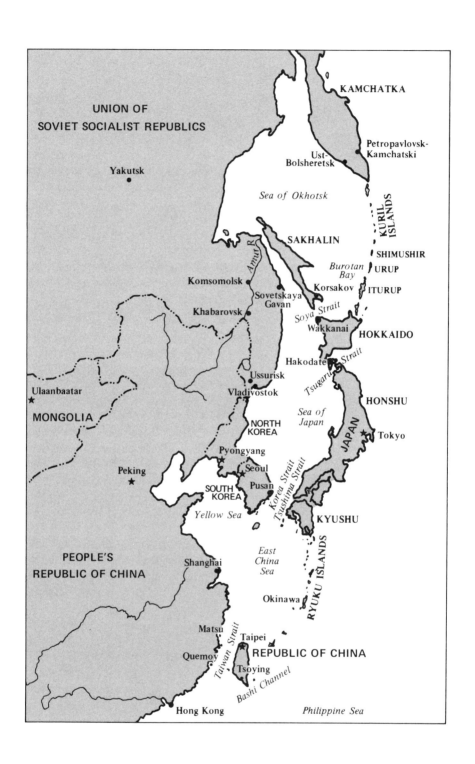

between the United States and Europe. At that time, the United States was exporting over $20 billion in goods and services to Asia, an activity that was translated directly into employment for over 625,000 Americans.

In East Asia, Japan alone operates the world's second most productive economic system—and thus has overtaken the Soviet Union. In fact, in dynamic East Asia, the nonsocialist nations of the northeast are by far the most dynamic. Quite apart from the awesome economic performance of Japan, both the Republic of Korea (ROK) and the Republic of China on Taiwan (ROC) annually exchange more than $10 billion in goods and services with the United States.

To better appreciate what such figures signify, one need but recall that in the early 1950s Japan, South Korea, and Taiwan all languished with per capita incomes of less than $150. Less than three decades later, the per capita income in Japan exceeded $8,800, that of the Republic of China exceeded $2,000, and that of the Republic of Korea was about $1,500. Together, Japan, South Korea, and the Republic of China have sustained rates of economic growth that have exceeded those of any other region in the world. Moreover, growth has not been purchased at the expense of the subaltern classes. Income distribution has been surprisingly egalitarian in all three nations; income is distributed more equitably in the Republic of China than in some developed socialist economies.[3]

Together the three nonsocialist nations of Northeast Asia possess substantial economic power and are the leading trading partners of the United States in East Asia. Japan is now the foremost trading partner of the United States in the Pacific, and it is the single most important market in the world for U.S. agricultural produce. The Republic of China is the seventh, and the Republic of Korea the eleventh, most important trading partner of the United States. Taiwan will remain, in the immediate future, one of the larger markets for U.S. agricultural exports in Asia. Moreover, both South Korea and Taiwan— collected around Japan as newly industrialized communities—serve as growth engines that stimulate the economic development of the remaining nonsocialist nations of Southeast Asia.

Japan is a major importer of resources from the Association of South East Asian Nations (ASEAN) and supplies many of the capital goods required for the development of these countries. Since the mid-1970s, the Republic of China has begun the export of whole plants and has become a major supplier of basic producer goods, as well as manufactured raw materials such as steel and petrochemicals, to Southeast Asia. All the indicators suggest increased interregional cooperation between the Southeast Asian nonsocialist economies and those of Japan and the newly industrialized systems of South Korea and Taiwan.

More significantly, in terms of the most enduring U.S. policy goals, the economies of the nonsocialist countries of Northeast Asia are fundamentally market-governed systems, essentially compatible with those of the United States and the European Economic Community. In fact, the nonsocialist economies of Northeast Asia are fully integrated into the international market system of industrial North America and the Atlantic community of nations.

Finally, all three systems are oriented toward defense rather than offense. The armed forces of Japan are configured for the protection of its national territory and are constrained by constitutional enactment from developing the potential that might be used to impose its foreign policy initiatives upon other nations. The armed forces of the Republic of Korea and the Republic of China are similarly defensive, in terms of both inventory and policy. Even though they are unconstrained by national policy, neither could launch a successful attack against any neighbor. The immediate neighbors of both are equipped with military capabilities that are formidable, if not overwhelming. North Korea, by any determinate estimate, is possessed of military power that threatens the integrity of South Korea.[4] South Korea, without the intervention of a major military power, could not, at this time, contain a North Korean armed assault. Similarly, the Republic of China is threatened by the armed forces of the People's Republic of China (PRC). Communist China deploys a military force that exceeds that of the Republic of China by a ratio of 10:1 in every category of military capability.[5]

Given at least these considerations, the three major nonsocialist nations of Northeast Asia (Japan, the Republic of Korea, and the Republic of China) constitute a major asset with regard to the secular foreign policy interests of the United States in Asia. If these concerns can be conveniently identified with opportunities for trade and investment, the nonsocialist nations of Northeast Asia will be seen to be of utmost importance.

The concern with the peace and stability of Northeast Asia is not the special product of U.S. benevolence. The interests of the United States in East Asia require that no single nation or combination of nations become so powerful in the region or subregion as to enable it to enjoy special privileges denied the United States. Nor do Americans wish to see the market economies of Asia in general, and those of Northeast Asia in particular, devolve into centrally controlled command economies—not only because that might impair access to the investment and trading markets but because it would probably dampen any future hope for political democracy. In effect, animated by its own policy interests, the United States seeks, and has sought, to sustain a reasonable balance of power in East Asia in general, and in Northeast Asia in particular.[6]

Normatively, the United States has been committed to the establishment, maintenance, and fostering of open economic and political institutions. United States foreign policy has been, and continues to be, based on the convictions that (1) market economies are intrinsically superior to command economies in satisfying the immediate and long-term material interests of populations, (2) open political institutions allow the participation of citizens, which itself makes possible more effective welfare distribution, and, finally, (3) the existence of market economies and open political institutions contributes to regional and international stability, increased economic and cultural exchange, and a general enhancement of the quality of life.

The performance of the three major nonsocialist nations of Northeast Asia has shown these policy goals to be attainable and has afforded evidence to support these assumptions. Since the early 1950s, no socialist developmental economy has been able to register such sustained rates of growth over so long a period, nor to make the transition from a traditional agrarian system to industrial maturity in so short a time and with so little sacrifice.

What this means, in part, is revealed in a comparison of the particulars of income distribution in developing nations. During the 1970s, the average share of total income of the 40 percent of the population receiving the lowest income in all developing countries was 12.5 percent—and in half of all developing countries the income share of total income of the lowest two quintiles of the population was only 9 percent. In Japan, however, that share was 21 percent, in South Korea it was about 16.9 percent, and in the Republic of China it was 21.9 percent. Japan began its postwar economic growth at a more advanced stage of development, but the same cannot be said for South Korea or the Republic of China, both of which began their trajectories of growth circumstanced very much like the less developed nations of Asia and Africa.[7]

The United Nations has identified those nations in which the lowest 40 percent of the population receives more than 17 percent of available total income as "low inequality" economic systems.[8] In fact, as we have suggested, the nonsocialist nations of Northeast Asia have enjoyed sustained and intensive economic growth with remarkable equity.[9] They have shown that developing economies can remain governed, by and large, by market signals, can operate within the international money economy, and enjoy more substantial civil and political liberties than those provided to populations enduring "proletarian dictatorship" and "people's democracy." Their record provides compelling evidence to counter the principal theses of "dependency theory," which maintains that developing countries that remain involved in the international money market are destined to lapse into patterns of negligible growth, with high unemployment, mass impoverishment, and gross maldistribution of welfare benefits.[10]

In effect, the major nonsocialist nations of Northeast Asia provide a number of substantial benefits to the United States. As previously mentioned, they are currently economic partners of considerable importance. They pay at least lip service to democracy; Japan is manifestly democratic in practice. They provide an attractive alternative nonsocialist model of development for those nations that remain partially, or substantially, underdeveloped. And finally, as we shall see, they are strategic security assets in the intense competition with the Soviet Union.

Throughout the remainder of this century, Northeast Asia will play a critical role in the global strategy of the competing superpowers, the Soviet Union and the United States. Politics, economics, military power, history, and the struggle for alternative futures will all come into play in the northeast quadrant of East Asia. It is there that the interests of four of the world's major powers (the People's Republic of China, Japan, the Soviet Union, and the United States) intersect. This is an area dense with armaments and afflicted with memories of recent conflict—a subregion in which there are conflicting territorial claims and divided states competing for advantage.

Today, Northeast Asia has one of the largest concentrations of military power of any comparable region in the world.[11] The two largest land armies in the world—those of Communist China and the Soviet Union—are locked in immediate confrontation along the Sino-Soviet border. Two of the world's largest combat air forces patrol the skies, and two of the world's largest navies patrol the waters, of Northeast Asia. The United States maintains bilateral security arrangements with both Japan and South Korea, and the Soviet Union and the People's Republic of China maintain similar arrangements with North Korea. Air units of the U.S. Air Force are stationed in South Korea and Japan, and the U.S. Navy services its vessels in Japan, makes regular port calls to South Korea, and plies the waters of the Japan and East China seas. Moreover, since the early 1950s, Communist China has threatened to overwhelm the Republic of China by force of arms, and the United States, in domestic law, has affirmed that the security of Taiwan remains a matter of "grave concern" for Americans. Yet the United States has also allowed itself to be drawn into an increasingly intimate relationship with the "pragmatic" Communists of Peking.

Given its manifest economic power, the concentration of arms within its boundaries, and the complexity of conflicting interests, Northeast Asia reveals itself to be one of the most important geostrategic pressure points in contemporary international politics. In the past, such regions have been centers of unexpected political change, the vast movement of peoples, the rise and disintegration of political systems and cultures, and armed conflict.[12]

Within this complex security environment U.S. strategists are obliged to formulate policy. Although the clear outlines of such a policy have not yet been drawn, several things appear to have been generally recognized. The majority of policymakers seem to accept, in principle, the contention that "the cornerstone of peace and prosperity in Asia . . . is . . . Japan, for it is the control over the industrial power of Japan . . . that is the determinant of whether the

Pacific Basin continues its present dynamic development or sinks once again into a cockpit of Great Power contention."[13]

Given Japan's critical role in stabilizing all of East Asia, and the fact that Japan's economic might is not coupled with a corresponding military capability, the security of Japan turns largely on the credibility of U.S. treaty guarantees and the insulation of its exposed flanks. At least some Japanese thus see South Korea not only as their second largest export market but as a shield from the influence and overt pressures of both the Soviet Union and Communist China.[14] The Soviet Union already deploys substantial military might just north of Hokkaidō. A Soviet presence on the Korean peninsula would make the defense of the Japanese home islands, even with U.S. assistance, much more difficult.

In all this, Japan remains confused by Communist Chinese intentions.[15] The U.S. effort to establish an enduring rapprochement with Peking has reduced the measure of suspicion with which the Japanese have pursued relations with Communist China. The United States has tended to perceive the growing Sino-Japanese rapprochement as a contribution to stability in East Asia. But the Japanese have considerable reason to be chary of Peking. Communist China, as we shall subsequently consider, entertains subsea territorial claims in the Sea of Japan and the East China Sea that conflict with the offshore mineral rights and fishing claims of Japan. Moreover, by employing blandishments or pressure, Peking would like to draw Japan more firmly into an open alliance against the Soviet Union—an alliance that could only increase the threat of Soviet military adventure against Japan.

Sino-Japanese relations, for at least these reasons, remain characterized by ambivalence. Both the Soviet Union and Communist China, in pursuit of their own national and security interests, will attempt to extend their influence over their neighbors. To resist that influence, Japan finds support in an independent South Korea. A united Korea, allied with either the Soviet Union or Communist China, would render the Sea of Japan far more difficult to defend and would expose all of Japan to air attack and naval investment. Increasingly exposed, Japan might well be compelled to enter into a client relationship with either a patron Soviet Union or a patron Communist China, to the ultimate detriment of U.S. interests in Asia and the long-term stability of the region. The extinction of the Republic of Korea could well contribute to the "finlandization" of Japan.

To the south of Japan lies the Republic of China. Not only is Nationalist China Japan's fifth largest trading partner, it also sits astride the most important waterways to Japan. Seaborne traffic from Europe and the oil ports in the Persian Gulf reaches Japan through the Taiwan Strait or the Bashi Channel, off the southern coast of Taiwan. Bulk carriers, container ships, and tankers either negotiate the waters of the Taiwan Strait or, if too large, traverse the

Bashi Channel, to pass eastward of the Okinawa chain on their course to the Japanese home ports.

Should the island of Taiwan fall under the dominance of the Soviet Union or mainland China, the flow of vital shipborne traffic to Japan would come under the control of powers whose geopolitical interests differ critically or substantially from those of the United States. The flow of resources and energy supplies, so essential to the viability and growth of the Japanese economy, would be subject to interdiction at the discretion of Moscow or Peking. The very threat of interruption of free trade with Europe and the Persian Gulf could significantly reduce Japan's freedom of action. Under the pressure of such threat the government in Tokyo might very well accede to the demands leveled by any power that could influence the movement of resources or energy supplies.

How sensitive Japan is to that trade flow was revealed in 1974 when the Arab nations, threatening to restrict the sale of crude oil to Japan, insisted that Tokyo change its declared policy toward Israel. In response to that threat, Japan quickly complied, even though such a change conflicted with the avowed policies of the United States toward Israel. However much Japan depends on the United States to oversee its most fundamental security interests, Tokyo remains vulnerable to the constraints that would follow from any restriction of passage through the Taiwan Strait and the Bashi Channel.

Japan, the Republic of Korea, and the Republic of China share substantial economic and security interests. By 1976 Japan was providing about 67 percent of the total overseas investments in South Korea. As we have seen, South Korea is now Japan's second largest export market (after the United States). These investments and commodity exports involve broad sectors of both economies and the innumerable small transactions that are conducted attest to the intensity of the interactions. The Republic of China, Japan's fourth largest export market, is only second in importance to South Korea. Japan provides the bulk of the foreign investments on Taiwan, and in 1975 over 30 percent of the total of Taiwan's imports originated there.

Geographic proximity, common security concerns and economic interests, political alignments, historical connections, and similar international trade and investment modalities all combine to create strong ties among the three major nonsocialist nations of Northeast Asia.

On the flanks of Japan, South Korea and the Republic of China provide a market supplement and an investment outlet involving over 50 million people (about 18 million on Taiwan and over 36 million in South Korea), equivalent in size to about half of the domestic market of Japan itself. Both have sustained an average real economic growth rate of about 10 percent per annum, and together they purchase about 75 percent as much from Japan as does the entire European community, the world's largest single market.

Japan, South Korea, and the Republic of China make up an "iron triangle" of about 170 million people enjoying high growth rates and a level of productivity that is the second highest in the world. All three nations are capable of deploying substantial military force. The Republic of Korea is armed with the largest military force in noncommunist Asia. Japan, at the moment, denies that it maintains an export-oriented arms industry, but both the Republic of Korea and the Republic of China are capable of producing a wide range of conventional weapons for export. All three have the technical capability and the scientific talent to develop advanced weapon systems, including nuclear weapons and the delivery systems necessary for their strategic and tactical use.[16]

In substance, the three nonsocialist nations of Northeast Asia constitute a vital triangle with regard to the security arrangements in East Asia. Japan is the linchpin of those arrangements, and South Korea and the Republic of China are essential to its defense perimeter, affording Japan the freedom of maneuver that allows it to maintain its diplomatic independence and military viability and to function as a force for stability and economic growth. In the foreseeable future, both South Korea and the Republic of China will remain threatened by adversaries possessed of massive military superiority. Should either nation succumb, the position of Japan could be seriously threatened. Japan, under such threat, would no longer be the secure ally critical to U.S. security postures in East Asia. Should Japan be compelled, in response to such changes, to withdraw basing privileges for the forward deployment of U.S. forces in the West Pacific, timely and effective Western response to Soviet military moves in the entire region could be seriously impaired.

Making foreign policy in such unstable circumstances will, at best, be difficult for the United States. So many forces interact in the security environment of Northeast Asia that no single policy recommends itself without qualification. Nonetheless, policy must be formulated and initiatives undertaken, for there is good reason to believe that the future of Asia may well be determined by whatever the United States chooses to do, or not do, in the immediate future.

2 | The Security Threat: The Soviet Union

Soviet military capability is the single most important factor in any consideration of the complex security environment of Northeast Asia. The Soviet Union enjoys superiority in both conventional arms and nuclear arms capabilities when compared with any Asian nation, and in Afghanistan it has demonstrated both the will and the ability to mobilize, marshal, and transport the general-purpose forces necessary for the military occupation of foreign soil. It has shown itself prepared to put its military in harm's way should its interests so require. During the brief Sino-Vietnamese War of 1979, Soviet naval vessels made their appearance offshore in Southeast Asia in support of their Vietnamese allies—within strike range of Communist Chinese aircraft based in Hainan.

Since that time Soviet missile cruisers, destroyers, and frigates, supported by oilers and supply and intelligence-gathering vessels, have made regular entry into Camranh Bay, Haiphong, and Danang—signaling a Soviet intention to continue its presence in Southeast Asia. From midsea anchorages in the South China Sea and facilities in Vietnam, Soviet naval units have made their way north, through the Taiwan Strait. They have conducted antisubmarine warfare exercises off the coast of the Japanese home islands and adjacent to the Okinawa chain. Soviet military aircraft have been increasingly active in Japanese airspace in the North, and military activity in the Kuril Islands indicates a progressive buildup of Soviet forward deployment capabilities in that subregion.

In Northeast Asia, the Soviet Union has long since constructed permanent military bases. Around the shores of the Sea of Okhotsk and on the western shore of the Sea of Japan, the Soviet Union has articulated an impressive complex of military establishments, including the major naval bases at Vladivostok and Sovetskaya Gavan. There are military facilities at Possiet, Novgoradsky, Shkotovo, and Tynkin, and a massive air base at Ussurisk. Smaller airfields, naval shipyards, submarine pens, early warning stations, and hardened storage complexes dot the Soviet Maritime Province, Sakhalin Island, and the Kamchatka peninsula. On the Pacific coast of the Kamchatka peninsula the Soviets have fashioned one of the largest ballistic missile nuclear submarine bases in the world.

Much of this has been part of the continuing intensive military buildup begun by the Soviet Union in the early 1960s—the most impressive undertaken by any nation in peacetime since the rearmament of National Socialist Germany in the mid-1930s.[1] Estimates of the cost to the Soviet Union vary from analyst to analyst, but however calculated, Soviet outlays have for years exceeded U.S. military expenditures.[2]

Soviet military expenditures probably have increased at a rate of 3 percent per annum since 1970, whereas U.S. military expenditures, in real terms, have been declining. According to the Central Intelligence Agency's estimates, Soviet military spending in 1976 was about $120 billion compared with U.S. outlays of about $102 billion.[3] Thus, the Soviet Union, with an economy about 55 percent as productive as that of the United States, expends about 20 percent more of its national resources on the military than does Washington.[4] Given the fact that the Soviet Union allocates far less to personnel costs (about 25 percent of its military budget, compared with about 62 percent of the U.S. military budget) and more to weapon systems procurement than does the United States, such assessments understate the rate of Soviet force level enhancement.

The almost unanimous view among U.S. and West European government officials and military analysts is that the level of Soviet military capability today affords Moscow parity with the United States and places the USSR on the threshold of general strategic and conventional arms superiority. Since at least the early 1960s, the leadership in Moscow has maintained that Soviet security requires that its armed forces "establish superiority over the enemy in modern weapons . . . [and] the material prerequisites of victory. . . . It is especially necessary to maintain constant superiority over the enemy in firepower, troop mobility, and maneuverability."[5]

The pursuit of military superiority has not only involved the quantitative and qualitative improvement of Soviet general-purpose and special services forces, but has prompted the deployment of troops, weapon systems, and support adjuncts to the Soviet Far East. From 1964 through 1977 the Soviet Union allocated about 15 percent of its entire national defense budget to forces deployed in the eastern territories.[6] Conjoined with such deployments has been the independently budgeted construction of a vast system of transport and communication. The Baikal-Amur Mainline Railway, which will connect the Soviet Far East with the European heartland, is over 2,000 miles in length, beginning at Ust-Kut on the Lena River and terminating at Komsomolsk on the Amur. Approximately two and a half times the length of the Alaska pipeline, the line traverses seven mountain ranges, a series of broad rivers, and more than 1,300 miles of permafrost. It is estimated to have cost over $5 billion by 1980 and is one of the most ambitious public works projects in history.

The development of the infrastructure in the Soviet East was a necessary adjunct to the expansion of ground, sea, and air forces in the region. By the late 1970s about 25 percent of the Soviet Union's conventional forces were being deployed in the East, including at least 38 motorized rifle divisions, 6 or 7 armored divisions, and 2 airborne divisions, supplemented by about 2,500 first-line combat aircraft. The command, communications, and supply ancillaries for these forces have been hardened to withstand nuclear blast effects and have been connected with a network of hard-surface roads that are passable throughout the northern winters.[7]

Over 700,000 troops man the defensive positions of the military districts of Soviet Central Asia (about 8 or 9 divisions), Siberia (4 divisions), Transbaikalia (12 divisions), and the Far East (20 divisions). Although few hard statistics are available concerning the Soviet forces in the East, it is estimated that the ratio of troops to tanks and armored fighting vehicles is 20:1, which makes the Soviet forces in the eastern provinces among the most heavily armored and mobile in the world. Armored forces include the newest Soviet battle tanks, the T-64/T-72 and T-80, all of which are protected by heavy laminated steel armor that is almost impenetrable. These main battle tanks are armed with 125-mm smoothbore tank guns, as well as 12.7-mm heavy machine guns for suppression fire. All are fully equipped with the most modern laser range-finding devices and infrared night lights. Each tank is capable of laying its own smoke screen to foil optically sighted antitank weapons.[8]

The four Soviet tactical air armies, designed for close ground support in the East, operate a wide range of aircraft, including the most modern MiG-23s, MiG-25s, Su-19s, and Su-17s. The MiG-25 is one of the Mach 3-capable aircraft that entered Soviet service in the 1970s—with a maximum speed of over 2,100 miles per hour, a service ceiling of about 75,000 feet, and an absolute ceiling of almost 100,000 feet. Armed with a twin-barrel, 23-mm cannon and four AA-6 Acrid air-to-air missiles, the MiG-25 is uninterceptible except by the most sophisticated antiaircraft weapons and the most advanced aircraft of the United States Air Force.

The Sukhoi Su-19, currently in service in the Soviet Far East, is equally impressive with a maximum speed of about 1,600 miles per hour and an ability to deliver 16,000 pounds of ordnance. It has the widest variety of avionics and the most advanced and multipurpose armaments available in the USSR. The Su-19 can launch air-to-air missiles, antiradar missiles, and pilot-guided "smart bombs." It is the most modern Soviet aircraft to be developed specifically as a fighter bomber for ground support missions.[9]

An entire range of medium and heavy bombers, transport aircraft, and helicopter troop transport and gunships supplements these aircraft on station in the Soviet East and provides the flexibility that renders the ground forces maximally combat capable.

These forces are supplemented by an array of Soviet nuclear weapons. About 30 percent of all Soviet strategic missiles are deployed along the route of the Siberian and Baikal-Amur Mainline railroads, and tactical nuclear weapons delivery is provided by FROG-7 rockets with an estimated range of 60 kilometers. The FROG-7 launchers are fully truck mobile and, even when carrying conventional high explosives, provide effective battlefield fire support. As tactical nuclear weapons they are critical military assets.

Soviet strategic missiles in the Far East, both land based and submarine launched, can target all the major cities of Asia and North America. The strike range of the smaller Soviet SS-N-5 missiles extends as far south as Taipei, Taiwan, and includes all the Japanese home islands as well as the northeast quadrant of mainland China. The newest SS-20 surface-to-surface missiles, with a range of over 3,000 miles, can target Asia as far south as Borneo, Thailand, and southern India. Finally, Soviet long-range aircraft can attack any site in Asia, in half of Australia, and in much of northwestern North America.

The constellation of forces available to the Soviet armies in the Far East thus far exceeds the requirements of static defense. As discussed in Chapter 3, there is nothing currently in the Communist Chinese inventory that could threaten the integrity of the Soviet eastern provinces. The massed foot infantry of the Communist Chinese People's Liberation Army (PLA), facing the overwhelming superiority of Soviet forces, could only serve as defensive cannon fodder; these troops are fundamentally incapable of penetrating Soviet defenses or of maintaining themselves outside the immediate range of mainland China's thin support structure.

Although it is an empirical fact that the Soviet buildup in East Asia occurred at the same time that Sino-Soviet relations soured (during the early and mid-1960s), the correlation may have been more coincidental than causal. The Soviet Union commenced its general buildup at that time, and it would seem that the general enterprise would eventually have included corresponding force enhancements in East Asia whatever the relations with the People's Republic of China might have been.

Under any conceivable set of circumstances, the Soviet Union could not allow the vast reaches of the Soviet Far East to remain undefended. That entire territory constitutes the most vulnerable, as well as the most valuable, region in the Soviet Union. Whereas 80 percent of the Soviet Union's energy in 1980 was consumed in the heavily industrialized and urbanized West, about 80 percent of its recoverable energy resources are located in the East.[10] Whatever the supply available to the Soviet Union (and estimates of that availability vary), it has been determined that oil, natural gas, and coal are to be found in abundance in the Soviet East. The Samotlor oil field in western Siberia has reserves estimated to be more than twice as large as those of Alaska's North Slope. The Urengoy field is estimated to be the world's largest natural gas reserve, and the Kansk-Archansk coal deposits are thought to contain approximately 1.2 trillion tons of recoverable coal.

These crucial energy resources in the Soviet eastern provinces are supplemented by vast stands of timber, as well as by gold, copper, and nickel deposits, all of which bring in the hard currency foreign exchange that has become critical for underwriting the expensive high-technology purchases that the Soviet Union now requires to sustain and enhance its economic productivity. For years the Soviet Union has had to import high-technology equipment to further the efficiency of its economic enterprise—and such purchases will continue and probably increase in the future.

This Asiatic resource abundance, so critical to the future of the Soviet Union in terms of energy supplies and hard currency potential, is located in a region with one of the lowest population concentrations in the world[11]—a region that was threatened by anticommunist interventionist forces on the eve of the Bolshevik Revolution and by imperial Japan in the 1930s and 1940s; it is now threatened by Communist China.

Under almost any conceivable relationship that might exist between the USSR and Communist China, the political and military leadership of the Kremlin would commit substantial general-purpose and strategic forces to the region east of the Urals and extending to the Pacific coast.[12] The enormous expense incurred by the leadership in Moscow to construct the infrastructure capable of sustaining modern warfare in the Soviet East is evidence enough of the Soviet intention to maintain a balanced and effective military force there, capable of undertaking both nuclear and conventional operations. Such a force is capable of providing the nucleus of an offensive ground assault against Communist Chinese positions, staging interventionist incursions on the Korean peninsula, or launching a sea and airlifted attack against the Japanese home islands.

That the Soviet buildup in the Far East was undertaken without degrading the forces of the Warsaw Pact nations indicates that it is part of Moscow's program of achieving parity with the armed capabilities of the West and Communist China combined.[13] Lieutenant General DeWitt C. Smith, Jr., has pointed out that the Soviet army in Asia "is an army that has been built without any reduction of Soviet forces in the West," and is nonetheless "nearly as modern as [those] in the West."[14] In fact, not only were the Soviet forces in the eastern provinces built up without reducing force levels in Eastern Europe, but during the buildup in the East the number of Soviet divisions facing the West was actually increased from 26 to 31—and each division was larger in absolute number, and considerably upgraded, compared with its earlier counterpart.[15]

It would seem that the Soviet buildup in East Asia was not simply the consequence of the Sino-Soviet confrontation, but rather was part of a general Soviet program of force enhancement that would have occurred whatever the relations between Moscow and Peking. The forces required to contain the Communist Chinese would need very little of the advanced weaponry that currently characterizes Soviet military might in East Asia. The forces in that region exceed defense requirements by a considerable margin; that they constitute the core of the offensive capability is nowhere more evident than in the expense and energy Moscow has employed in the construction of its naval capabilities in the region.

The People's Republic of China does not possess an oceangoing navy. Its large number of small vessels are designed for little more than coastal defense. In time of war, Soviet aircraft could destroy the port and storage facilities of mainland China with little fear of interception. The more than 100 advanced strike aircraft now in the Soviet Far East naval inventory could devastate the ship traffic destined for mainland Chinese ports. Standoff air-to-surface missiles launched by Soviet aircraft could be targeted against merchant vessels with every expectation of success. Thus, even without the imposition of a Soviet naval blockade, it would appear that Communist China could not sustain its international ship traffic under conditions of a frontal conflict with the Soviet Union.

All that notwithstanding, the Soviet Union has undertaken to vastly increase its naval capabilities in East Asia. Since the early 1970s, the total tonnage of the Soviet Far East Fleet has been increased from 700,000 to about 1.2 million tons. During the same period the fleet tonnage of the U.S. Navy has declined from 1.1 million to 600,000 tons.[16] When the Soviet navy undertook the three-week naval exercise identified as "Okean II" in 1975, it demonstrated a sophisticated blue-water war-making capability that impressed Western observers. Four task forces of the Soviet Pacific Fleet undertook simulated attacks in the Sea of Japan, the Sea of Okhotsk, and off the Caroline Islands and the Philippines in the South China Sea. The entire operation was directed by computerized data flow originating in satellite surveillance. Worldwide, almost instantaneous communications coordinated the tracking and target acquisition required for simultaneous cruise missile launches and air strikes from widely separated sites.[17] None of this would be necessary to counter a Communist Chinese threat.

In 1980 the Soviet Pacific Fleet order of battle listed about 78 major surface combatants in service, including one aircraft carrier (the *Minsk*), 11 missile cruisers, 25 destroyers, and 41 frigates—all missile capable.[18] These are supported by about 125 submarines, about 50 of which are nuclear powered. The submarine fleet includes *Delta*- and *Yankee*-class boats capable of launching strategic nuclear ballistic missiles. The *Hotel*- and *Golf*-class boats supplement that force and are capable of the sea-launch of missiles with a range of about 1,000 kilometers. Cruise missile–capable submarines of the *Echo*, *Juliet*, and *Whisky* (*Long Bin*) classes pose serious threats to surface vessels, and a formidable force of about 65 attack and patrol submarines constitutes a significant challenge to all seaborne traffice in the region.

The Soviet naval forces in East Asia include a modest but growing amphibious capability. Among the 70 or more Soviet landing ships now available, the newest *Ropucha* class has made its appearance alongside the *Ivan Rogov*, the most modern of the Soviet navy's amphibious warfare ships. The *Ivan Rogov* can transport at least a battalion of naval infantry, as well as up to 40 tanks and support vehicles, and it affords the Soviet Union an appreciable long-range, long-endurance assault capability. It is reported to be capable of carrying state-of-the-art conventional or air-cushioned personnel landing craft; the latter can transport about a platoon of naval infantry at speeds in excess of 65 kilometers an hour.[19] In effect, the Soviet Far East Fleet is now able to undertake combined sea, air, and land operations against the shore in East Asia.

Except as collateral support for a Soviet attack against the northeastern provinces of Communist China, it is unlikely that such attacks would figure in an anti-Chinese military plan. Rather, seaborne infantry would probably be deployed as forward assault elements that could secure the Sōya Strait north of Japan in the event of a general conflict in the Pacific. Soviet general forces in the Kuril Islands are estimated to number 10,000 troups, and Buroton Bay on Shimushir Island now hosts a submarine base of the Soviet Pacific Fleet, while Kunashir and Iturup are the sites for radar and surveillance installations. These forces protect the critical straits through which, in the event of a general conflict, Soviet naval units would have to make exit to the open Pacific from the inland Okhotsk Sea, which serves as a major servicing and marshaling center for Soviet Far East naval forces. By the mid-1980s, the Soviet Union will have completed construction of its fourth major naval base in East Asia at Korsakov harbor opposite the Japanese home island of Hokkaidō. Korsakov will be equipped to provide major service facilities for Soviet destroyers, amphibious craft, and attack submarines.

Soviet control over the critical water passages leading from the Sea of Japan and the Sea of Okhotsk would be essential in any general conflict in the Pacific. If denied egress to Pacific waters, the Soviet Far East Fleet could be contained in the offshore waters of East Asia. The three major waterways affording such passage (the Sōya, Tsugaru, and Tsushima straits) are all exposed to Western interdiction. The Soviet Union has immediate control over only the Sōya Strait in northern Hokkaidō and in the event of conflict would probably attempt to secure the entire passage.

Soviet occupation of the Kuril Islands at the close of the Second World War provided potential control over all water passages from the inland waters to the Pacific. In the judgment of Soviet analysts, "the Kurile Islands no longer separate the USSR from the Pacific Ocean. On the contrary, they open a free outlet to it, which is of tremendous importance. Exit to the open ocean has been provided."[20] In fact, the Soviets now fully control only the Kuril Strait— between the Kuril Islands and the southernmost tip of the Kamchatka penin- sula—which spans no more than 10 kilometers at its widest point and might easily be mined by an enemy in time of conflict. To assure passage for its major naval combatants from both the Sea of Okhotsk and the Sea of Japan to the Pacific, the Soviet Union would have to secure the waters along the northern coast of Hokkaidō—at present defended only by small Japanese garrisons centered at Wakkanai. Forty kilometers from Wakkanai, major Soviet naval, air, and land forces are positioned, and given the increasing amphibious and airborne capabilities of the Soviet military, Wakkanai would be one of the first targets of attack in the event of a general conflict.

The other major waterway used by Soviet naval vessels to travel from the inland waters to the Pacific is the Tsushima Strait, between Japan and the Republic of Korea. Between 1971 and 1975 the Japanese reported that of the annual average of 283 transits made by Soviet naval vessels through the Sōya, Tsugaru, and Tsushima straits in that period, an annual average of 123 were made through the Tsushima Strait.[21] In time of major conflict, the Soviet Union would be compelled to attempt to gain control of that waterway as well. Moreover, in the event of a limited conflict on the Korean peninsula between the forces of communist North Korea and the noncommunist South, the Soviet Union might feel it necessary to intervene in order to protect its interests in the Tsushima Strait. A Soviet military force on the Korean peninsula would not only assure Soviet naval vessels free passage to the Pacific, it would be able to outflank Communist Chinese forces in Manchuria and would afford the USSR an appreciable advantage.

Aside from that, the very presence of United States forces in Japan and South Korea renders a Soviet buildup in East Asia a perfectly comprehensible necessity, given Moscow's goal of attaining overall military superiority vis-à-vis the West. In effect, the expansion of Soviet military power in East Asia cannot be reasonably interpreted simply as a response to Sino-Soviet tensions. The Soviet Union probably would have undertaken its force enhancements in East Asia even if relations between Peking and Moscow had remained amicable. The deployment of Soviet troops, and the emplacement of Soviet special forces, might have varied in terms of locale and structure, but the reinforcement and expansion probably would have taken place in any case.

The entire massive infrastructural development that has taken place in the East would have been necessary to supply Soviet naval and air capabilities to East Asia. The long oceanic supply routes from the Baltic and the Black seas to the Soviet Maritime Province and the surrounding territories are far too exposed to Western interdiction to allow the USSR to forgo strengthening its logistic capabilities in the Northeast. The strengthening of those capabilities would include increasing air defense assets, hardening critical command and control facilities, and dispatching service troops. In substance, it is hard to see how much different the Soviet buildup in East Asia might have been had there been no tensions between the People's Republic of China and the USSR.

Thus the Sino-Soviet conflict did not precipitate the Soviet buildup in East Asia, nor does mainland China "tie down" forces that would otherwise be deployed elsewhere. The Soviet forces in East Asia are there because Moscow believes those forces necessary to meet a variety of contingencies—only one of which is the potential threat from Communist China.

The Soviet Union and the Warsaw Pact nations probably have conventional military superiority over the North Atlantic Treaty Organization forces in central Europe[22] and substantial superiority over the forces of mainland China in East Asia;[23] they still retain 40 general-purpose divisions in reserve for contingencies.[24] In general, the principal disability suffered by the Soviet armed forces is their limited seaborne war-making capability. In a time of general conflict, one of the missions assigned to Soviet naval forces would be that of neutralizing the supply capabilities of the Western merchant fleet— inflicting disabling ship losses along the long sea-lanes of communication that the Western forces would have to maintain. To impose an unacceptable attrition rate on Western supply vessels, the Soviet Union would have to maintain a submarine force of appreciable size, as well as long-range, land-based aircraft, located in facilities that would allow easy and early access to supply routes. This requires the ready availability of bases, facilities, midsea bunkering, and anchorage in the waters of East Asia, as well as assured free passage through the choke points that confine the major naval assets of the Soviet Union in the Sea of Okhotsk and the Sea of Japan.[25]

The acquisition of Soviet access to facilities in Vietnam seems to be part of the program of naval force projection and submarine servicing in East Asia. The anchorage maintained in the Macclesfield Bank in the South China Sea seems to serve the same purpose, and the assignment of over half of its inventory of Tupolev Tu-26/30 Backfire bombers to the Far East Fleet apparently constitutes a supplement to that program.

The Backfire can travel at twice the speed of sound at high altitudes; furthermore, it can air-launch either of two sophisticated air-to-surface missiles that travel to their destinations at almost three times the speed of sound and that can reach surface targets within a range of about 800 kilometers.[26] Together with the large complement of attack submarines on station in East Asia, the assignment of Backfires to East Asia indicates a determination on the part of the Soviet Union to interdict the strategic supply lines of the West in the Pacific in the event of war.

It would be difficult to interpret the Soviet decision to supply its East Asian forces with this newest and most capable of long-range bombers as an effort to intimidate the mainland Chinese. The Soviet forces along the borders of mainland China hardly need such a force enhancement, for any conflict with Communist China would not require such a large number of sophisticated and expensive long-range aircraft. The performance of the Tu-26/30 argues for a long-range offensive role.

Communist China is not the sole object of Soviet military concern in East Asia. In the last analysis, Moscow must prepare for a confrontation with the United States and its allies. The most sophisticated Soviet forces in the East are configured for conflict with the West—not with mainland China. The major components of its naval and air forces would be largely unnecessary in the event of frontal conflict with the Communist Chinese. Soviet amphibious forces are probably designed for action against Japan, in an effort to secure free passage through the choke points off the Japanese home islands. Its submarines and long-range, land-based aircraft constitute threats to the West's long lines of supply and communication. Similarly, Soviet penetration into Southeast Asia is probably part of an effort to establish submarine and surface combatant servicing facilities there, rather than an attempt to "surround" Communist China.

Given the force levels available to the Soviet Union, Communist China, at best, poses little more than an inconvenience; it does not immobilize the Soviet Union in the region, nor does it seem to inhibit Soviet initiatives there. In fact, Moscow has acted more aggressively against Afghanistan than it has against any other country in the recent past—irrespective of the border that Afghanistan shares with the People's Republic of China. The Soviet Union has proceeded to reinforce its relationships with Vietnam, Cambodia, and Laos, even though mainland China has attacked Vietnam and has vociferously objected to the Vietnamese-dominated "Indochina confederation." And Moscow still anchors its naval vessels in the Macclesfield Bank, ignoring Peking's insistence that it is "sovereign Chinese territory."

The military forces of the PRC do not offer very much in terms of security to the nonsocialist nations of Northeast Asia. Even if mainland China made its foot-mobile infantry available for the defense of the nonsocialist nations of Northeast Asia against Soviet attack, their inability to utilize sophisticated weaponry, and their overall lack of military credibility, would make them dubious assets. More significantly, none of the nonsocialist nations of Northeast Asia would welcome a Communist Chinese presence on the ground. Given the decisional history and the ultimate intentions of the leadership in Peking, the intervention of Communist China in the defense of Northeast Asia would be almost as much of a threat to the nonsocialist nations of the subregion as would an attack by the Soviet Union itself.

The Republic of Korea and Japan have every reason to fear the increasing Soviet military strength in East Asia. The Soviet Union has steadfastly refused to discuss Japan's claims to the northern territories now occupied by the forces of the USSR. Moreover, the Soviet Union has insisted upon an exclusive 200-mile maritime economic zone surrounding its territories that severely restricts Japanese fishing in the Sea of Okhotsk and off the Kuril Islands. As of September 1976, a total of 1,500 Japanese fishing boats and almost 13,000 fishermen had been seized by Soviet vessels for "intruding" into the Soviet's self-proclaimed exclusive economic zone around the Kuril Islands, the Kamchatka peninsula, Sakhalin Island, and the four northern islands that Japan still insists constitute national territory. In fact, almost 75 percent of the Japanese vessels captured by the Soviet forces were removed from the waters surrounding the islands of Kunashir, Iturup, Habomai, and Shikotan, over which the Japanese government still claims sovereignty.

In all probability Moscow will continue to use its control over the Japanese northern territories to influence Tokyo's policies. Should the Sino-Japanese rapprochement take on features that the Soviet Union could interpret as threatening, there is little doubt that Moscow will put increasing pressure on Tokyo by more intensively policing the fishing in the northern waters off Hokkaidō. The Soviet Union is well aware that it now deploys a superior ground force, and that it probably enjoys air power advantage in the subregion. The increasing Japanese concern for national security is evidence that Japan is equally aware of that superiority.

For the Republic of Korea, the general situation is much more complicated and will be dealt with in more detail in Chapter 5. But it is clear that should the Democratic People's Republic of Korea in the North decide to embark on a military adventure in the South, either the Soviet Union or Communist China could find itself drawn into the conflict—each in pursuit of its own security and national interests. It is obvious that should the Soviet Union so choose, it could probably occupy the entire Korean peninsula.

If the leadership in the North should decide to attack the Republic of Korea for whatever reason, the Soviet Union might intervene in order to insulate the peninsula from Communist Chinese penetration. Should that eventuate, only the direct interposition of U.S. force might save South Korea from extinction.

Since both Communist China and the Soviet Union support the communist regime in the North, South Korea must depend on the guarantees provided by the United States for its national security. For the time being, both Peking and Moscow seem content to tolerate the present arrangements on the Korean peninsula, if only to ensure that the other obtains no advantage in any armed conflict. But the situation, as shall be argued in Chapter 5, is very volatile.

The intervention of the armed forces of Communist China in any likely conflict scenario could only compound the problems that attend the defense of Northeast Asia. As for the Republic of China on Taiwan and the islands still controlled from Taipei, the People's Republic of China—rather than the Soviet Union—constitutes a forbidding security threat. Thus the PRC reveals itself as being of major concern to the entire subregion, for the defense of Japan and the Republic of Korea turns in large part on the security of those territories.

3 | The Security Environment of the People's Republic of China

Ever since the "normalization" of relations between the United States and the People's Republic of China, the armed forces of Communist China have been the object of intense scrutiny. The apparent inspiration for normalization of diplomatic relations between the United States and Communist China—for over two decades the bitterest of opponents—was Washington's intention to reap "substantial benefit to the free world in terms of the strategic balance, the NATO–Warsaw Pact balance, and the balance in Asia." It was argued that "the flow of Western technology made possible by the shift in U.S.-Chinese relations may strengthen PRC military capabilities to the point where the Soviet Union is increasingly forced to pursue a conservative, defensive, and détente-oriented strategy."[1]

In the early 1970s, the United States government found itself faced by increasing public opposition to an East Asian policy that had involved the nation, to little apparent purpose, in one of the most protracted and costly wars in its history. Congressional opposition mounted against the massive flow of U.S. arms to foreign countries and the forward positioning of U.S. troops in Asia. In an environment where defense spending was increasingly restricted by popular and congressional resistance, President Richard Nixon seemed to imagine that formalizing diplomatic relations with the People's Republic of China in order to pursue "parallel strategic interests" might provide a "counterweight to the Soviet and Warsaw Pact buildup."[2] The idea of adding all the military assets of the PRC to the inventories of the United States and its allies, at so little cost, was greeted with considerable enthusiasm.[3]

By accommodating itself to Peking (so the argument proceeded), the United States could restore some semblance of equilibrium to the military balance, which at that time was disadvantageous to the Western powers. "While it may be possible to postulate a Soviet conquest of NATO and the strategic destruction of the United States in isolation," it was argued, "it is infinitely harder to postulate a Soviet 'conquest' of both the West and China in the 1980s or 1990s."[4] In one stroke, the United States would relieve itself of the threat of Soviet assault. Moreover, rapprochement with the West would afford the mainland Chinese similar security against Soviet attack, allowing the more "pragmatic" leadership in Peking to devote itself to the pursuit of "modernization." These circumstances—an increased sense of security and a preoccupation with the complex problems of economic development—would domesticate the PRC. The leadership in Peking would have little incentive to act aggressively against any of its neighbors.[5]

The unlikelihood that so much could be purchased at so little cost in the real world of international politics prompted a review of the capabilities of the Communist Chinese armed forces. If those forces were to constitute a significant supplement to the security of the West and provide a critical counterweight to the Soviet Union in the global military balance, they would have to possess some dramatic properties.

That mainland China operates the world's largest military establishment is not in dispute.[6] The People's Liberation Army (PLA), which includes all Communist Chinese arms and services, is composed of approximately 4.7 million men. The general-purpose forces are composed of about 190 main force divisions, divided into 40 army corps. These forces are made up of about 121 foot infantry divisions, 12 armored divisions, and 3 airborne divisions— supplemented by support elements. The main forces are augmented by "local" forces composed of 85 infantry divisions and 130 independent regiments. In addition to the main and local forces there is the common militia, which nominally includes anywhere from 50 to 200 million participants.

Of this mass, only the main force divisions are equipped to combat an enemy attack directly. The local forces are armed for local self-defense, and the militia possesses little more than small arms. The common militia actually provides manpower reserves and simple labor power for the field forces. In frontal conflict with the Soviet Union, it would be the main force units that would engage the enemy and would be expected to defend the territorial integrity of the homeland. Local defense units and the militia are too lightly armed to be expected to resist armored assault, massed artillery attacks, aircraft strikes, and chemical warfare initiatives.

The most distinguishing feature of the main force PLA is that it is foot mobile. Although the Communist Chinese have about 11,000 tanks in inventory (approximately the same number as utilized by the armed forces of the

United States, and about one-fourth the number in service with the Soviet military), the ratio of active personnel to available tanks leaves the PLA largely foot mobile. If the category "armored vehicles" is taken to include both tanks and the 3,500 armored personnel carriers the Communist Chinese can deploy, the ratio of personnel to armored vehicles in the PLA is about 240:1 compared with a Soviet ratio of personnel to armored vehicles of 20:1. In effect, much of the PLA has very limited strategic and tactical mobility.

The 20,000 field guns and rocket launchers (a relatively large inventory) and the 6,000 heavy mortars of the Communist Chinese army are almost all obsolescent. Almost all the towed artillery pieces are of 1950s vintage and are used almost exclusively for training purposes in the Warsaw Pact armies. Much the same is true of the truck-mobile rocket launchers. The BM-13 and the BM-14, the most common launchers in the PLA, are used for training exercises in modern Soviet-supplied armies. What becomes apparent is that the Communist Chinese forces conspicuously lack armored mobility and effective firepower in the field, both of which would be necessary should they be forced to contend with a modern military force.

These disabilities of the general forces are compounded by the fact that the air force of the PLA (the PLAAF), although large in absolute numbers (at least 5,300 combat aircraft), remains critically deficient in modern weapon platforms, modern weapon systems, and modern electronic warfare ancillaries. If confronted by any modern machines, it is doubtful that the PLAAF could contest tactical air control over the battlefield, much less obtain general air supremacy. Without even tactical air control, the foot soldiers of the PLA could expect only episodic air support. Hampered by a lack of armored mobility and by inadequate firepower in the field, the infantry units of the PLA would suffer grievously from the air strikes that certainly would be launched with relative impunity by any modern adversary.

On the seas, the Communist Chinese deploy the world's third largest navy, in terms of combatant units. None of these combatants, however, is larger than a destroyer, and most of them are coastal defense craft ranging from small gun, torpedo, and missile boats to frigates armed with surface-to-surface missiles. These surface combatants are supplemented by the world's third largest fleet of attack submarines. The approximately 100 attack boats in the navy of the PRC are conventionally powered, Chinese-constructed replicas of Soviet submarines of the 1950s. (There are about 80 *Romeo*- and 20 *Whisky*-class, diesel-powered boats in the inventory.) All the vessels of the PLA navy (PLAN) are of Soviet designs that are at least a generation old. The machine properties and capabilities of such vessels are well known to Soviet experts—and subject to relatively simple neutralization. Because the Soviet Union supplied the ship-to-ship missiles now in service on Communist Chinese vessels (the SS-N-2 Styx), there is little doubt that all Soviet naval vessels of any size are equipped with electronic countermeasures designed to foil them. And since all the submarines in service with the PLAN are of similar Soviet derivation, the naval command of the USSR is fully aware that they would be easy targets for antisubmarine warfare interdiction outside the hospitable shallow coastal waters of continental Asia.[7]

Other than the surface and subsurface combatants, there are approximately 800 shore-based aircraft assigned to the PLAN. They provide the air defense for the combat vessels of a fleet without shipboard antiaircraft capabilities. The force is composed of about 100 torpedo bombers, 50 light bombers, and about 600 fighter aircraft including mainland-built MiG-15s, MiG-17s, and MiG-19s. The PLAN is by and large a coastal defense force; its dependence on land-based, short-range fighter air cover ties it close to the shore.

Beyond these conventional forces available to Peking, there are strategic nuclear forces under the control of the Second Artillery, the nuclear missile arm of the PLA. By the early 1980s, the offensive nuclear weapons available to the PRC possessed a modest but growing potential.

The Second Artillery deploys about 50 CSS-1 *Tong Feng* medium-range ballistic missiles with an estimated range of 1,800 kilometers and an explosive impact of 15 kilotons. These are augmented by about 85 CSS-2 intermediate-range ballistic missiles with an estimated range of 2,500 kilometers and an impact of 1–3 megatons. Four intercontinental ballistic missiles with a range of approximately 7,000 kilometers and an impact of 1–3 megatons, coupled with a true intercontinental ballistic missile having an estimated range of 13,000 kilometers and an impact of 5–10 megatons, deployed in small but unknown numbers, make up the long-range strategic nuclear inventory of the PRC.

The PLA is believed to possess a stockpile of several hundred fission and fusion nuclear devices that are available for gravity drops by tactical fighter and bomber aircraft. The PLAAF has about 100 Tupelov Tu-16 Badger medium bombers in inventory, having an operational radius of about 3,000 kilometers, that could be used for nuclear weapons delivery.

In substance, then, the People's Republic of China is possessed of not negligible military capability. More to the point, however, is how effective its capability might be when confronted by that of the Soviet Union. The Soviet forces along the Communist Chinese border, although substandard in terms of combat readiness, are clearly superior to those of the PLA. Even though the manpower available to the PLA exceeds that available to the Soviet command, the armor, aircraft, artillery, and chemical warfare capabilities of the USSR are decisive when compared with those of Communist China.

At sea, the Soviet advantages are even more pronounced. As we have seen, the Soviet Far East Fleet deploys at least one aircraft carrier, 11 *Kresta-* and *Kara*-class missile cruisers, 25 destroyers including those of the *Kotlin* and

Krivak classes, 41 frigates, and about 700 other vessels, including about 125 submarines. All these combatants are equipped with state-of-the-art weaponry (including cruise and surface-skimming missiles under autopilot control with a range of approximately 55 kilometers).

Shaddock-type missiles, installed on *Kresta*-class cruisers, have a standoff range of about 320 kilometers, autopilot guidance, and active radar and/or infrared terminal homing properties. Nothing even remotely comparable is available in the PLAN. Without shipboard antiaircraft defenses, devoid of antisubmarine warfare capabilities, armed only with limited-range missile capabilities, and possessed of no electronic countermeasures to deflect anti-ship missile attack, the PLAN is hardly a match for the Soviet navy in East Asia. About 95 percent of the submarines in service with the PLAN, approximately 96 percent of its land-based strike aircraft, over 30 percent of its major surface vessels, almost all of its mine warfare vessels, and all of its fast attack craft, radar, and electronic systems, are of twenty-year-old Soviet design. They are not only obsolescent, they are open to Soviet neutralization since all of their properties are known to the PLAN's most threatening antagonist.

That Communist China could defend itself against the Soviet Union with a pre-emptive or retaliatory nuclear strike was a suggestion entertained for only a brief period during the euphoria that confused U.S. strategic judgment immediately after the normalization of diplomatic relations between the United States and mainland China. Given the targeting precision that Soviet nuclear weaponry is known to have attained, it is estimated that less than half the current Soviet inventory available in East Asia would be necessary to effectively destroy all "hard" targets, and critical "soft" targets, in Communist China. The hard targets would comprise substantially all PLA launch sites, including those burrowed into mountainsides. Communist Chinese hardening technology, designed to resist nuclear blast effects, is significantly behind that of the West but is particularly inferior to that of the Soviet Union. All PLA fixed silos have been hardened to about 600 pounds per square inch (psi) overpressure, as opposed to about 1,000 psi for those of the United States and 4,000 psi for those of the Soviet Union. Similar disabilities afflict other hardened targets housing the military command, control, and communications infrastructure. Should Peking contemplate any nuclear exchange with the Soviet Union, it would have to anticipate incalculable retaliation.

The Soviet Union could probably destroy not only the hardened targets exposed to its nuclear attack, but Peking could also expect its most important industrial centers, major railheads, communication hubs, and the 150 airfields capable of servicing jet aircraft to suffer similar devastation. More ominous still is the fact that should Peking decide, for whatever reason, to gamble on a pre-emptive nuclear strike against the Soviet Union, it would have to anticipate that such an attack might have negligible military effect. The PRC's nuclear deterrent system was established in the early 1960s, and all its delivery systems are liquid fueled. Liquid fuel is very difficult to store and deteriorates very rapidly. The guidance systems on such vehicles are equally sensitive in storage and require constant and proper maintenance. Given the shortfall in PLA skilled personnel and the time such delivery systems have been in storage, it is highly probably that errors and malfunctions would preclude effective launch of a large proportion of the Communist Chinese missiles. Those considerations, coupled with the fact that the PLA lacks testing experience and possesses few means of effective target acquisition, suggest that any missiles that might achieve launch probably would not reach their targets.

Although the PLA has a small but operational photointelligence capability, the inaccuracy of target data, the questionable target acquisition capabilities, and the primitive guidance properties of the delivery system do not afford Communist Chinese missiles much precision in terms of impact area. The "circular error probable" (cep) of Communist Chinese missiles is 4 kilometers (this means that only 50 percent of arriving warheads can be expected to fall within a target circle having a radius as large as 4 kilometers), making such strikes largely ineffective against any hardened Soviet targets. The cep of Soviet and U.S. missiles is 0.5 kilometers.

In general, the known history of liquid-fueled missiles strongly indicates that some number of those successfully launched would fail en route to their targets. Others would be destroyed by Soviet antiballistic missile defenses. Those that did impact would have little effect on hardened sites, and it is not at all certain that any would penetrate to a meaningful target—military or civilian.

In 1981, the PRC successfully orbited three experimental satellites in one launching, suggesting that the mainland Chinese have the potential for developing a solid-fuel-powered, multiple independent re-entry vehicle (MIRV) that could be employed with nuclear delivery systems. MIRVing its missiles might be a partial answer to the inaccuracy of PLA targeting, and solid-fuel propulsion would offset the problems of liquid-fuel power. Nonetheless, it will be some considerable time before the PLA can deploy MIRVed missiles in sufficient numbers to appreciably alter the present military balance along the Sino-Soviet border.

The smaller Communist Chinese nuclear devices, used for tactical strikes, are of equally dubious value for defense against any pre-emptive attack. Since the PLA would have significant targeting problems with strategic nuclear missiles, the precision of guidance systems would become increasingly critical as the size of the target and the size of the warhead diminished. Given their guidance problems, Communist Chinese tactical nuclear weapons could only be used with any effectiveness against massed troops and matériel, not hardened launch sites. But this would mean that conflict was imminent or in progress. If such were the case, then any Communist Chinese first use would initiate an all-out Soviet nuclear attack. The Soviet Union possesses such an overwhelming advantage in terms of numbers and delivery capabilities of strategic and tactical nuclear weaponry that any PLA recourse to their use would hardly be prudent.

Any attempt to air-deliver nuclear weapons would require that the obsolete aircraft of the PLAAF penetrate airspace defended by the most modern early warning and antiaircraft system in the world, as well as by some of the world's most advanced high-performance interceptor aircraft. The probable result would be the destruction of such a force before a significant Soviet target could be struck.

Because of its enormous superiority in early warning surveillance, electronic warfare capabilities, surface-to-air missilery, conventional air defense, and interceptor aircraft, the Soviet military would enjoy every advantage. The long lead time necessary for the launch of PLA liquid-fueled vehicles (the CSS-2 requires 48 hours of firing preparation before launch), as well as the doubtful targeting and low probability of delivery that would accompany an attack by the small number of devices available, would probably give the Soviet military ample lead time to devise effective countermeasures. The Soviet Union would then have every justification for destroying all Communist Chinese armed forces in the forward deployment areas, as well as all major strategic targets, without the political and diplomatic opprobrium that would attend Soviet first use.[8]

Given such an assessment, it is difficult to understand in what sense the nuclear military capability of the PRC serves either as a deterrent to Soviet aggressive behavior or as an asset in the strategic security calculations of the West. By 1980, even with its ballistic missile deployment in East Asia, the Soviet strategic strike capabilities threaten all the land-based nuclear weaponry of the West. The PLA does not pose a serious nuclear threat to the Soviet Union, and little of the Soviet nuclear potential is employed exclusively in covering Communist Chinese targets. In fact, the proportion of Soviet weapons needed to counter the Communist Chinese nuclear threat is smaller now than it was in the 1970s. By 1980, Soviet strategic nuclear delivery technology had improved with such rapidity that a counterforce strike against the nuclear weapons of the PLA would have involved only a negligible part of Soviet capabilities.

The U.S. suggestion, tendered at the time of the normalization of diplomatic relations between the PRC and the United States, that the strategic forces of the PLA could be rapidly improved to the point where they would have a disabling impact on Soviet strategy, is now recognized to have been totally unrealistic. The mainland Chinese may not be able to put together a survivable nuclear deterrent (not to speak of a first-strike-capable system) anytime during the present century.[9] The successful firing of a submarine-launched ballistic missile in 1982 suggests a more flexible Communist Chinese nuclear capability, but until there is series production of such platforms, the strategic situation will not have been appreciably altered.

The Communist Chinese strategic nuclear system requires massive upgrading to reduce malfunction to a minimum, an improvement in system accuracy in order to render its missiles point-target capable, and a set of passive and active defense measures that would contribute to overall survivability. Under any set of circumstances, satisfying these requirements would require a very long lead time because of the evident problem of keeping pace with an opposing system that is constantly evolving new and improved defensive and offensive capabilities. The PLA would ultimately have to solve the problem of the vulnerability of land-based systems, given the targeting capabilities of Soviet weaponry and the fact that the PRC does not yet have a substantial seaborne or subsea missile-launching capability.[10] To solve any of these problems, even granting the existence of mainland Chinese determination and available technological talent, would require substantial financial commitments that the PRC presently seems reluctant to make.

If such are the circumstances revealed by a consideration of the strategic nuclear capabilities of the PRC, an assessment of its non-nuclear conventional capabilities offers little more that might serve as grounds for optimism. There is no reason to believe that the Soviet Union contemplates an attack on Communist China, but it is equally clear that should such an attack be made, the vast armies of the PLA probably could not contain Soviet forces.

By 1980 the configuration of forces along the Sino-Soviet border provided the Soviet Union with a repertoire of military options that offered more than a reasonable chance of rapid success. Should the Soviet Union undertake an attack across the borders of the PRC, the open spaces and thinly populated stretches of Sinkiang and Inner Mongolia are optimum terrain for rapid armored and motorized infantry assaults—the standard Soviet mode of attack. Such a campaign would be supported by air strikes against strong points and air cover for attacking ground troops.

The communications system from central China to Sinkiang is very fragile; the major system of transport is a single rail connection that traverses the Kansu corridor. Sinkiang is a vast arid region ringed by mountains, and thus is similar in large measure to the desert reaches of the Middle East. The topography and the thin communications and transport infrastructure make the region susceptible to classic desert warfare maneuvers. Severance of the rail connection through the Kansu corridor would make regeneration of PLA ground forces extremely difficult for the Communist Chinese, and the Soviet employment of mobile armored vehicles and firepower, combined with its air supremacy, would make the entire region largely indefensible by the mainland Chinese.

Effective air defense of the Communist Chinese forces in the field is precluded by the fact that PLAAF aircraft, given their obsolescence and given the lack of skilled manpower in the Communist Chinese military, seem to suffer greater maintenance problems, and consequently have more downtime, than aircraft in other air services. The propulsion systems of the PLA MiGs, for example, require overhaul after only 100 hours of in-flight time, whereas the F-4s in inventory in Western air forces remain in operation without such major servicing for ten times as long. Moreover, supplies of repair parts for PLAAF aircraft are limited and their delivery is unreliable. Finally, the training of Communist Chinese pilots seems singularly inadequate; less than 100 annual flight hours per pilot (the norm) were scheduled as late as 1978.[11]

In a combat situation, the pilots of the PLAAF could expect only limited ground intelligence and control assistance—the Communist Chinese radar system is notoriously thin. There have been some suggestions of an attempt at upgrading, but for the time being the system appears to have a very limited capacity for detecting low-flying aircraft; thus Soviet attack aircraft making entry into Communist Chinese airspace under 5,000 feet would arrive on target virtually undetected. PLAAF pilots would have literally no early warning time. Once the aircraft did engage in combat, the lack of on-board electronic countermeasures to deflect Soviet air-to-air missile attacks, launched from outside the range of PLAAF guns, would rapidly decrease the numbers of aircraft available for the continued defense of the Communist Chinese homeland.[12]

Should any PLAAF aircraft that survived such encounters attempt to attack Soviet ground formations, they would have to contend with one of the most formidable antiaircraft defense systems of modern times. Surface-to-air missiles launched from SA-2, SA-6, and SA-9 sites would constitute grave threats to such attacking aircraft. The SA-6 Gainful surface-to-air missile was employed by the Egyptians in the Arab-Israeli War of 1973 and scored notable successes against the most experienced of Israeli air units. A fully mobile missile, equipped with sophisticated fire control features and in-flight guidance adjustment capability over the missile-borne semiactive homing system, the SA-6 has a 60-kilometer high altitude and a 30-kilometer low altitude range, and a high first-shot kill probability. Supplemented by the short-range SA-9 Gaskin and by about 10,000 radar-controlled antiaircraft weapons, the air defenses of any Soviet invasion force would be virtually impenetrable by the PLAAF. In the judgment of Western analysts, "the Chinese air force is likely to prove almost completely ineffective against any concerted air defense." Worse still, it is "unlikely that China's air force could successfully protect the PLA from attack and interdiction [from Soviet aircraft]."[13]

With assured air superiority along the entire northern borders of the People's Republic of China, the Soviet forces would exploit their advantages in armor and mobility. In 1980 Soviet forces enjoyed about a 3:1 superiority in tanks and a 10:1 superiority in armored fighting vehicles and personnel carriers. Calculation of qualitative superiority shows the differences to be even more pronounced.

As we have seen, the Soviet Union has deployed some of its most advanced armor along the Communist Chinese border. The T-64/T-72 and T-80 main battle tanks, protected with special laminate armor and armed with 125-mm smoothbore guns, outclass the best that the PLA can marshal in opposition. The PLA's main battle tank, the T-59, is a copy of an obsolescent Soviet T-54 that was supplied to the PRC by the USSR in the late 1950s and early 1960s. The T-59 is armed with a 100-mm gun, but it lacks the power traverse, stabilization of the main weapon, and infrared sighting devices that were standard on the original Soviet models. In an open field engagement, where first-hit capability is critical, such shortcomings would significantly reduce the survivability of this equipment.[14] In the open terrain characteristic of large expanses of Sinkiang and Inner Mongolia, such armor would have little chance against the technologically and numerically superior Soviet tanks. The Soviet T-72, for example, firing fin-stabilized, armor-piercing rounds, could easily breach the shielding of the PLA main battle tanks from standoff positions beyond the maximum range of the Communist Chinese on-board weapons.[15]

In the early 1980s there were reports of a new PRC main battle tank, the Type 69, appearing in service. The T-69 utilizes the same chassis and turret as the T-59 but has incorporated a weapons platform stabilizer, a 105-mm smoothbore main weapon, an automatic laser range finder, and an infrared night light, all of which are calculated to improve the combat effectiveness of PLA armor. It will be some considerable time before the PLA can replace the older T-59s with the more modern T-69s, and even then its armor will remain inferior quantitatively and qualitatively to Soviet tank formations. Given the continual improvement of Soviet inventory, the PRC's efforts, at best, will only marginally improve its position. Exposed to Soviet air strikes and attacks by antitank helicopter gunships, the armor of the PLA would suffer grievous attrition rates.

The difficulties the PLA would experience in attempting to contain Soviet armored thrusts would be compounded by the critical shortfall in modern antitank weaponry that afflicts Communist China's armed forces. The PLA inventory includes largely outdated and ineffective antitank grenade launchers and recoilless rifles, whose limited range and lethality preclude any significant defense against Soviet armor.

The Type 56 antitank grenade launcher, with which PLA units are amply supplied, has a maximum range of 160 yards. Soviet tank crews would have to be singularly inept to allow antitank teams to make so close an approach in open country. In cluttered terrain such weapons might have some impact, although the current series of Soviet main battle tanks are so heavily armored that it is doubtful that such weapons could inflict significant damage. The D-44 85-mm antitank gun and 75-mm recoilless rifle in service with the PLA are ineffective except at murderously short range, thus exposing antitank teams to heavy suppression fire. The shielding of the Soviet main battle tanks would probably frustrate them in any event.[16] There are some reports of a PRC copy of the Soviet Sagger antitank guided missiles having entered PLA service in 1978 or 1979, but they are apparently much more primitive than the Soviet original, and of dubious effectiveness.[17]

The PLA will have to rapidly enhance its antitank capabilities if it is to attempt to impede a Soviet armored invasion across the extended Sino-Soviet border. Even below the threshold of nuclear exchange, the Communist Chinese forces are outclassed by Soviet forces. Bereft of the hope of air support, outgunned and outmaneuvered by mobile forces, armed with obsolete weapons of minimal effectiveness, the foot soldiers of the PLA would be disadvantaged in any frontal engagement. Any attempt to employ the human wave attacks that proved so costly in Korea against an aggressor that can lay down about 5 million pounds of ordnance on a battlefield in 30 minutes would result in a grotesque casualty rate.

Any fall back to "people's war" tactics would be all but impossible given the relatively thin population concentrations in Sinkiang and Mongolia. Only in Manchuria might the irregular warfare of classical Maoist military doctrine make secure occupation more difficult. But the Japanese managed to pacify Manchuria in the late 1930s and early 1940s, and there is little reason to believe that the Soviet Union could not accomplish as much.

In 1945, the Soviet army overwhelmed the Japanese Kwantung army in Manchuria in a lightning armored attack that averaged a 50-kilometer daily advance. At that time, the Soviet Union transported a combat-ready force of about 750,000 troops across Siberia in about four months to launch an armored blitzkrieg in Manchuria. Today the USSR has vastly improved capabilities—and although it is evident that the effort would be burdensome, it seems equally clear that the transport, upgrading, maintenance, and resupply required for the campaign could be provided. The land, sea, and airlift capabilities of the Soviet military are sufficiently robust to ensure the victory of such a venture.

From whatever aspect one considers the land, air, and sea capabilities of the PRC in any threat environment involving the Soviet Union, its weaknesses are clear. All the armed services of the PLA suffer from obsolescence of matériel, weapon systems, and combat units. The infrastructure, in almost every respect, is inadequate to sustain modern warfare. The lack of skilled manpower makes maintenance, and research and development, extremely difficult.

Although the Soviet Union has a range of potentially successful military options, including strategic and tactical nuclear strikes against mainland China, the most plausible operations would probably include active support, at a variety of gradually escalating levels, of "national liberation" uprisings in Sinkiang, Inner Mongolia, and/or Manchuria. This might include anything from providing military supplies to insurgents, to allowing them sanctuary in Soviet territory, to staging a lightning armored invasion of the border regions to whatever depths chosen in support of their activities. Such support could be either punitive or designed to afford the Soviet Union a bargaining advantage with Peking and would not require the permanent occupation of Chinese territory.

In *The Coming Decline of the Chinese Empire*, Victor Louis, long identified as a publicist for the Kremlin, suggests just such a scenario. Louis insists that the outlying regions of the People's Republic of China, including the vast territories of Sinkiang, Inner Mongolia, and Manchuria, are today populated by those whose ancestors were conquered by the oppressive might of "feudal China." He anticipates their imminent uprising "against sinification and for their self-determination and independence." Hundreds of thousands of Uighurs, Kirghiz, and Kazaks have crossed the borders into Soviet Central Asia, according to Louis, there to receive military training that will equip them to "fight for independence" against a Communist Chinese regime more oppressive than any that preceded it.

A reasonably well-trained and adequately equipped guerrilla army of 60,000, Louis maintains, "should be quite enough to tie down . . . as many as 1.5 million Chinese troops. If we add to those 60,000 [who will cross over the border into the PRC from Soviet Asia] the hundreds of thousands of insurgents who are usually carried away by the wave of an uprising, it will be easy to imagine the scale of the new Vietnam that China is very likely to get into." The ultimate result, in Louis's judgment, would be the creation of an "entire chain of independent state entities" between the Soviet Union and a residual China vastly reduced in size and economic viability. A successful Soviet-supported national liberation struggle that detached Manchuria from Communist China would immediately reduce the PRC's electric power generation by half and cost it 70 percent of its iron ore and 30 percent of its coal deposits. A similar success in Sinkiang would reduce the total land surface of Communist China by 20 percent and remove substantial reserves of oil and coal.[18]

Such an enterprise would be far less hazardous and costly for the Soviet Union. Moscow's support of an indigenous liberation movement would conceivably generate little hostility among Third World nations and make it difficult for interested third parties to intervene. It would neutralize any Communist Chinese military threats on the Sino-Soviet border, surround the USSR with Soviet satellites, and reduce China to the status of a third-rate political power without the necessity of Soviet occupation.

The suggestion that the PRC might attempt a similar strategy—supporting anti-Soviet efforts on the part of minority populations within the Soviet Union —is implausible. Even though the Communist Chinese might exploit anti-Soviet sentiments and support local insurgents, Moscow would in all probability retaliate with localized armed incursions into the territory of the PRC. Given Moscow's clear advantages, such punitive raids would take a heavy toll of Communist Chinese forces. In effect, the USSR seems to have the option of exploiting national liberation insurgencies in the region whereas the PRC does not.

It has become increasingly obvious that the military capabilities of the People's Republic of China offer little that might serve as a counterweight to overall Soviet military advantages or that could contribute to the security of the West. In a general conflict the Soviet Union could probably withdraw troops from the Sino-Soviet border without fear of attack. There is every reason to believe that the Communist Chinese would not involve themselves in a general conflict unless directly subjected to armed aggression. Even if they were disposed to attack, there is no way that the PLA could long sustain operations outside the borders of continental China. The PLA military, in all its services (land, sea, and air), is manifestly and necessarily a defensive force when opposed by a modern army. Whatever offensive capabilities it possesses could not be used to any effect against the Soviet Union.

If mainland China were attacked by the Soviet Union, it is doubtful that the United States, or the West in general, would or could intervene effectively. Neither Western inventory nor Western productive plant could provide the mass of weaponry and supplies that would be required to rehabilitate PLA combat units mauled by superior Soviet forces. In fact, there is very little that the United States, or the West in general, could do to alter the military balance that obtains along the Sino-Soviet border. "What difference would hypothetical American military assistance to China make . . .? After the battle was joined practically none. But even with a long buildup and with opportunity for Chinese assimilation it is difficult to visualize U.S. assistance making a major difference in the military capabilities of the PRC relative to those of the Soviets."[19] Even if the West attempted to supply the sophisticated weapon systems that would alter the military balance, mainland China has neither the abundance of human skills nor the infrastructure that would allow it to absorb and employ such complex systems. Therefore, any military assistance afforded the Peking regime could not possibly be used effectively against the Soviet Union. The net result of such an assessment is that "the range of Soviet strategic options regarding China is sufficiently robust to demonstrate that Western nations would be ill-advised to put too many hopes in the deterrent capacity of the Chinese in the years ahead."[20]

There can be little doubt that Moscow would prefer not to have a truculent Communist China on its extended borders, but it is equally apparent that such a China would do nothing to force the Soviet Union "to pursue a conservative, defensive, and détente-oriented strategy." Soviet moves in Afghanistan and Vietnam provide sufficient evidence that the Kremlin has not found itself inhibited by the hypothetical "Chinese threat." The leadership in Peking has long been aware of Communist China's military ineffectiveness as a counterweight to the Soviet Union. In December 1978 Su Yu, then vice-minister of defense, lamented:

> If and when war breaks out between China and Russia, it will not be enough for us to depend on our own strength. If we work at renewing our strength it is only about twenty or thirty years that we will be able to see some results. At present, even though we have the atomic bomb, still, in comparison with our opponent it is . . . a mudball in comparison with a stone. Our mudball could annoy and humiliate Russia, but with her stone Russia could deliver our death blow.[21]

By 1980 Soviet force deployments in East Asia were sufficient to counter any Western or Chinese moves—with a strategic reserve that allowed Soviet initiatives in Southwest Asia and the Persian Gulf. In the military game between the two superpowers, the People's Republic of China is an "unarmed giant," incapable of undertaking initiatives against, or defending itself against those undertaken by, the Soviet Union.[22] It is unlikely that the PRC would come to the assistance of the West in any general conflict, and any effort by the West to come to its aid in the event of Soviet attack would undermine Western security without offsetting Communist China's disabilities.

On the other hand, none of this precludes the possibility that the leadership in Peking might employ its armed forces in adventures against one or another of the nations of Northeast Asia. Communist Chinese military capabilities are sufficient to sustain a number of initiatives against South Korea and/or Taiwan, and possibly Japan. These nations remain essential parts of the residual defense system in the West Pacific that has survived the retrenchment that followed the Nixon redirection of U.S. security policies in East Asia.

4 | The Security of Japan

Japan, not China, should be the focal point of American policy
toward Asia.

Donald C. Hellman,
"Japan and North East Asia," in Myers, ed.,
A U.S. Foreign Policy for Asia.

The Americans presumably recognize that Japan's industrial
potential is a major asset to the democracies as a whole. A drastic
change in Japan's industrial-economic system would lead to a
gradual collapse of the internal structure of many Pacific nations
whose economies are closely interwoven with those of Japan and the
United States. If, assuming the worst, Japan were coerced to change
its system, the impact would be global. . . . Finally, Japan is
geographically situated at critical choking points vis-à-vis the Soviet
Pacific Fleet whose unrestrained expansion might destabilize the
balance of power in the Pacific.

Makoto Mamoi,
"Alternative Strategies for the Defense of Japan,"
in Weinstein, ed., *U.S.-Japan Relations*
and the Security of East Asia.

Concern for Japan's security has evolved largely in response to changes originating in the international arena. Japan's security policies have been essentially reactive—initially accommodating U.S. initiatives, and subsequently responding to external changes in its own security environment.

At the close of the Second World War, the United States imposed a constitution on defeated Japan that compelled that nation to abjure warfare as an instrument of national policy. Article IX of the imposed constitution affirmed that "the Japanese people forever renounce war as a sovereign right. . ." and furthermore committed Japan to "nevermore maintain" land, sea, or air forces.[1]

The Korean War, which drew off U.S. forces from the Japanese homeland and hardened the lines of conflict during the period of the cold war, prompted the United States to urge "defensive" rearmament of Japan. Beginning with formation of the police security forces, designed to maintain domestic order, and the subsequent creation of a nucleus of general forces and specialized maritime and air contingents for national defense, Japan gradually reconstructed its military capabilities and established the Self-Defense Forces (SDF).

The reconstruction of the Japanese national SDF, however, was constrained by several important considerations. Whatever weapon systems those forces were to deploy, they would have to qualify, in some sense, as being "defensive," rather than having manifest "war potential," in order not to violate the renunciation of war strictures of Article IX of the postwar Japanese Constitution. Since there is no generally accepted definition of what might constitute "war potential," the suggested acquisition of any weapon system has invariably aroused protracted and acrimonious discussion among the Japanese.

In the early 1950s, when Japan's SDF lacked jet aircraft, for example, it was because such systems were considered instances of "war potential." By 1982, however, the Japanese Air Self-Defense Force (ASDF) had deployed F-4 Phantoms and F-15 Eagles—jet aircraft possessed of impressive range and payload capability—and they are considered solely defensive. On the other hand, aircraft carriers and long-range attack submarines remain proscribed as systems that constitute "war potential."[2] In 1969 the then director general of the Japanese Defense Agency, Yasuhiro Nakasone, announced the Fourth Defense Program, which committed Japan to the construction of two 8,000-ton helicopter cruisers for the Maritime Self-Defense Force (MSDF). Their construction was deleted from the program in the very first stage of review, however, on the grounds of their "war potential."

After Japan promulgated its Defense Agency Establishment and Self-Defense Forces Laws in 1954, weapons procurement should have been a function of the military missions assigned to the newly created military forces. But because the responsibilities of the Japanese SDF have never been made clear, a great deal of confusion continues to surround the acquisition of weapon systems.

Thus although the general public now supports the continued existence of the SDF, many Japanese still conceive of the tasks of those forces largely in terms of disaster relief and domestic public service rather than as providing military defense against external attack. The fact is that in 1975, about one-quarter of the Japanese polled indicated that they were not prepared to resist (other than passively) an enemy invasion of the Japanese home islands. If a large minority of the Japanese public still regards active resistance to external attack as either inappropriate or ill-advised, it is not difficult to understand why Japan's military leaders lack clear direction and why the SDF do not have a set of reasonably specific functions.

The MSDF has one of the most modern collections of antisubmarine-capable convoy escort destroyers in the West Pacific—but it can deploy neither the air cover assets nor the open-water replenishment vessels that would make such a force serviceable outside the immediate confines of the Japanese home islands. The particular function of Japan's naval force remains uncertain. The MSDF is clearly inadequate to defend the long sea-lanes of communication that sustain the economic life of Japan, and given its limited antiship missile capability, whether it could defend the Japanese coast from a determined amphibious invasion is doubtful. Similar kinds of problems confront the other Japanese armed services.

In effect, there is no determinate role for the armed forces of Japan because there is no national consensus concerning Japan's overall security policy. The gradual expansion of Japan's military capabilities has not been governed by a coherent defense program. In 1981–82, the SDF included about 250,000 men under arms, divided among three services: the Ground Self-Defense Force (GSDF), the MSDF, and the ASDF.

The general-purpose forces of the GSDF are composed of about 12 infantry divisions and one armored division—supported by engineer, quartermaster, demolition, special service, artillery, and antiaircraft units. There are about 1,000 heavy, medium, and light tanks and about 650 armored fighting vehicles in the inventory of the GSDF. Given the sophisticated rail and road system of Japan, such forces enjoy optimal mobility.

Japan's MSDF is composed of 14 submarines, 34 destroyers, 16 frigates, and about 86 lesser craft—the largest component of which consists of 42 mine warfare vessels. Given its relative dearth of on-board air defense weapon systems and the absence of air cover potential and antimissile electronic countermeasures, as well as its limited surface-to-surface missile capability, the Japanese MSDF has no more than modest coastal defense capability.

The ASDF counts 44,000 men in its ranks and deploys about 350 combat aircraft in 6 combat air wings, one composite air division, and a reconnaisance squadron. Most of the first-line combat aircraft are F-4 Phantoms, but they are being supplemented by the most advanced air superiority aircraft in the inventory of the U.S. Air Force: the McDonnell Douglas F-15 Eagle.

The Japanese SDF constitute an organizationally sound, compact, modern, and superbly maintained defense system. They are financed by a budget that is at least the equivalent of about 1 percent of Japan's gross national product, which is, in absolute terms, the seventh largest military budget in the world. The GSDF, composed of 180,000 men, about 1,000 tanks, and 350 aircraft, possesses greater firepower than did the entire Japanese Imperial Army of the

Second World War. The combat aircraft of the GSDF, combined with those of the ASDF and the MSDF, provide Japan with the world's fourth-largest air force—deploying about 1,400 combat machines.[3] Although Japan has a substantial defensive capability, what it does not have is a security policy to guide military planners and define the missions to be discharged by the forces available.

That Japan has failed to evolve a national defense and security policy is the consequence of a number of factors that together have produced a pervasive apathy with regard to planning for national defense. In the first place, since 1950 Japan's security has been the responsibility, by and large, of the United States. The Japan-U.S. security treaty that was concluded in 1951 contained an explicit commitment by the United States to "ensure the peace and safety" of Japan. The presence of U.S. forces on the ground in Okinawa and U.S. naval vessels off bases such as Sasebo and Yokosuka, conjoined with U.S. nuclear potential, have since provided the deterrent threat that has assured the safety of the Japanese home islands. Second, the horrors of the Second World War have left the Japanese with a positive dread of the consequences of armed conflict; they have been content to leave international power politics to others. The Japanese still choose to conceive of their nation as a "cultural state," divested of the attributes of a "war making state,"[4] and assume that their nonaggressive behavior will insulate them from external attack. Thus, most Japanese devote precious little time to reflections about their nation's security. This indisposition is reinforced by the knowledge that Japan has not been the victim of unprovoked aggression since the thirteenth century.[5]

More significant, perhaps, is the fact that it has become very difficult to imagine how Japan, employing only its own resources, might adequately defend itself against any modern aggressor because Japan suffers from a number of very serious geostrategic disabilities, the most fundamental of which is that the home islands possess no strategic depth. With a land mass slightly smaller than the state of Montana, and a configuration that determines that no point in Japan is more than 75 miles from the coast, Japan is exposed to assault from every point of the compass. Japan's dense population is heavily concentrated around Tokyo and the Osaka-Kōbe prefectures. (In 1975 over 50 percent of the entire Japanese population was concentrated in those two locales.) The bulk of Japan's industries, infrastructures, and life-support facilities are similarly localized in those two regions. The entire nation is a mammoth precision mechanism—a sensitive network of structures. Any attack, even a conventional assault below the nuclear threshold, could have a devastating effect on the whole.

National paralysis would be the probable and almost immediate consequence of precision air strikes against the Japanese home islands by any reasonable sophisticated air force. Precision attacks on the power grids that sustain the densely populated urban conglomerate, or on the rail and road infrastructure, for example, would disrupt the entire life of the nation to a degree that would threaten its survival. Selective conventional air attacks could sever the complex and sensitive network of delicate life-support structures and thus would effectively cripple the entire political community.

Much of Japanese territory is within range of Soviet aircraft. From their bases in the Soviet Maritime Province, MiG-21s and Il-28s could undertake attacks on Hokkaidō and the coast of northern Honshu. The entire Japanese archipelago is within range of the Tu-16s in Soviet inventory, not to mention the Backfire bombers and the medium-range ballistic missiles that are operational in the Soviet East. Soviet naval vessels offshore could target every major urban and industrial center in Japan for air-launched cruise missile attack.

This vulnerability is compounded by the fact that Japan possesses scant, if any, strategic reserves. Any conflict that was protracted beyond a few weeks would cause shortfalls in almost every arms, spare parts, fuel, and replenishment category.

Any effort to construct an "autonomous" conventional defense of its home islands would exact an incredible financial and human capital toll from the Japanese. In such an eventuality, Japan would require, for example, an early warning radar and over-the-horizon detection system against air attack that would, at best, afford the ASDF twenty minues lead time to prepare an adequate defense. The enormous expense required for the construction of such a system would purchase only negligible advantage. Interdiction of any such attack, launched by a modern air force, would require a much larger interceptor force, and a much more elaborate antiaircraft system, than is currently being deployed.

Survival beyond the first attack would require a sufficiently large stockpile of strategic matériel to ensure continuation of response capabilities during the first postattack period, and this stockpile would itself require storage capacity that is in remarkably short supply in Japan. To sustain its civilian population and its military capabilities over any extended period, Japan would have to provide for the security of its sea-lanes of communication, which are now traversed by a merchant fleet that is the largest in the world. Their defense would require a navy possessing blue-water endurance capabilities and composed of far more combatants than Japan would be able to put together (at anything less than disabling cost) in the twentieth century.

In effect, for the foreseeable future, Japan will not be able to engage in any war without the massive and immediate support of a major military power. Since the 1950s Japan, lacking strategic depth and denied the right and the opportunities of forward defense, has been compelled to depend upon the deterrent capabilities of the United States to ensure its defense against external attack.

Japan's best defense is to avoid armed conflict entirely, and that defense is based on the threat of armed intervention by the United States should Tokyo find itself subject to aggression. Unfortunately, the credibility of the United States as the guarantor of Japan's security was allowed to erode considerably during the 1970s. That erosion began with the announcement of the Nixon Doctrine in 1969, signaling Washington's general disposition to partially disengage its military forces from East Asia. The rapid contraction of popular support for U.S. involvement in military activities in Southeast Asia, combined with increased congressional resistance to the Nixon administration's defense policies, compelled President Richard Nixon to undertake an alteration of the established U.S. policy of "containment of the expansion of communism in Asia."

Under the Nixon Doctrine the United States reduced the forward deployment of U.S. ground forces in East Asia, while retaining a substantial air and naval presence in the region. The immediate defense of noncommunist Asia was assigned to the Asians themselves; the United States was prepared to support their efforts with the transfer of arms and the assurance of collateral support.

Whatever the intentions of the Nixon Doctrine, one of its major consequences was the perception, among Asians, of a weakening U.S. resolve to defend the integrity of East Asia. The United States was understood to have embarked upon a "withdrawal" from the troubled West Pacific. This perception (whether correct or incorrect) was reinforced by a series of "shocks" to which noncommunist Asians were subjected by the Nixon and subsequent administrations.

However much U.S. behaviors may have eroded the confidence of the Japanese people and public officials in Washington's determination to defend the peace and integrity of Japan, Tokyo has no other credible option but to remain within the U.S. security system. Even the leader of the Japanese Socialist Party, whose officials allude regularly to an "unarmed and neutral" Japan that will one day "abrogate the U.S.-Japan security treaty," has felt compelled to declare that "for the Japanese people, life without the United States is inconceivable."[6] The People's Republic of China, for example, can offer little that might serve as a credible deterrence against an attack on Japan by any major power. The only real alternative to dependence on the United States as a security partner is dependence on the Soviet Union, and that would require a massive change in Japan's external international relations, at the cost of revisions in Tokyo's critical trade and investment policies.

Furthermore, any suggestion of such a change would necessitate a radical disengagement of the United States from Northeast Asia and probably from much of the West Pacific—to the detriment of its economic and strategic interests. The United States is deeply involved in the economy of the Western Pacific Basin; furthermore, basing facilities in Japan will be necessary if U.S. armed forces are to contain Soviet ground forces along the Asian rimland in the event of a general conflict. Those bases will also be required if U.S. forces are to close the Japanese choke points in order to confine Soviet naval forces in the inland waters of the seas within the archipelagic barrier that stretches from the northern Japanese islands to Indonesia.

The fact that the United States has so much invested in its security relationship with the Japanese did not stop Richard Nixon from announcing his plans to visit Peking in the hope of achieving a rapprochement with the PRC without having first discussed the entire issue with the Japanese. Moreover, Nixon's announcement was followed by the first suggestions that the United States was planning to withdraw its ground forces from the Korean peninsula. Because any rapprochement with the People's Republic of China would probably involve a termination of or a significant weakening of the defense relationship between the United States and the Republic of China on Taiwan, Tokyo was suddenly faced with the prospect of the withdrawal of U.S. military and security support from both Japanese flanks—the Korean peninsula and Taiwan.

For the remaining decades of the present century, the defense of Japan will involve a credible nuclear deterrence provided by the United States, and will require the ability to undertake a conventional sea denial strategy with a reasonable expectation of success. For a sea denial strategy to enjoy that expectation of success requires the security of the Korean peninsula and the island of Taiwan. Why that should be so is not difficult to understand.

The possibility that the Japanese home islands will be the direct object of military aggression outside the context of a general conflict is very remote. Although the Soviet Union has the capability, it is doubtful that it would have, under any foreseeable circumstances, the motives for such an adventure. Even if the motives should materialize, the U.S. conventional and nuclear deterrent remains sufficiently credible to make such an isolated enterprise extremely hazardous.[7]

In any general conflict that did not immediately escalate to a nuclear exchange, Japan would have to prepare for a conventional defense. That defense would necessarily involve an attempt to bottle up the Soviet Pacific Fleet in the inland seas. Conversely, the Japanese could expect an almost immediate effort by the Soviet Union to secure at least two of the three major waterways that allow egress from the inland seas to the open Pacific.

Unless the demands of the general conflict drew off U.S. forces, they would immediately be transported to northern Hokkaidō to assure control of the

Sōya Strait, and a friendly South Korea would ensure a U.S. military presence on both shores of the Tsushima Strait. Once the shores of the straits were secured, transit by Soviet submarines could be impeded by sophisticated sonar surveillance, and the shallow waters of the straits could be easily mined.[8] Soviet surface ships, confined to the narrow passages of the straits while attempting to make transit, would find themselves at grave risk. Control of these waterways would significantly reduce Soviet naval activities in the Pacific, minimize the threats to Japanese sea-lanes of communication, and limit the damage to the home islands. Until well into the 1990s, neither Japan nor the United States will have enough naval assets in the West Pacific to provide both coastal defense and convoy protection for the large numbers of merchant ships that would be required to sustain the Japanese islands for the duration of the conflict. Japan's continued participation in the conflict and its ultimate defense would depend on the continued integrity of its vital trade connections with the international community.[9]

Even if most of the Soviet navy were confined to the inland waters as a result of U.S. and Japanese control of the major choke points in the Tsushima and Sōya straits, Soviet naval forces operating out of Vietnamese bases and bunkered at midsea anchorages like the Macclesfield Bank would still constitute a threat to sea passage. Facilities on Taiwan would be essential to neutralization of that threat. Even before the Soviet threat fully materialized, the Japanese were aware of the importance of Taiwan in the defense of Japan. As early as 1969, Prime Minister Eisaku Satō expressed Japan's concern for the integrity of both South Korea *and* Taiwan, viewing both nations as critical to the defense and security of Japan.[10] In 1972 Foreign Minister Masayoshi Ōhira reaffirmed that concern and indicated that there was every reason to believe that Japan would remain preoccupied with the independence and pro-Western alignment of both for the foreseeable future.[11]

Defense of the Tsushima Strait, the major waterway employed by the Soviet Pacific Fleet to exit the inland waters, is notably enhanced by the presence of anti-Soviet forces on both shores. To that extent, an anti-Soviet South Korea is crucial in the defense of Japan. Tokyo's security interests require that the situation on the Korean peninsula not be altered by military means to the advantage of the North and that the portions of the peninsula essential to securing the Tsushima Strait retain a U.S. military presence.

That Tokyo should insist on continued United States support for Seoul as an essential guarantee of Japan's security is thus easily understood.[12] Japan's security in any conventional conflict will depend largely on the control of the critical water passages out of the inland seas—and a friendly South Korea is vital to obtaining and maintaining that control.[13] Taiwan is equally important to the defense of Japan, for it occupies crucial space along the major sea-lanes to Japan. As has been indicated, the bulk of Japan's sea traffic passes within the immediate range of support or interdiction forces on Taiwan. The Bashi Channel and the Taiwan Strait are utilized by much of the sea traffic from Europe and the Persian Gulf to Japan. In a general conventional conflict, access to the basing facilities on Taiwan could be of substantial importance in defending the trade routes to Japan.

The U.S. withdrawal from Vietnam and its apparent ambivalence concerning the security of both the Republic of Korea and the Republic of China on Taiwan were interpreted by many Japanese as evidence of a declining U.S. interest in the security and defense of Japan.[14] Without the active or passive support of South Korea and Taiwan, the defense of the seas around the Japanese home islands, as well as Japan's extended trade routes, would become all but impossible.[15] Anti-Soviet forces on both shores of the Tsushima Strait would be essential to closing that waterway to Soviet combatants, and the facilities on Taiwan would be critical to the defense of the sealanes to the south and east.[16]

When the United States embarked on its policy of rapprochement with the People's Republic of China, Japan was compelled by domestic and international pressure to undertake a similar policy at the expense of its relations with the Republic of China on Taiwan. Nonetheless, Tokyo has proceeded toward normalization of relations with Peking with considerable caution and dexterity. In order to continue the gradual rapprochement with Peking yet not sacrifice its economic and security interests, Tokyo has agreed to recognize mainland China as the seat of the "sole legal government of China" while not acknowledging the Communist Chinese claim to sovereignty over Taiwan. Tokyo's explicit policy has remained one of "avoiding commitment as to Japan's legal position on the status of Taiwan."[17]

The reasons for the general Japanese reluctance to accede to Peking's claims to sovereignty over Taiwan are not difficult to appreciate. Even if Peking were to assure Japan a continuance of its profitable trade and investment relations with Taiwan (a not unlikely prospect), should Taiwan devolve into an "autonomous province" of Communist China, Tokyo would have little assurance that, in any general conflict in the Pacific, the facilities on Taiwan would be made available to the United States for the defense of Japan's vital sea-lanes.

Should mainland China gain control over Taiwan by whatever means, the United States and its allies would, in all probability, lose access to the basing facilities on Taiwan. There is every reason to believe that in any conflict between the Soviet Union and the United States, the People's Republic of China, if given the option, would choose to remain neutral (unless it were directly subjected to military aggression)—opting to "sit on the hillside and watch the tigers fight." The authorities in Peking are fully aware that mainland

China could only suffer grievous damage in any such conflict because its military forces are inadequate to defend its national integrity.

Should the United States be deprived of access to the basing facilities on Taiwan, the scant resources of the U.S. Seventh Fleet and the Japanese SDF would be further diluted, rendering more difficult the attempt of these forces to maintain surveillance and convoy defense along the trade routes between U.S. bases in the Philippines and in the Ryukyu archipelagic chain. Air cover for the exposed routes would have to be provided by the few aircraft carriers that would be operational in the West Pacific, rather than by the land-based aircraft on Taiwan.

The Republic of China on Taiwan, irrespective of its "derecognition" by both the United States and Japan, has made it quite clear that in any contest between the United States and any combination of communist powers, it would cast its lot with the United States and Japan. Its not inconsequential military forces as well as its air and naval bases would thus be available to those two nations. Japan has every reason to appreciate the significance of this kind of commitment; its survival in any general conflict in the Pacific might very well depend upon it.[18]

The Republic of China on Taiwan maintains excellent air base facilities at Ching Chuan Kang and Tainan. During the Vietnam War, a wing of C-130 transport, and KC-135 tanker, aircraft was stationed at Ching Chuan Kang and provided tactical airlift support for U.S. forces and refueling facilities for B-52 bombers carrying out missions in Southeast Asia. The 405th Fighter Wing of the Thirteenth Air Force was stationed in Tainan for a considerable time, and the repair and refurbishing facilities there remain excellent.

Antisubmarine patrol and fighter support aircraft based on Taiwan would materially enhance the defense capabilities of U.S. forces in the West Pacific. Combined with access to the ship repair and submarine servicing facilities in the major ports of Taiwan, such enhancements would significantly increase the range and endurance of the limited U.S. naval forces in the entire theater and would improve Japan's ability to survive the first high rate of attrition of its merchant ships that is to be expected during the initial phase of a general conventional conflict.

By 1980, about 2,000 vessels were arriving in Japan's ports each month. During the first phase of a general conflict, this number would be markedly reduced, both through attrition and as a result of refusal by carriers to enter the war zone. Japan has stockpiled some strategic materials that would last for approximately 45 to 90 days of consumption, and efforts are being made to increase reserve oil stocks so they will last at least 180 days. With some enhancement of storage space, resupply by the United States, and a reduction of nonessential production, the Japanese economy could conceivably continue to function reasonably well for about 4 to 6 months under wartime constraints. Thereafter, industrial output would rapidly decrease unless sea traffic could be substantially restored by an adequate defense of the sea-lanes. This would involve both the Japanese MSDF and the U.S. Navy, utilizing the basing facilities available along the entire exposed length of Japan's sea-lanes.

All this considered, it becomes perfectly obvious why, when Japan was preparing to sever diplomatic relations with the Republic of China on Taiwan in 1972, Taipei's ambassador was assured that the "Taiwan clause," contained in the Satō-Nixon communiqué of 1969, remained valid. Foreign Minister Takeo Fukuda insisted that "the maintenance of peace and security in the Taiwan area was . . . a most important factor for the security of Japan."[19]

Thus while Japan has pursued its "normalization" of relations with the communist government in Peking, it has retained its concern for the security of Taiwan, not only because of its profitable trade and investment relations with that island, but because Taiwan "occupies a strategic position on the routes to the south and the southwest"[20] that would be vital to Japan's security and survival. Because of its economic, ideological, political, and diplomatic interests, the government of the Republic of China on Taiwan is inextricably locked into an anti-Soviet posture, and its active support of Japan and the United States in any conflict in the West Pacific is all but assured. Whereas the communist authorities in Peking have every reason to avoid involvement in any conflict short of military attack, the authorities in Taipei can expect only to suffer by pursuing neutrality. The domination of the West Pacific by the Soviet Union or Communist China would jeopardize the future of the Republic of China on Taiwan. Its survival is irrefutably dependent upon the survival and vitality of the United States and Japan.

Like the Republic of Korea, the Republic of China on Taiwan is a secure defense partner. With the assurance of their support, Japan and the United States can significantly increase their capability to confine most of the Soviet Pacific Fleet to its home waters and materially improve their ability to neutralize those elements that do escape to the open Pacific. Japan, the Republic of Korea, and the Republic of China on Taiwan thus constitute a security triangle of considerable significance in the defense of the West Pacific and, specifically, the security of Japan.

What emerges from this assessment is the outline of a reasonably coherent security policy for the defense of Northeast Asia. It is evident that the immediate threat to the region emanates (and will emanate for the foreseeable future) from the Soviet Union. The military forces marshaled by the Soviet Union are primarily directed not against the People's Republic of China, which poses little serious threat, but against the forces of the United States and its allies.

The threat that those forces pose remains essentially conventional in nature. Because the major military powers fully realize that nuclear conflict would result in universal devastation, recourse to nuclear exhange is most unlikely. As a consequence, the United States and its allies must prepare for non-nuclear contingencies—including limited conflict below the level of nuclear exchange.[21] To ensure that any potential violence is either averted or restricted to the non-nuclear level, the United States will have to undertake a significant reallocation of its deterrent capabilities to locales where they can effectively threaten vital Soviet interests in East Asia.

Soviet capabilities in East Asia are localized in three sites: Petropavlovsk-Kamchatski on the Kamchatka peninsula, Khabarovsk on the Sino-Soviet border, and Yakutsk in the interior of eastern Siberia. The positioning of strategic bombers and missiles in the western Aleutian Islands, the stationing of amphibious forces in Alaska, and the preparation of an Arctic and sub-Arctic military capability by the United States would pose a credible threat to Petropavlovsk-Kamchatski and a concomitant threat to the rest of eastern Siberia.[22]

Petropavlovsk-Kamchatski is the only Soviet naval facility that opens directly on the Pacific Ocean. Soviet submarines based there have an unobstructed passageway to the major Pacific shipping lanes. Although they are snowbound from December to April, the naval vessels of the Soviet fleet can make their way from port with the assistance of icebreakers at any time of the year.

Petropavlovsk-Kamchatski is protected by four naval air stations and a newly constructed major air base. It is supplied by a major highway leading to Ust-Bolsheretsk and a seaport facing the Sea of Okhotsk, but the bulk supplies required for sustained conflict have to be transported by sea. With the report of new Soviet antiaircraft and antiship missile systems having been emplaced around the naval base by the early 1980s, it is clear that the Soviet command is acutely aware of the logistical fragility of its military capabilities in East Asia.[23] Although smaller submarine and support bases have been built at Buroton Bay on Shimushir Island in the Kuril chain, the entire subregion remains vulnerable to air strikes and the sea-lanes remain open to interdiction by missile attacks and mines.[24]

The most immediate requirement for a credible anti-Soviet deterrence strategy in the Northwest Pacific is the re-establishment of a permanent naval, air, and missile attack capability in Aleutian and Alaskan waters strong enough to jeopardize the extended Soviet positions in eastern Siberia and on the Kamchatka peninsula.[25] At the same time, Japan should enhance its tactical naval and air capabilities in the region. The obvious obligations of the Japanese SDF would be the timely mining and blockade of the Tsushima,

Tsugaru, and Sōya straits and the provision of an air defense capability that could inflict initial prohibitive losses on incoming Soviet tactical fighters and bombers entering the surrounding Japanese airspace.

At the United States–Japan Security Conference in Hawaii in June 1981, the U.S. delegation provided an outline of a force structure to serve these purposes that would include an increase in the number of destroyers in the Japanese MSDF from 34 to approximately 60. The number of submarines would increase from 14 to approximately 25. The major shortfall in Japanese capabilities is the relatively limited active mine warfare potential. Although the MSDF has a large and well-maintained fleet of minesweeping platforms, such vessels make relatively inefficient minelayers—their limited deck and storage space restricts their effectiveness. The Japanese have only one *Souya*-class minesweeper support ship in service that can carry and deploy 200 buoyant mines. The most immediate alternative available is the utilization of aircraft for the airdrop of mines.

In this latter regard the Japanese have already planned for an interim procurement of 40 Lockheed P-3 Orion aircraft, 3 to be directly imported. Some will be assembled in Japan from knockdown kits and some will be built under license by Kawasaki Heavy Industries. The United States has recommended that the Japanese ultimately acquire 125 of these aircraft, which could serve both a minelaying and an antisubmarine warfare function. This, in turn, would necessitate the provision of a secure airspace within which the antisubmarine and minelaying P-3s could operate. To that end the U.S. recommendations have been for the acquisition by the Japanese of approximately 350 high-performance interceptors—primarily F-15 Eagles—to augment the strength of the ASDF. The F-15, with a maximum combat radius of 1,600 miles, an air speed of Mach 2.5, and a climb rate superior to that of the Soviet MiG-25 Foxbat, is a most formidable combat aircraft. As a fighter interceptor, it mounts the General Electric M61A1 Vulcan 20-mm cannon that fires at variable rates of 4,000 to 6,000 rounds per minute. This armament is supplemented by 4 of each of the latest AIM-9L infrared homing Sidewinder and AIM-7F Sparrow air-to-air missiles, both of which possess a high first round kill capability. The fire control radar of the F-15 provides a target detection range of more than 100 miles and can target enemy aircraft in cluttered environments when the target is no more than 50 feet off the ground. For a nation like Japan that has only limited low-level radar surveillance, such aircraft are necessary as weapon platforms if a credible defense is to be mounted against low-flying intruders.

The F-15 is thus not only an air defense supplement for the protection of minelaying P-3s as well as of the home islands, it is an important first-line defense against Soviet Backfire bombers, whose high speed, ordnance-carrying properties, and standoff missile-launch capabilities constitute a serious threat not only to the Japanese home islands, but to the sea-lanes in the West Pacific. Basing F-15s in Korea and Japan, and potentially in Taiwan, affords the United States and its allies an early interception force enhancement in the reactive defense of Northeast Asia that would be necessary in the event of a general conflict in the region. Such an enhancement would complicate Soviet risk assessments throughout the area and would significantly reduce the possibility of misadventure on Moscow's part.

The shortage of aircraft carriers in the West Pacific is a serious disability.[26] Because the possibility that Japan will embark on a program of major surface ship construction in the foreseeable future is very remote, the provision of as large a number as possible of high-speed, long-range fighter interceptor and fighter bomber aircraft bases along the extended archipelagic chain from the Japanese home islands to the Philippines is necessary to partially offset the singular lack of air defense capabilities that characterizes the Japanese MSDF and the seriously depleted U.S. Seventh Fleet.

The rapid development of a Soviet blue-water naval capability in the Pacific has significantly altered Japanese perceptions of their nation's security, because it means that only a combined effort by the United States and Japan could ensure Japan's survival in the event of a general conflict. Soviet naval and air activities around Japan were given unusual prominence in the 1981 Japanese Defense White Paper, and Tokyo continues to manifest concern about the security of South Korea and Taiwan—both essential to an anti-Soviet interdiction and sea denial strategy.[27]

The specific defense of the Japanese home islands against air attacks turns on the availability not only of an adequate number of fighter interceptors, but of an effective air defense radar system to detect incoming aircraft. The Japanese base air defense ground environment system, with 28 monitoring sites installed in 1967, provides medium- and high-level detection capabilities that feed information to defending Nike and Hawk missile units with fighter interceptor backup support. The system is reasonably adequate for such detection but is inadequate to detect low-flying aircraft (as established by the undetected landing of a Soviet MiG-25 at Hakodate by a defector in 1976). The radar network has been supplemented by the acquisition of Grumman E-2C Hawkeye airborne warning and control aircraft, which can monitor low-flying incoming aircraft and vector intercepts to the proper vicinity, but the system clearly requires modernization and improvement.

The only system that might exact an unacceptable toll from incoming aggressor aircraft is one resulting from thorough integration of these assets with the U.S. air defense forces, which have more extensive early warning properties. The probability of such losses might deter conventional air attacks against the densely populated cities of Japan. In addition, the projected expansion of the Japanese ASDF to the level that would make it qualitatively one of the most advanced interceptor forces in Asia should be supplemented by passive civil defense preparations; to date Japan has done very little to adequately prepare its population for civil defense.

The land defense of those sites that would probably be targets of amphibious assault by Soviet landing forces is being strengthened. The GSDF is budgeted to receive about 300 heavy tanks by 1984, to be supplemented by an unknown number of 155-mm and 203-mm howitzers, along with over 100 armored fighting vehicles. The stationing of Soviet ground troops in the northern islands in 1978, and the deployment of about 70 amphibious vessels, some with the properties of the *Ivan Rogov*, in the Far East in the same year have aroused Japan's concern for the adequate ground defense of its northern territories.

The 1976 Japanese Defense White Paper stated that the GSDF would be expanded to a level of thirteen infantry divisions and two mixed brigades—sufficient to contain any amphibious assault against the northern home islands for a minimum of three days, until U.S. power could be fully brought to bear.[28] The principal concern troubling the Japanese is the possibility that a general conflict would occupy U.S. naval and air forces elsewhere and that U.S. reinforcements might come too late or prove insufficient.

There are several strategies that might be invoked to mitigate such a concern. The United States has certain strategic advantages in the North Pacific region. The economic and transport infrastructure of Alaska and the U.S. Pacific Northwest is robust when compared with that of the USSR in eastern Siberia, and with some rationalization of the U.S. force structure, Alaska and the Aleutian Islands, now largely defense liabilities, could be transformed into defense advantages. Strategic air bases and launch sites in Alaska and the Aleutians would serve as major deterrents to any Soviet adventure, as has been suggested. A Marine division, permanently headquartered in Anchorage (rather than at Camp Pendleton, California) would afford ready manpower, suitably trained, to counter the presence of a Soviet division in the Kuril Islands. Finally, to attempt to restore Tokyo's confidence in the disposition of the United States to protect the Japanese home islands, it might be necessary for Washington to acquire at least a symbolic U.S.-Japanese force integration for the tactical defense of Japan. Such force integration, particularly at the level of first-line combat operations, would be an attempt to assure the Japanese that in any military operations undertaken in such contingencies, Americans would be in the first combat operations, alongside their Japanese allies.

These joint tactical combat operations would require a more unified command structure than currently obtains. The Japanese SDF do not have a system for integrated command and control of ground, air, and sea forces. This could be accomplished with minimal budget costs, and such a system could interface with that of the U.S. defense command. The immediate command and control advantages could be supplemented by integration with the U.S.–South Korean system so that the entire subregion would have a unified information and surveillance capability. It seems clear that a U.S. Northeast Asia Command, with subordinate participation on the part of Japan and South Korea, has become a strategic requirement.

In this regard, in the late 1970s and early 1980s there was some evidence of an increased measure of defense cooperation by the United States, Japan, and South Korea. The establishment of a Japan–U.S. Security Consultative Committee in 1978 constituted a first step in the direction of a more unified and coordinated command structure. Similarly, joint exercises in South Korea and Japan involving elements of the armed forces of the United States are part of a gradual integration of command and control capabilities in order to respond more efficiently to regional crises. An improvement in air defense tracking information links between South Korea and Japan would be of mutual benefit and would provide the Japanese ASDF command with increased early warning capabilities. The integration of such command and control would send clear signals to the Soviet Union and would decrease the risks of misadventure by reducing the probability of success of any attacks against Japan in times of general conflict.

All these security efforts have the advantage of shifting the focus from resource input (that is, Japan's preoccupation with the share of GNP allocated to defense expenditure) to specific performance goals. The major concern in Northeast Asia is not only the quantity of military hardware available, but its combat effectiveness. Establishing a Northeast Asia Command, integrating forces, sharing military intelligence, and linking surveillance capabilities, for example, are moves toward the improvement of military effectiveness—they are not necessarily budget items.

It seems reasonably clear that in the foreseeable future, Japan will not radically expand its armed forces. There will be only an incremental change in the number and quality of combatants and weapon systems. Neither the Japanese public nor the Japanese political establishment seems prepared to fundamentally alter the security policies that have been followed since the 1950s. But this does not mean that the security of Japan and of Northeast Asia would not benefit significantly from a more rationalized defense posture. Such a change would not require much greater financial commitment than is already anticipated in the Japanese defense budgets for 1984–1989.

The increasing measure of concern regarding the security of Northeast Asia, and the assumption by Yasuhiro Nakasone of the office of prime minister in 1982, affords Japan and the United States the opportunity to arrive at a bilateral consensus concerning defense policy in the region. According to the Japanese Midterm Program Estimate provided by the National Defense Council in April 1981, an expenditure of $18.2 billion for front-line combat equipment is anticipated between 1983 and 1987. By fiscal year 1984, Japanese defense costs are expected to exceed the limit of 1 percent of GNP that has constrained such outlays in the past.

Although the 1981 plan includes procurement of 72 P-3s (rather than the 125 recommended by the United States) and 75 F-15s, to bring the total of F-15s to 155 (rather than the approximately 300 recommended by the United States), it will afford Japan a credible, though not ideal, sea denial and air defense capability for protecting the four home islands and allow it responsibly to discharge its proposed defense functions in the immediately adjacent waters.

In a general conflict, the F-15 fighters, supplemented by four squadrons of refurbished F-4 aircraft, E-2C early warning aircraft, an improved ground radar system, and integrated command and control capabilities, would provide a significant first contact opposition to Soviet aircraft entering Japanese airspace. These defense assets could obstruct the air routes over the Japanese home islands and the Sea of Japan, should any Soviet Backfire bombers attempt to reach the open waters of the Pacific. An alternative route to the southwest would be left open for such aircraft, however—across northern China and over the East China Sea and the Ryukyu Islands. Japanese interceptor strength is insufficient to defend this region as well as the home islands, and the Japanese defense command apparently has no plans to undertake base construction on Okinawa or on other islands in the southern chain.

The United States does maintain three squadrons of F-15s on Okinawa, but contingency plans reportedly make those assets subject to deployment to the Indian Ocean region under certain circumstances. In a general conflict, that would allow Soviet Backfires free passage. In such an eventuality, air defense assets in Taiwan could be of major strategic significance. Unfortunately, the decision by the Reagan administration not to allow the ROC purchase of high-performance aircraft has undermined this defense alternative. Once again, it is evident that the defense of the Northeast Pacific requires comprehensive planning—and in that planning, the potential security role of the Republic of China on Taiwan is of considerable importance.

The Reagan administration has begun to analyze Japanese capabilities from the standpoint of roles and missions. Among U.S. military experts there has been a decrease in the emphasis on how much is being spent by the Japanese and more emphasis on the specific responsibilities Japanese forces should assume. Should the Japanese be prepared to undertake those responsibilities, the forces available for minelaying and for antisubmarine and air defense missions could constitute important elements of a credible anti-Soviet security posture. The lack of an adequate defense of the area southwest of the home islands could be offset by increased ROC capabilities (an issue to be addressed in Chapter 6).

The proposed Japanese buildup could be accomplished with relatively modest increments in Tokyo's 1982 defense expenditures (about 10–11 percent per year). In 1983–84 this would require an increase of about $600 million over the sum already allocated. Given a national budget of $210 billion, such an increase should not be disabling or politically objectionable.

It seems reasonably clear that Prime Minister Nakasone would like to accommodate the United States by increasing military expenditures and is also seriously concerned about the security of Japan. He does, however, operate within the constraints of bureaucratic prerogatives and public attitudes of skepticism and widespread indifference. But there is increased recognition, at least among Japanese strategists, that Japan must assume more responsibility in defense of the region than it has in the past. This has become evident not only because of the Soviet military buildup, and the transparent inability of the Communist Chinese to offer a credible deterrent counterweight, but because of the relative drawdown of U.S. forces in East Asia in general.

United States security policy in East Asia in general, and Northeast Asia in particular, remains unclear. Nonetheless, the elements of a reasonable policy have emerged—more in accordance with the dictates of necessity than by calculation. Japanese military leaders have significantly contributed to that emerging security policy by emphasizing the critical role to be played by South Korea and Taiwan in any comprehensive defense of the home islands in a general conflict.

In the Japanese Comprehensive Security Report of 1980, the defense agencies of Japan explicitly recognized both that the Soviet Union represents the "only potential threat to Japan" and that unqualified U.S. military superiority in the Pacific had been lost by the late 1970s.[29] Japan realizes that it requires a comprehensive security policy, predicated on collaborative dependency on the United States and the security of South Korea and Taiwan.

For the United States, the recognition that Japan, South Korea, and Taiwan constitute a critical security triangle in Northeast Asia is the deductive consequence of any rational assessment of U.S. economic, political, and military interests in East Asia. The economic systems of all three nations are essentially market governed and are components of an international money market that is critical to the survival of the noncommunist states of Southeast Asia. Japan's pluralistic political system remains the model nonsocialist democracy for the remaining Asian nations, however impaired their current democratic practices may be. Any threat to the economic or political viability of Japan would be a threat to the continued economic and political development of all the noncommunist Asian nations.

Japan and the newly industrialized nations of Northeast Asia provide compelling evidence that open-market pluralistic and semicompetitive political systems have substantially more to offer Asians than do alternative socialist and communist systems. (Whatever their present disabilities, South Korea and Taiwan offer more welfare benefits and political and civil liberties than do their communist counterparts.) Moreover, the dynamic economies of these noncommunist nations provide the United States more trade and investment outlets than could any alternative arrangements which might only hinder trade. Whatever trade difficulties the United States has experienced with the Japanese, U.S. economic difficulties would be compounded by the alienation of Japan and by its withdrawal from the anti-Soviet alliance. The Soviet Union would be the only conceivable beneficiary—to the detriment of the strategic and economic interests of the United States and of its vision of an expanding arena for open-market economies and pluralistic political systems.

For the foreseeable future, the security of Japan will remain a critical concern for the United States. Both forward deployment in East Asia, however limited, and denial of access to the open waters of the Pacific by the Soviet Pacific Fleet are in the fundamental strategic interests of the United States. To accomplish the latter, and to ensure the survivability of Japan and South Korea, control of the critical choke points off the Japanese home islands and South Korea is essential. To that end, the sea-lanes of the West Pacific must be secured, and that requires the provision of basing facilities along the entire Asian archipelagic chain, at the center of which is Taiwan.

The limited resources of the U.S. Seventh Fleet, which is obliged to cover about 50 million square miles of open water, must be supplemented by the ocean-going assets of the Japanese MSDF—limited by its lack of air cover and open-water replenishment capabilities. The tactical employment of these limited-endurance forces requires access to extensive basing facilities and collateral assistance by the naval forces of potentially allied nations in the region. Similarly, the lack of shipborne air defense assets requires air bases along the island chain that stretches from the Japanese home islands to the Philippines. Taiwan is the critical midpoint of that chain.

Once the United States has formulated a clear and coherent security policy, the Soviet Union will be faced with a deterrence strategy that will make military adventure in Northeast Asia a high-risk undertaking. That, in turn, can only benefit the People's Republic of China. Peking will have to recognize that the maintenance of the status quo in the Taiwan Strait remains in its ultimate best interest and will have to accept the seriousness of the U.S. and Japanese interest in the security of Taiwan.

Under the circumstances prevailing in Northeast Asia, the U.S. commitment to the security of both South Korea and Taiwan serves the interests of both the United States and the PRC. The defense of Japan against Soviet military threats turns largely on the security of its flanks, and the security of Japan, given mainland China's manifest military disabilities, serves the ultimate interests of Peking.

Given the constraints that exist in Northeast Asia, formulation of a security policy for the region is an onerous political, diplomatic, and military task. That it is possible to put together such a strategy seems reasonably clear. That its formulation will be difficult and will require all the energies of the U.S. foreign policy establishment seems equally evident.

5 | The Security of the Republic of Korea

Besides [Japan's] concern over the continuing Russian buildup and mounting tensions, [its] nascent interest in defense issues is currently focused on three areas . . . .: (1) any possible threat to [Japan's] vital sea lanes, particularly through Southeast Asia, (2) the future of Taiwan, which is economically and strategically very important to [Japan], and (3) the future of Korea, which is of central importance to [Japan's] defense.

Hideaki Kase,
"Northeast Asian Security: A View from Japan,"
in Foster, Dornan, and Carpenter, eds.,
Strategy and Security in Northeast Asia.

The Korean peninsula is the sole place in East Asia where the vital interests of all the major Pacific powers intersect. Both the Soviet Union and the People's Republic of China have defense and security treaties with the Democratic People's Republic of Korea (DPRK)—North Korea—and the United States maintains a similar relationship with the Republic of Korea (ROK) in the South. The United States–Japan security treaty implicitly links the security of the ROK with U.S. access to basing facilities on the home islands of Japan. Military activity on the Korean peninsula would mean that U.S. bases in Japan would be used for staging, servicing, and dispatch of aircraft and troops for the combat zone. Moreover, ever since the Satō-Nixon communiqué of 1969, the Japanese government has regularly reinterated its preoccupation with the integrity of the ROK and the peace and security of the entire Korean peninsula.

On August 19, 1974, the foreign minister of Japan affirmed that "it is vital to Japan that the Korean peninsula as a whole must maintain peace and security"; on September 15, 1975, during the eighth Korea-Japan ministerial meeting, the Japanese insisted that relations with Korea were "crucial" for the mainte-nance of peace and security in Northeast Asia. On August 6, 1975, President Gerald Ford and Japanese Prime Minister Takeo Miki, in a joint communiqué, announced that "the security of [South] Korea was essential to the maintenance of peace on the Korean peninsula, which in turn was necessary for the peace and security of East Asia, including Japan." In elaborating on the clause in the United States–Japan security treaty that required prior consultation before the U.S. military could employ bases in Japan for the forward projection and deployment of troops to the Korean peninsula, Prime Minister Miki maintained that it would be inconceivable that Japan would hesitate to allow such activities should an actual Korean crisis develop.[1] The fact that the four major powers have security investments in the Korean peninsula makes it one of the most potentially dangerous places in the world today.

None of this was appreciated in 1950 when the United States signaled its indisposition to concern itself with the security situation on the Korean peninsula and left South Korea with only limited defense capabilities. Washington policymakers remained indifferent to evidence of Soviet preoccupation with the military and political developments in the subregion, heavily discounting any possibility of conflict in Korea for two main reasons. First, the Soviet Union had suffered grievously during the Second World War, and it was deemed unlikely that Moscow would choose to test the fragile stability that existed in East Asia after the conclusion of the war in the Pacific. Second, the PRC, having recently defeated the armies of the Kuomintang on the Asian mainland, would be in no better position than the USSR to underwrite adventure on the Korean peninsula.

So convinced was the political leadership in Washington that military conflict was impossible on the Korean peninsula that the first reports of a North Korean invasion of the South were discredited. Only when official confirmation was received from the United States ambassador in Seoul did Washington respond. There was a swift reversal of U.S. policy, and on June 25, 1950, one day after the commencement of the North Korean invasion of the South, the United States called for an emergency meeting of the United Nations Security Council. On the same day, the Security Council declared the armed attack on South Korea, by seven divisions and 150 tanks from North Korea, a "breach of the peace" and invoked the assistance of all members of the United Nations in protecting the integrity of the Republic of Korea.

On June 30, President Harry S. Truman dispatched U.S. military support to the ROK. Ground forces were deployed to assist in the defense of South Korea and air attacks were ordered against specific military targets in North Korea. A naval blockade was emplaced along the entire Korean coast.

Between 1950 and 1953 (when the fighting was stopped by an armistice), the United States forces, under the mandate of the United Nations resolutions of June 25 and 27, 1950, fought a limited war to re-establish the antebellum status quo. At the commencement of U.S. intervention, political and military strategists in Washington dismissed the threats issued by Peking that the PRC would become involved if Communist Chinese interests were threatened—again because mainland China had only recently defeated the armed forces of the Kuomintang, and its economy, support structure, and armed forces were assessed to be unequal to any such task.[2]

For all that, the Communist Chinese did become massively involved in the fighting, and the "volunteers" of the People's Liberation Army, despite staggering losses in manpower, succeeded in driving back the forces of the United States and the United Nations to the 38th parallel.

Peking recognized that the loss of the Korean peninsula to potentially hostile forces would open the passage to the critical industrial heartland of Manchuria, where mainland China's most productive plants were located. The Japanese had employed Korean staging areas for the invasion of Manchuria in 1931, and the Soviet Union, in the closing days of the Second World War, had used the Korean corridor as a military conduit in defeating the Japanese Imperial Army in Manchuria. A secure Korean peninsula was clearly essential to the credible defense of northeastern China.[3]

The Soviet Union, which was allied with the PRC and the DPRK, provided a considerable part of the war matériel employed by the communist forces in their struggle with United States and United Nations forces. The USSR was aware that the presence of potentially hostile forces on the peninsula would threaten its forward positions in the Soviet Maritime Province and eastern Siberia, and control of the entire coastline of Korea by hostile forces would help seal Soviet merchant and naval vessels in the inland waters of continental Asia and directly threaten the survival of the major naval base at Vladivostok.

In those three years of battle, the United States suffered almost 34,000 battle deaths, over 100,000 nonfatal battle casualties, and over 20,000 combat-related deaths. Almost 4 million Koreans lost their lives, and the total cost of the war ranged (according to varying estimates) from $20 to $80 billion.[4] The capital of the South, Seoul, changed hands four times during the fighting and at the end of the war was left a shattered ruin. Whole regions of the peninsula were devastated by the conflict. Approximately 120,000 South Koreans were executed by the Communists from the North during their occupation of the South—an act that sowed the bitter seeds of enmity that have nourished the pervasive anticommunism of the South ever since.

What the Korean War made evident was the full measure of the security investment Communist China, the Soviet Union, and the United States had, and have, in the Korean peninsula. For the United States, the original motivation for the mutual security arrangement with the Republic of Korea was to "contain world communism." The Soviet Union, the PRC, and the DPRK were conceived as a monolithic threat to the freedom and security of the noncommunist nations of East Asia, and the United States committed its renewed military capabilities to its containment. The Republic of Korea and the Republic of China on Taiwan were shorn up as forward outposts of the "free world" and included in a defensive alliance that covered a region stretching from the Japanese home islands to the southernmost Pacific. The defense of the ROK had become part of a grand strategic design.

Since the uneasy armistice that ended the fighting on the Korean peninsula, the United States has poured vast quantities of economic and military aid into South Korea—first to sustain its population and its precarious security and subsequently to fuel its rapid economic and industrial growth. Since the end of the Korean War, the Republic of Korea has received more direct aid and concessional loans from the United States than any other country in the world save Israel and South Vietnam.

Through the years the association between the United States and the Republic of Korea has matured into a mutually profitable trade and investment relationship. In the 1970s the U.S. supplied about 22 percent of all the direct foreign investment active in the Korean national economy and purchased about 30 percent of all South Korean exports; U.S. goods made up about 26 percent of all of South Korea's imports. The ROK is now the twelfth largest trading partner of the United States.

Since 1965, with the normalization of relations between the Republic of Korea and Japan, there has been a rapid increase in direct Japanese investment in the economy of South Korea. When U.S. economic assistance grants ceased, their place was taken by direct Japanese investment. By the early 1980s Japan, alone, was providing about 64 percent of all foreign investment capital active in the South Korean economy; Japanese investment in South Korea will soon exceed $10 billion. Although Japan has assiduously cultivated trade with much larger markets in mainland China and Brazil, the ROK remains its second largest trading partner—second only to the United States. Bilateral trade between Japan and the ROK will soon exceed $10 billion, with Japan purchasing about 26 percent of all South Korean exports and Japanese goods making up about 34 percent of all South Korean imports.[5]

While the national economy of the Republic of Korea was undergoing massive structural changes, the relationships among the United States, the Soviet Union, the People's Republic of China, and Japan—all involved in the security of the Korean peninsula—were undergoing equally significant changes. By the mid-1960s the Sino-Soviet dispute had become public knowledge, and by the end of the decade the Nixon administration had made its overture to Peking. Shortly after Washington began its tortuous course toward normalization, Tokyo began to normalize its relationship with Peking, and in 1978, Japan entered into a peace and friendship treaty with the PRC.

The first response was a flurry of diplomatic activity on the Korean peninsula. In the early 1970s Seoul and Pyongyang began a series of bilateral talks designed to reduce the mutual enmity and the risk of war on the peninsula. Both sides were less than accommodating and the net result was that by 1973 interest had subsided.

Throughout all this Pyongyang found itself singularly disadvantaged by cross-pressures. North Korea has maintained security relations with both Peking and Moscow since 1961, when the three nations signed amity, cooperation, and mutual assistance treaties. Since its independence in 1948, North Korea has been a recipient of both Soviet and Communist Chinese economic and military aid: about 48 percent of all aid it has received from communist countries has originated in the Soviet Union, and 30 percent has originated in the PRC. Thus Pyongyang has had reason to attempt to maintain good relations with both its communist neighbors.

In the first half decade of its independence, North Korea was substantially "sovietized"—its party structure, its military force structure, and the organization of its economy were virtually carbon copies of those of the Soviet Union. With the advent of the Korean War and the intervention of the mainland Chinese, Peking's influence was added to that emanating from Moscow. As a result of the massive support provided by the Communist Chinese, North Korea no longer found itself entirely dependent on Moscow to ensure its survival. The new situation allowed Kim Il-sung to deal with some problems of internal political control with far more independence than he might otherwise have. As long as North Korea was inextricably tied to Moscow, a Moscow-oriented faction within the North Korean hierarchy could always appeal to the Soviets over the head of Kim in the event of a policy dispute. In effect, as long as North Korea was abjectly dependent on Moscow, Kim Il-sung's policies would always be subject to a potential Soviet veto. The Communist Chinese support was accompanied by formation of a Peking-oriented faction, however. The Moscow faction did not always agree with the Peking faction and Kim often served as mediator between them. The tensions that resulted ultimately indicated the necessity for the purging of both factions if policy deliberation was not always to bog down in dispute and if Kim was to be master in his own house.

The empirical evidence strongly suggests that from the signing of the armistice that ended the Korean War until the early 1960s, the North Korean central administration, under the leadership of Kim Il-sung, was preoccupied with creating a unanimity of ideological opinion in the DPRK essential to the political dominance of Kim himself.[6] The purging of the Pak Hon-yong and the Ho Ka-i factions not only made possible that political dominance, it also allowed Pyongyang the independence that permitted it to pursue a self-serving balance between Communist China and the Soviet Union.

North Korea early signaled its disposition to pursue its own domestic and foreign policies. In December 1955, Kim Il-sung outlined the cardinal features of a policy of *juche* ("self-reliance") that would allow the DPRK to appeal to one or another, or both, of its communist patrons as circumstances and Pyongyang's interests dictated without being totally captive of either.[7] By this time the Soviet Union no longer dominated North Korea's deliberations as it once had. Communist Chinese military intervention in the Korean War had irreversibly altered that. Moreover, the death of Stalin in 1953 had created confusion among all the members of the Communist International.

In North Korea the confusion that followed Stalin's demise was compounded by the fact that the declamations against the "cult of personality" by the new leadership in Moscow were used against Kim Il-sung by his political opponents in 1956, when he was busy with the effort to make his political position unassailable. As an effective counter, Kim found it expedient to emphasize the independent course that North Korean politics would henceforth follow.[8]

North Korea, of course, would remain within the "socialist camp," but the developing circumstances allowed Pyongyang considerable discretion in making policy choices. Thus throughout the early 1960s, North Korea continued to refer to the socialist camp as the "socialist countries led by Communist China and the Soviet Union" in order to signal its balance and its equidistance from both.

Unhappily, events very quickly upset Pyongyang's "balanced" approach. The Bucharest Conference in June 1960, the Moscow Conference in November 1960, and the Twenty-second Soviet Communist Party Congress in June 1961 made the extent of the Sino-Soviet disagreement abundantly clear. The communist countries, North Korea among them, were increasingly obliged to select one of the two major "socialist" powers as a preferred patron. Pyongyang found itself pressured to choose either the aggressive revolutionism of Peking or the "revisionism" and the "peaceful coexistence" of Moscow.

Between 1960 and 1965 Pyongyang leaned toward the mainland Chinese. As a consequence, the Soviet Union suspended economic assistance to North Korea after 1962, and Kim Kwang-hyop, who had been sent to the Soviet Union in that year with a request for military aid, returned to Pyongyang empty-handed. Only when Communist China's aggressive foreign policy in Indonesia resulted in debacle in 1965 did the North Korean leadership reassess its position.

The situation in Vietnam contributed to Pyongyang's reassessment. Despite Peking's revolutionary rhetoric, it soon became evident to Pyongyang that Hanoi depended heavily on Soviet military and economic aid to sustain its war effort against South Vietnam and the United States. As a consequence, when Premier Aleksei Kosygin visited Pyongyang in February 1965, he was welcomed, and in March, when the Twenty-third Soviet Communist Party Congress was held in Moscow, the North Korean delegation, headed by Choe Yong-gon, fully participated even though the Communist Chinese refused to attend. In May 1965 and again in March 1967, the North Koreans concluded military aid agreements with the Soviet Union; in February 1966 the two nations concluded a long-term economic and technical agreement.

At about this time, the traumatic Great Proletarian Cultural Revolution ravaged mainland China. In 1967 the Chinese Red Guards attacked Kim Il-sung, and in 1968 border incidents were reported between the North Korean and Communist Chinese military. Pyongyang nevertheless attempted to maintain some degree of equilibrium between its two communist neighbors—especially following the Satō-Nixon communiqué in 1969, stating that the security of South Korea was a critical concern of both the United States and Japan.

After Chou En-lai visited Pyongyang in April 1970, bilateral relations between the DPRK and the PRC gradually improved witout impairing the relationship between Pyongyang and Moscow. When the North Koreans brought down an unarmed U.S. observation plane in 1969, the mainland Chinese were quick to support Pyongyang's position that the action was a legitimate defense of its national sovereignty. The Soviet Union offered support on similar grounds three days after the Chinese response. Since that time, North Korea has assiduously sought to preserve a balanced neutrality in the Sino-Soviet dispute and has maintained good relations with both Moscow and Peking. Throughout the efforts at rapprochement that followed Kissinger's initiative with regard to Peking, for example, the North Koreans refrained from any criticism of Communist China's "revisionism" in foreign affairs, reserving their hostility for the "American imperialists." For their part, the mainland Chinese have continued to identify the North Koreans as their "no. 1 allies" in Asia, "close comrades in arms who shared life and death and joys and sorrows and overcame trials."[9] The Soviet Union has continued to support North Korean foreign policy positions and supplies the DPRK with the military equipment necessary to maintain its force structure. It has, however, withheld the advanced weapon platforms and ancillary equipment that would make the North Korean military a truly independent modern force.

Nonetheless, the Soviets have expressed their continued confidence by using the North Koreans as conduits for the distribution of military equipment to those Third World nations that do not wish to publicize a direct Soviet connection. Burundi, Libya, Mozambique, Sierra Leone, Tanzania, Togoland, Syria, and Zaire have used North Korea as a transit point for Soviet military supplies, and North Koreans have served in the military of these countries as Soviet surrogates. Moreover, the Soviets have obtained Pyongyang's permission to use the port of Najin, on the northeast coast of Korea, as a naval supply and refurbishing facility.[10]

Pyongyang shares a land border with both the USSR and the PRC and continues to bear substantial economic indebtedness to the Soviet Union and to have equally significant diplomatic indebtedness to the PRC. Both Moscow and Peking continually express their support of Pyongyang's insistence on the withdrawal of all foreign troops from Korean soil—a reference to the presence of the U.S. Second Division in the South. But both Moscow and Peking seem at least resigned to the continued U.S. presence if for no other reason than that neither can control the policies of a remarkably independent North Korea. The presence of U.S. forces in the region acts as a major deterrent to any military adventure against the South by Kim Il-sung. As long as neither Moscow nor Peking wants war on the peninsula, and as long as neither can control Pyongyang, both are prepared to allow the responsibility for that control to remain in Washington.

That the communist regime in North Korea might choose to disturb the troubled peace of the Korean peninsula remains a worrisome possibility. Since its inception, the regime in Pyongyang has staked its legitimacy on its insistence on early reunification of the divided nation.[11] By the early 1980s, the prospects of such reunification under conditions that would be acceptable to Pyongyang seemed to be diminishing for a variety of reasons.

Vast economic changes have taken place on the Korean peninsula since 1955. From 1945 to 1965, North Korea's economic performance was measurably superior to that of the South. In the first two decades of his party rule, Kim Il-sung managed to tranform the preindustrial and underdeveloped segment of the peninsula under his control into a reasonably well-organized and politically stable industrial community while the South continued to languish in economic stagnation.

In 1967 the gross national product of North Korea was about $2.1 billion while that of South Korea was $4.2 billion. Given the small North Korean population (about half that of the South), its per capita annual income was somewhere between $162 and $220 compared with a meager $143 in the South. Between 1947 and 1967, the national income of the North increased at an annual rate of 12.7 percent. Thereafter, the growth rate decelerated. During the same twenty-year period, South Korea's economic growth rate averaged approximately 9 percent per annum. In 1967 it peaked at 15 percent. The gross national product of South Korea was by then four times that of the North and its per capita income had improved dramatically.

While conditions in the South improved, North Korea was accumulating more and more foreign debt. Despite the constraints imposed by its economic circumstances, North Korea was expending about 17 percent of its gross national product on military procurement and support—a sum that was in 1981 just short of $1 billion. In that year South Korea, although it spent only about 6 percent of its gross national product on defense, could afford to disburse almost $1.5 billion for its military improvement program. It is estimated that because of its economic circumstances, North Korea cannot possibly allocate more than $2–3 billion annually for military purposes—

whatever the external environment. South Korea, on the other hand, with a gross national product that was in 1981 about five times that of the North, could match and even exceed Pyongyang's investments with relative ease.[12]

What this suggests is that the military advantages North Korea enjoys at the moment will probably gradually diminish and it will no longer have the kind of military superiority that frontal invasion requires. If North Korea has a military solution to the problem of a divided peninsula, it will have to make the effort soon or entirely forsake the option.

From 1970 to 1980, North Korea systematically marshaled its resources in preparation for a military victory on the Korean peninsula. It militarized its economy and developed the capabilities for manufacturing its basic weapon systems and all but the most sophisticated arms. It also hardened all its major military facilities and their command and control adjuncts. In this ten-year period the standing forces of the North Korean military were almost doubled, from about 393,000 to 782,000, a force that significantly exceeds the 601,600 troops serving under the South Korean flag.[13]

The organizational structure and the combat tactics of the North Korean armed forces have been modeled after those of the Soviet army. North Korean units are prepared for a brief and mobile conflict, initiated by a heavy barrage of artillery and spearheaded by armored thrusts. More than a third of Pyongyang's maneuver battalions—approximately 100,000 troops—are composed of special service forces, commandos, and both airborne and seaborne units. About 180 An-2s of the North Korean air force can airlift about 2,500 troops behind South Korean lines, and the amphibious capabilities of the North were enhanced in the early 1980s by the provision of about 90 personnel landing craft. All of these forces, when used in conjunction with Soviet-supplied river-crossing equipment, constitute a major threat to the forward defense of Seoul, which lies a scant 40 kilometers from the North Korean border.

North Korean heavy artillery and long-range mortars are emplaced in hardened positions along the demilitarized zone that separates the two Koreas at the 38th parallel. After the initial withering barrage, Pyongyang could launch an armored thrust, employing the 3,000 tanks it has in inventory. Its 300 relatively obsolete T-34 Soviet-designed tanks are supported by about 2,500 T-54/55/62 battle tanks of Soviet design. In every measure of military effectiveness of its armor in inventory, North Korea possesses an advantage of at least 3:1 over the South.

Given the topography of the peninsula, armored thrusts, led by infantry transported by over 1,000 personnel carriers and fighting vehicles, would travel along the mountain corridors into the South, following the same routes used during the Korean War. Three major corridors would be followed: two merging into one at Uijongbu, sixteen miles north of Seoul, and the other further west near Panmunjom and traversing Musan. The T'aebaek mountain range would divide the South Korean defense forces into two contingents; the smaller would be deployed in the West and the larger would be deployed in the East in the defense of Seoul.

Highly mobile North Korean artillery and truck-mobile 122-mm multiple rocket launchers would follow the advance echelons of the invading North Korean forces. South Korean defenders would find themselves caught between barrages emanating from the hardened artillery positions along the demilitarized zone, fire from special forces, ordnance laid down by mobile artillery, and rocket launcher assault along their flanks and from the rear. Under such circumstances, it is estimated that almost 20 percent of the South Korean defenders would be decimated in the first 90 seconds of any such conflict. Within 48 hours after initiation of the conflict, North Korean tanks would approach Seoul, where about 25 percent of the population of South Korea resides and where most of its manufacturing plants are located.[14]

South Korean defenses at the choke points along the main invasion routes from the North are themselves in hardened fortifications, and the army of the ROK is equipped with several hundred wire-guided antitank TOW missiles that have a high first round kill probability. Precision-guided munitions afford its infantry a low-cost, if high-risk, antiarmor defense capability that would complicate the North Korean strategy. South Korean artillery and air strikes could exact a heavy toll from invading armored units, particularly when the F-16s and antitank helicopters acquired in the early 1980s are fully integrated into the force structure of the South.

Although the Pyongyang air force is numerically larger than that of South Korea, the South Koreans probably enjoy a qualitative advantage. Of the approximately 700 combat aircraft in the North Korean inventory, about 300 are MiG-15/17s. The MiG-15 is of Korean War vintage, and the MiG-17 is not much less obsolescent. Only the 120 MiG-21s in service qualify as modern fighter interceptor aircraft. The principal advantage enjoyed by the air force of North Korea is its ability to launch preemptive raids on South Korean airfields without fear of detection.

North Korean airfields are positioned so close to the demilitarized zone, and South Korean surveillance and early warning capabilities are so limited, that the MiGs of the North Korean air force will be on target before the defense forces of the ROK can respond. Once engaged, however, the South Korean air force can be expected to acquit itself well. Its F-5Es are marginally superior to the MiG-19s that make up the bulk of the North Korean air force. Certainly the new F-16s are superior to the aircraft in service with the North Koreans. Some effort is being made to upgrade the air intelligence and early warning capabilities of the South, and the relatively primitive ground communications system that in the mid-1970s made it impossible for units to communicate over intervening mountains is gradually being replaced by microwave communications networks.

The principal logistical problem that would affect the defense capabilities of the South is that the road and rail system, which would be burdened with the transport of supplies from the major port of Pusan and from storage facilities in the South to the combat area, is very thin. Pre-positioning large stocks of ordnance close to the potential combat zone would be hazardous because of the high risk that the forward areas might be overrun in the first engagements.

Besides the logistical difficulties, there is some suggestion that the armed forces of the ROK do not have in storage a supply of conventional munitions that will be adequate for the heavy indirect mortar and artillery bombardment necessary in the kind of antiarmor interdiction warfare that is anticipated.[15]

To attempt to solve some of its more urgent defense problems, the government of South Korea has embarked upon a series of Force Improvement Plans. The first plan, completed in 1980, was designed largely to promote military self-sufficiency. The industries of the South now produce almost all the standard military equipment necessary for the defense forces, and the guns of the M-48 tanks in inventory have been upgraded to meet the performance specifications of the more modern M-60A1 tanks of the United States forces. In addition, artillery pieces and antitank TOW missiles are being produced in South Korean factories. The latter, used in conjunction with advanced Fairchild Republic A-10A aircraft, provide the defense forces of the South with a considerable antitank capability that could be used effectively at the choke points along the invasion corridors from the North. Moreover, the fledgling aircraft industry of the South is beginning to coproduce not only F-5Es, but Hughes 500MD helicopters that can be equipped and used as antitank weapon platforms.

According to a U.S. assessment of the military posture of the South Korean armed forces made in 1982, they "are well trained, well led, and fairly well equipped, but their ability to deter and, if necessary, to defeat North Korean aggression will depend upon continued modernization and timely air, naval, and logistical support. Uncertainties still exist in both these areas. The economic downturn in South Korea has slowed the pace of programmed force improvements, and worldwide force levels are such that a major crisis elsewhere would severely hamper U.S. ability to assist [South Korean] forces in repelling aggression."[16]

Under the circumstances existing in the early 1980s, North Korea could launch a surprise armored invasion of the South with a reasonable probability of success—even if the 30,000 U.S. troops were to remain as a deterrent force. Even locally available U.S. air assets could not be expected to stop a determined North Korean attack. Most of the North Korean military facilities are in hardened sites invulnerable to conventional air strikes.

Should the United States be occupied with a crisis situation elsewhere and be unable to intervene massively early in the fighting, or should the United States withdraw the Second Division from the peninsula, the authorities in Pyongyang might very well undertake a lightning invasion of the South in an attempt to finally resolve the problem of reunification, and there is a serious possibility that the South would be overrun. Until such time as the armed forces of the South are capable of effective autonomous defense, that option will remain open to the independent leadership in the North—for in the last analysis, neither Moscow nor Peking controls Kim Il-sung.

North Korea will probably continue to enjoy some of its advantages until approximately 1990. But its economic difficulties, its outstanding foreign debt of over $2 billion, and its default on its Western European and Japanese debts all suggest that Kim Il-sung's efforts to maintain the North on a virtual war footing cannot be long sustained. If North Korea intends to exercise its military option with any real probability of success, it must undertake that adventure in the near term.

For both the Soviet Union and the People's Republic of China, such an adventure would create special problems, for neither wishes to see the other become more deeply involved on the Korean peninsula. And yet to ensure the success of its venture, Pyongyang would have to depend on the support of its communist patrons—particularly the Soviet Union. Only the Soviets are capable of providing the advanced aircraft and the modern battle tanks necessary to counter any possible U.S. intervention.

Communist China would be loath to see any further Soviet penetration into the Korean peninsula for at least the following reasons. First, Peking would perceive an established Soviet presence on the peninsula as a threat to its security in Manchuria. Should the Soviet Union obtain secure access to the peninsula during such a conflict by providing Pyongyang with advanced military equipment and the attendant technical support teams, the defense positions of the Chinese People's Liberation Army in Northeast China would be compromised. Soviet troops would find themselves in the same corridors over which the Communist Chinese "volunteers" traveled after making their way across the Yalu to reach the fighting front during the Korean War. The industrial regions and the major energy-generating facilities of Manchuria would immediately be placed in jeopardy. Mainland Chinese troops would have to be redeployed to cover the border with Korea.

Second, by intervening in any military action on the peninsula, the Soviet Union could acquire full access to the naval facilities on the Korean coast—in much the same fashion as it has acquired access to those of Vietnam. This could put the Soviet Far East Fleet in a position to blockade marine traffic to some of the major ports of mainland China without fear of interdiction at the major choke points that restrict exit from the inland Sea of Japan.

Armed conflict between the two Koreas would bring with it the risk of direct involvement by both the United States and the Soviet Union. Moscow might very well be compelled to intervene if only to eliminate the possibility of the peninsula's being occupied by hostile forces that could bring pressure on the Soviet Far East provinces. Clearly, war on the Korean peninsula would not serve mainland China's strategic interests. War would adversely affect Peking's relations with both Washington and Tokyo and would bring with it the serious possibility of Soviet dominance of the subregion.

In all this, Peking finds itself in an awkward situation. As long as a reasonably stable peace continues on the peninsula, it serves mainland China's interests to court Pyongyang, to ensure that the Soviet Union does not exploit its bargaining position. Throughout the period of rapprochement with the United States and with Japan, Peking has not wavered in its support of Pyongyang's insistence on the reunification of the two Koreas. Irrespective of that rapprochement, Peking has persisted in identifying the United States as an "imperialist power" that remains a subsidiary enemy. Officially, Peking has continued to admonish the United States to stop interfering in Korea's domestic affairs. It has officially advocated the complete withdrawal of foreign troops from continental Asia, including Korea, and has insisted that Washington cease supplying military aid to the "dictatorial regime" in Seoul.

Since Peking has little to offer Pyongyang at the moment (short of political rhetoric), it continues to officially support Kim Il-sung's policies. Pyongyang, however, seems to appreciate the fact that only the Soviet Union is capable of contributing to the credibility of its military option and has, accordingly, sought to strengthen its ties with Moscow. As a case in point, North Korean representatives visited New Delhi in July 1980, when Sino-Indian relations were particularly troubled by India's recognition of the Heng Samrin regime imposed on Kampuchea in 1978 as a result of the Soviet-supported Vietnamese invasion. This North Korean initiative distressed the Communist Chinese authorities, to whom the Heng Samrin regime is anathema and who perceive Vietnam as an extension of Soviet power in Southeast Asia.

Moreover, Pyongyang has lavished praise on Castro's Cuba—much to the discomfiture of Peking. Finally, there is some evidence that North Korea's communist leaders have serious misgivings concerning Peking's increased identification with the general security interests of the United States and Japan, regardless of Peking's official commitment to Pyongyang.[17]

Thus the security situation on the Korean peninsula has become increasingly complex. In the near future, Pyongyang may find itself under increasing pressure to resolve the issue of reunification by force. It may also enjoy sufficient leverage to draw one or both of its communist patrons into its venture—if only because neither can countenance the other's gaining an advantage in the confusion that would follow.

Both mainland China and the Soviet Union clearly seem to appreciate how hazardous conflict on the Korean peninsula could be. The United States has suggested that in the event of conflict, the use of tactical nuclear weapons, already in storage on the Korean peninsula, might well be considered. Neither Moscow nor Peking seems anxious to test that possibility. It therefore seems evident that neither nation is prepared to precipitate armed conflict in Korea. The Soviet Union has displayed its reluctance by declining to provide the North Koreans with the advanced weapon systems that would increase the probability of success of any invasion attempt. For their part, the mainland Chinese seem to be willing to tolerate a U.S. military presence in the South as a stabilizing force.

It is clear that Pyongyang intends to continue pursuing its own political and/ or military policies. We have sobering historic evidence of what the consequences of that independence might be.

Although there are varying interpretations of the period, it now seems evident that neither Moscow nor Peking incited the North Korean invasion of the South in 1950. That military adventure of Kim Il-sung was apparently occasioned by domestic pressures (intense rivalry within the Korean Workers' Party in the North, complicated by the urging of South Korean–based guerrillas who had influential supporters in Pyongyang), which, combined with Kim Il-sung's commitment to an early reunification of the peninsula, precipitated the military misadventure that cost so much in terms of Korean, Chinese, and U.S. lives and money.[18]

Pyongyang's policy independence threatens the stability of the Korean peninsula. Irrespective of the interests of its patrons, North Korea persists in its commitment to the "national liberation" of the entire peninsula with perhaps more determination than ever, for it knows that its legitimacy as a political system and its credibility in the Third World depend in large part on the resoluteness of that commitment. The rapid buildup of its military forces since 1970, the construction of infiltration tunnels across the demilitarized zone, the continued infiltration of guerrilla and subversive elements into the South, and the propaganda and diplomatic efforts to isolate the Republic of Korea all suggest that given the appropriate external conditions, Pyongyang might be tempted to exercise its military option. Both Moscow and Peking would be compelled to respond, if only to protect their respective security interests. The Soviet Union would clearly have more to gain in terms of its position in Northeast Asia. Not only would it reap considerable advantages vis-à-vis the PRC by gaining military access to, or a firm commitment from, a unified Korea dominated by Pyongyang,[19] but a pro-Soviet Korea jutting into the critical Korea and Tsushima straits would all but ensure escape by Soviet naval vessels from the Sea of Japan to the less confined waters of the East China Sea and from there to the open Pacific in any general conflict.

In addition, a pro-Soviet Korea would provide a launching point for Soviet air, sea, and amphibious attacks against lightly defended Kyūshū in southern Japan. The Japanese Ground Defense Force, now largely configured for the defense of northern Hokkaidō, would have to be redeployed to cover two widely separated fronts. With the increased conventional military threat—stepped-up Soviet naval activities in the critical waters around Japan and along its extended trade routes to the south—Tokyo would find itself tempted to reduce the precariousness of its position as an advanced defense outpost for the United States and its allies by assuming an increasingly neutralist stance. One might well foresee an increasing "finlandization" of Japan as a consequence—with increased restrictions on U.S. basing rights in the home islands, leading to an eventual termination of the Japanese-U.S. security arrangements. "South Korea is the last U.S. outpost on the Asian mainland, and its loss could lead to a change in Japan's political orientation and have serious consequences for U.S. presence in Northeast Asia as a whole."[20]

The Japanese government has repeatedly and explicitly formulated its security policy on the basis of a set of necessary assumptions, among which the security of South Korea has figured very prominently.[21] A united Korea from which military threats against Japan could emanate would necessarily and fundamentally alter Tokyo's defense posture. Those who have argued that the Japanese preoccupation with the stability and security of South Korea is no more than a result of U.S. insistence[22] have relentlessly refused either to read Japanese assessments or to analyze the importance of the Korean straits to any credible defense of the Japanese home islands. The Japanese Defense White Paper published in July 1980 made clear Japan's abiding concern with the security of the Korean peninsula.

Should the loss of South Korea prompt a Japanese reassessment of its postwar security policy, the United States might well find itself confined to a mid-Pacific defense perimeter extending from the Aleutians to Hawaii. Its control over the maritime choke points around Japan would be negligible, and in any general conventional conflict the meager resources of the Seventh Fleet would have to contend with a Soviet naval presence throughout the entire Pacific.

Any perception of U.S. weakness with respect to the military security of South Korea might prompt the Soviet Union, mainland China, and/or North Korea to take a more militant stance. The Soviet Union, if given convincing evidence of United States withdrawal, could use the occasion to secure its position in Northeast Asia by underwriting a North Korean adventure. Mainland China, driven by its increasing energy needs,[23] might use its long and persistent dispute with Seoul over the potential oil resources in the territorial waters off South Korea to justify supporting a North Korean initiative, thereby gaining the favor of Pyongyang and preventing the Soviet Union from making further inroads on the peninsula.

A Korea unified under Communist Chinese influence would be only marginally preferable to one unified under Soviet influence. There is little reason to believe that Communist China, having displaced the United States from the Korean peninsula, would continue to perceive U.S. armed forces as a credible deterrent to the Soviet Union. As a result of this erosion of credibility, and the increased leverage over Japan its association with Korea would provide, the PRC would be able to initiate a rapprochement with the Soviet Union from a position of strength. Japan would increasingly become hostage to the interests of the two major communist powers in East Asia.

Unfortunately, the situation on the Korean peninsula remains fraught with potential conflict—and opportunities for mischief for both the Soviet Union and mainland China. In August 1981 the North Koreans fired a surface-to-air missile at a U.S. SR-71 high-altitude reconnaissance aircraft that was flying over international waters. When Washington protested, Peking refused to intervene in any way—out of loyalty to Pyongyang. It is clear that Peking wishes to maintain its relationship with Pyongyang, if for no other reason than to avoid allowing North Korea to move into the orbit of Soviet influence. North Korea thus remains a critical and immediate political problem for the authorities in Peking. There is little doubt that Peking's interests would be secured if it could secure the allegiance of Pyongyang and gain access to Japanese technological and investment resources to the exclusion of the United States.

The gunfire along the demilitarized zone between North and South Korea during 1981 simply highlighted the potential for conflict that exists on the peninsula. Kim Il-sung's formula for the resolution of tensions on the peninsula is tantamount to a virtual surrender by the government in Seoul. There is little prospect of a political or diplomatic solution to the Korean issue as long as he governs the North;[24] thus Korea will remain a locus of potential crisis for the foreseeable future. The one factor that stabilizes the situation is the presence of U.S. ground forces athwart the major invasion routes into South Korea. As long as these forces remain a credible deterrent to North Korean military adventure, neither the Soviet Union nor the People's Republic of China will be tempted to incite Pyongyang to such action.

The renewed U.S. commitment to maintain ground forces in South Korea as long as the danger of military conflict persists is part of the larger effort of the Reagan administration to restore the confidence of the Asian allies by reaffirming its commitment to East Asian security. Although it could be argued as late as 1975 that there was a "deepening trend toward isolationism in the United States,"[25] by the early 1980s it was evident that the majority of Americans felt that the nation must be more selective in making commitments, but "those [commitments] that are worthwhile and held to be strongly in the national interest must be defended with U.S. might." Moreover, a plurality of the general public (43 percent) held that the U.S. commitment to South Korea should be demonstrated by military intervention should North Korea undertake a military assault.[26]

As has been suggested, a defense of South Korea is a defense of one of those remarkable Asian nations that have shown that by adopting a form of open-market capitalism, and by participating in the international investment and trading community, a developing nation can, in fact, achieve a relatively high level of industrialization without sacrificing the well-being of its population. The 1983 plans for the revival of the economy of South Korea, necessitated by the severe dislocations of the 1979 recession, include an anticipated annual growth rate of about 7–8 percent and a decline of inflation to about 10 percent. A significant increase in domestic capital accumulation is predicted, along with a narrowing trade deficit. Export growth is expected to reach a level of about 20 percent per annum, which, along with a more balanced expansion of industry, will allow increased investments in social welfare services and increased defense expenditures.

Whatever the shortcomings of political democracy in South Korea, it is evident that the citizens of the South enjoy far more civil and political liberties than those locked into the totalitarianism of the North. Thus the Republic of Korea has demonstrated that economic and industrial growth with equity is possible in an environment that provides for at least some political freedom. In terms of the normative concerns of U.S. foreign policy, such a demonstration is of appreciable importance. In the early 1970s, academics in the United States held that only totalitarian controls could effect the mobilization of resources necessary to underwrite economic development. The performance of rapidly developing economies like that of South Korea has forced a modification of such views. The most dynamic developing economies of the modern world are those that are market oriented and that remain committed, at least in principle, to political pluralism. Although they may be flawed in practice, such political systems remain committed to political arrangements that Americans are prepared to defend. The conviction that authoritarian governments have the potential for transition to more open political systems—whereas totalitarian systems do not—inspires much of contemporary U.S. foreign policy.

The security of the Republic of Korea no longer figures as a simple constituent of an "anti-Soviet" or "anticommunist" grand strategy. The defense of the security of South Korea recommends itself as intrinsically supportive of overall U.S. interests. Countries with such open-market economies generally display the potential for establishing the kinds of political systems that Americans perceive as conducive to general economic well-being and political liberty.

Beyond that, the ROK is of not negligible economic interest to Americans. Trade and investment relations between the United States and the ROK have been mutually profitable since the late 1960s—but they were not when Americans were sent to defend South Korea on the battlefield.

Finally, the Republic of Korea is of major strategic importance in Northeast Asia. It commands the western shore of the Sea of Japan—essential to the defense of the Japanese home islands—and control of the waterways leading from it is necessary for the U.S. defense of the West Pacific in any general conflict.

The United States is being afforded the opportunity to display its determination to defend the security of the ROK. It seems clear that that defense requires the continued deterrent presence of U.S. troops on the ground. Although such troops can exercise little direct military influence, their presence is evidence of Washington's readiness to put U.S. lives in harm's way in the defense of its security commitments. The possibility that U.S. lives might be lost in any misadventure on the peninsula is a major consideration in any calculations made in Pyongyang, Moscow, or Peking.

But peace on the Korean peninsula is too important to allow its defense to remain solely a military concern. The United States is in a position to influence diplomatic and political initiatives in the subregion. There is some evidence that both the Soviet Union and the People's Republic of China would like to defuse the volatile situation on the peninsula. Cross-recognition of both Koreas by the major political actors in the region would go some distance in stabilizing the situation. Entry of both Koreas into the United Nations would further assist the process. Guarantees of the peace and security of the peninsula by the four major powers (Japan, the United States, the Soviet Union, and mainland China) would bring the process to substantial conclusion. With the establishment of a secure peace, the slow process of reunification of the divided nation could be undertaken.

The 1980s are the most critical period for the Korean peninsula. By 1990, barring unforeseen developments, the vulnerability of South Korea will be a thing of the past; it will no longer be exposed to North Korean military assault. If its economy performs anywhere near the anticipated levels, the likelihood of North Korean–inspired subversion should diminish as well.

With the Republic of Korea secured, the security of Japan will be enhanced. The political integrity and the military security of South Korea are fundamental to the stability and defense of Japan, and Japan's security is essential to the political stability and the military defense of the West Pacific. In sum, the security of Northeast Asia depends on a coherent and interconnected strategy that acknowledges the importance of the defense triangle that stretches from the Sōya Strait to the Tsushima Strait and to the Bashi Channel. It is on the basis of the integrity of this "iron triangle" that the defense of the West Pacific can be reconstructed.

6 | The Security of the Republic of China on Taiwan

The only sound policy for the United States to follow is to increase its conventional and nuclear strength in Asia sufficiently to defend successfully U.S. interests and those of its allies; to exploit but not become dependent upon the Sino-Soviet split; and to keep its strategic options open by retaining a littoral defensive position along the Western Pacific rim.

Taiwan, occupying a central position in that island chain defense, has been equated by Admiral Edwin K. Snyder, former head of the Taiwan Defense Command, "to about ten aircraft carriers." Secretary of State Alexander Haig has also referred to Taiwan as a "rather impregnable aircraft carrier." To withdraw U.S. support from Taiwan, or to deny it the arms necessary to defend itself, would not be strategically sound.

Martin L. Lasater,
The Security of Taiwan: Unraveling the Dilemma.

Of all the problems the United States inherited from the Second World War, the issue of the "two Chinas" is perhaps the most vexing and is currently the one having the most serious long-term consequences. For about a quarter of a century, the United States was allied with the Republic of China on Taiwan through a bilateral security treaty. When it entered into the security relationship with the United States in December 1954, the Republic of China on Taiwan was an impoverished traditional society much like the Republic of Korea. The United States subsequently championed the cause of the ROC in the international community and assisted the authorities in Taipei in putting together what proved to be one of the most successful economic development programs in recent history. Yet, for all that, the U.S. commitment to the Republic of China on Taiwan, like its commitment to the Republic of Korea, has been more an improvisation than a component of some determinate long-range policy.

In fact, in 1949 the United States had clearly signaled its disposition to disengage itself from any further involvement in the civil war that had ravaged China for almost a quarter century. In the summer of that year, communist forces were preparing an amphibious invasion that was expected to overwhelm the island with little difficulty. By the end of the year the Department of State had reconciled itself to the collapse of the final resistance against the communist forces of Mao Tse-tung.

The situation in the Taiwan Strait was dramatically altered by the invasion of South Korea by communist forces from the North on June 25, 1950. The leadership in Washington perceived that invasion as part of a broad-gauged communist offensive—orchestrated by Moscow—against the noncommunist nations of Asia, and in response reassessed its entire Asian policy. In the dramatic policy reversal that followed, the United States reasserted its concern with the security of the noncommunist Asian nations other than Japan and redrew the U.S. forward defense perimeter in Northeast Asia to include not only Japan, but the Republic of Korea and the Republic of China on Taiwan as well.[1] Bilateral security treaties followed that were calculated to provide for the defense of the noncommunist nations of Northeast Asia against aggression and basing facilities for the forward deployment of U.S. forces.

Thus the Mutual Defense Treaty between the Republic of China and the United States (March 1955) was designed to "declare publicly and formally" their "sense of unity and...common determination to defend themselves against external armed attack"; it also allowed the United States "the right to dispose such United States land, air and sea forces in and about Taiwan and the Pescadores as may be required" for the common defense.[2] Taiwan was to function as an "unsinkable aircraft carrier" in the Pacific rimland defense system.[3] Like the Republic of Korea, Taiwan was to be part of the line of forward posts that allowed the United States a defense in depth and provided advanced staging areas as part of the containment strategy of the immediate postwar period.

After this strategic posture was established in 1953, the United States insisted, for over two decades, that any demand that it "abandon" its "commitment to the defense of Taiwan...was not...and is not...open to negotiation."[4] As late as the Ford administration, the United States had reiterated its commitment to the defense of Taiwan on at least 52 formal occasions.[5] The association with the ROC was established so firmly and for so long that even those most favorably disposed toward the normalization of diplomatic relations with the People's Republic of China agreed that any accommodation with Communist China at the expense of the ROC would be considered by "many...a major crime even for the 20th century."[6]

When it became evident that the authorities in Washington were contemplating some sort of rapprochement with the PRC in an effort to counterbalance Soviet global advantages, the general public in the United States resisted, by a large plurality, the suggestion that Washington enter into diplomatic relations with Peking at the expense of Taipei. Forty-seven percent of those polled in 1977 objected to formalizing relations with Communist China if that normalization involved a "derecognition" of the ROC and a termination of U.S. security relations with Taipei. Only 28 percent of the general public favored recognition of Peking at the price of alienating Taipei.[7]

Among legislators in Congress, the resistance to entering into diplomatic relations with Peking at the expense of Taipei was perhaps even stronger. Of the 535 members of the House of Representatives polled in October 1978, 328 were strongly opposed or leaning toward opposition to such an eventuality; 56 of the 100 members of the Senate indicated their opposition. Moreover, between 1974 and 1978, 32 state legislatures (including those of New York and California, the most populous states) passed resolutions of one sort or another expressing support for the Republic of China.[8]

Given this reservoir of resistance to such a policy reversal, there must have been strong motives behind the Carter administration's resolve to recognize the PRC essentially on Peking's terms: the diplomatic derecognition of the ROC; the withdrawal of all U.S. forces from Taiwan; and the termination of the mutual security treaty between the United States and the Republic of China. In fact, so strong was the general reaction and so marked was the legislative resistance to the derecognition of the ROC that the relatively innocuous legislation suggested by the Carter administration (S.245), to provide for the ongoing relations between the United States and the "people of Taiwan," was completely overhauled by Congress and transformed into what has been described as a surrogate security arrangement written into domestic law.[9] The legislators, forced to grapple with the issue of "informal" relations between the United States and its former security partner, were critically concerned with the vulnerability of Taiwan after the withdrawal of U.S. guarantees. Senator Frank Church, chairman of the Senate Committee on Foreign Relations, spoke of the importance that the United States "must attach to the future security and well-being of the people of Taiwan."[10]

What emerged from all this was Public Law 96–8, the Taiwan Relations Act (April 1979)—a domestic law stating that "peace and stability in the [Taiwan Strait] area are in the political, security and economic interests of the United States" and that Washington would consider "any effort to determine the future of Taiwan by other than peaceful means, including boycotts or embargoes, a threat to the peace and security of the Western Pacific area and of grave concern to the United States" [Section 2 (b)]. The act committed the United States to the provision of "arms of a defensive character...in such quantity as may be necessary to enable Taiwan to maintain a sufficient self-defense capability" [Section 3 (a)].[11]

Whatever the personal or narrowly political determinants of President Carter's decision to normalize relations with Peking, some of the public reasons advanced as its rationale merit consideration. By 1978, many officials in Washington were prepared to regard mainland China as a military counterweight to the Soviet Union. The notion that the United States might profit from the deterioration of Sino-Soviet relations had been advanced as early as the first Nixon administration and received added currency as the threat from the Soviet Union military buildup increased. By the beginning of the Carter administration in 1977, such a notion was all but irresistible. It was clear that by pursuing a rapprochement with Peking, Washington could enter all of mainland China's military resources in the "assets" column of the anti-Soviet balance sheets.

The price to be paid for such a windfall was the derecognition of the Republic of China on Taiwan. For the first time in its history the United States was preparing to break diplomatic relations with a friendly power with whom it had been allied by security treaty. Although the price was high, the benefits were assessed to be abundant. Not only would the United States reap a security advantage, but there was the lure of the "vast Chinese market"—at a time when the United States economy was suffering massive foreign trade deficits and businessmen had few domestic investment opportunities.

Actually, the derecognition of the ROC in December 1978 and the termination of the U.S.-ROC mutual security treaty on December 31, 1979, were but the final acts of a drama that had begun with the first overture to Peking by the Nixon administration in 1971. When they became aware of the apparent readiness of the United States to come to some kind of agreement with the PRC after almost three decades of unremitting hostility, many nations began to alter their policies with respect to the "two Chinas."

In the early 1970s the Republic of China on Taiwan was an accredited member of the United Nations, and 68 nations maintained diplomatic relations with Taipei while only 53 nations had formal relations with Peking. At the end of the decade when, after more than six years of negotiations, the United States finally undertook to formalize relations with Peking, only 22 nations had ties with the ROC; more than 120 had entered into formal relations with the People's Republic of China.[12] Taiwan withdrew from the United Nations on October 25, 1971.

Tokyo had taken note of the changes in U.S. Far Eastern policy that followed in the wake of President Nixon's Guam statements in 1969. Implicit in the discussions concerning the disengagement from the West Pacific was a significant shift in U.S. China policy. But as late as January 1972 Foreign Minister Takeo Fukuda reassured the ambassador of the Republic of China that the "Taiwan clause" contained in the joint communiqué of Prime Minister Satō and President Nixon (November 1969) remained valid; Satō himself reaffirmed that an attack on Taiwan would constitute a "threat to the peace and security of the Far East including Japan."[13]

On February 27, 1972, the Shanghai communiqué, crafted by Nixon and Chou En-lai, was released. The United States proceeded to "acknowledge" that there was but "one China and that Taiwan is a part of China." The communiqué affirmed the U.S. "interest in a peaceful settlement of the Taiwan question by the Chinese themselves." Two months later Foreign Minister Fukuda announced that the reference to Taiwan in the Satō-Nixon communiqué of 1969 had ceased to be "relevant" after the articulation of the U.S. position in the Shanghai communiqué.[14]

What this seemed to mean was that although the Taiwan clause in the Satō-Nixon communiqué remained valid, it was not relevant to Tokyo's negotiations with Peking concerning normalization. The Japanese chose to interpret the Shanghai communiqué as a "tacit guarantee of peace in the Strait of Taiwan" that would allow Tokyo to seek improved relations with Peking without fear of causing a major security crisis in that area.[15] As a consequence of that construal, Japanese business interests, long attracted by the profit potentially to be gained from the mainland Chinese investment and export markets, were free to pressure the officials in Tokyo for the rapid improvement in Sino-Japanese relations that would afford them a competitive advantage in gaining access to such markets.

Japanese public officials were far more reserved in pursuing relations with Communist China for a variety of reasons—a concern for national security being not the least among them. Although popular support for the ROC in Japan had collapsed by the end of 1971 and enthusiasm for normalization with the PRC was running high, it was clear that Tokyo was not prepared to unequivocally dismiss the issue of Taiwan and, as a consequence, made no categoric commitments as to the status or future of Taiwan in the documents establishing diplomatic relations with Peking. The Japanese struggled to preserve as vague a definition of Taiwan's sovereignty as possible, and it seems evident that Tokyo has never abandoned its conviction that the security of the island is critical to the defense of Japan.[16] Although Tokyo has made it a studied policy not to take up the issue of Taiwan's security—allowing the United States to shoulder that particular burden—the Japanese have not explicitly renounced the concern embodied in the Satō-Nixon communiqué that Taiwan was important to the defense of Japan.[17] In fact, in 1976, while Japan was actively negotiating the peace and friendship treaty with mainland China, Foreign Minister Keniichi Miyazawa publicly asserted that Japan would not welcome any change in Sino-U.S. relations that might impair the strength of U.S. guarantees of the security of the Republic of China on Taiwan.[18] In 1980, the Research Institute for Peace and Security, one of the most prestigious of the Japanese security-oriented research agencies, reported that the Taiwan Relations Act, designed to govern U.S.-Taiwan relations after derecognition, had provided the foundation for "U.S.-Taiwan joint military maneuvers" and left open the possibility of U.S. Navy port calls and other forms of military cooperation "on a case-by-case basis"—all of which implied to the Japanese the possibility that "the United States and Taiwan will continue to endeavor to maintain some military relations, and consequently that the security of this area will be preserved for the time being."[19] In effect, Tokyo chose to interpret the "understandings" that followed from the Shanghai communiqué, as well as the formal statements of the United States on the occasion of the establishment of diplomatic relations with mainland China, as evidence that "the *de facto* continuance of Taiwan as an independent state" was assured "for some time to come." Tokyo noted that the United States was prepared to continue arms sales to Taipei and that, as a consequence, "Taiwan's existence...seems fairly well assured."[20]

Japan, partly in response to general public sentiment and the influence of interest groups, proceeded rapidly to normalize relations with mainland China as soon as the United States gave clear evidence of a fundamental change in its China policy. Japan expected to gain economic advantage from normalization, and for a brief period it seemed as though its expectations would be fulfilled. Nonetheless, there were sectors of the Japanese political and defense establishments that were (and remain) troubled by the changes—and they were not only individuals who owed political loyalties to Taipei for whatever reason. Many defense strategists, then and subsequently, emphasized the role the island of Taiwan could play in any defense of the shipping lanes in Japan. The argument proffered to allay their fears was that the United States had sufficiently secured the integrity of Taiwan to allow Japan to pursue its mainland Chinese connection. The Japanese could exploit the trade and investment opportunities offered by Communist China without preoccupation because the Taiwan Relations Act provided the guarantees for Taiwan's increasingly fragile security.

The behavior of other Asian countries revealed a similar set of concerns. As a case in point, the Republic of the Philippines severed diplomatic relations with the Republic of China on Taiwan for essentially the same reasons as those that prompted Japan's subsequent derecognition. It chose, however, to make its security concerns more explicit. When the United States terminated its security treaty with Taiwan in 1979, Manila complained that that action cast still further doubt on the credibility of the United States as a defense partner—a credibility already impaired by the consequences of the Nixon Doctrine of 1969.[21]

To noncommunist Asian leaders, U.S. behavior appeared more and more confused. Those leaders judged it only prudent to attempt to mollify real or potential enemies in the region. As confidence in the United States as a security partner diminished, there was a scramble to placate Moscow or Peking, or both at the same time.[22]

Japan and the Philippines felt compelled to normalize relations with Peking, even at the expense of Taipei, once Washington had signaled a fundamental change in its East Asian policy. Tokyo, Manila, Singapore, and Bangkok, too weak to act as major powers, had the responsibility of making whatever arrangements would best serve the interests of their respective populations. The noncommunist nations of East Asia felt that if the impact of the Vietnam War on U.S. policy, reflected in the retrenchment implicit in the Nixon Doctrine, reduced their security, they had the right (and some were driven by necessity) to make some accommodations with Moscow, Hanoi, or Peking.

Most of the noncommunist nations of East Asia made it quite clear that they understood Washington's behavior. Most recognized that the balance of global power had shifted and that the United States no longer enjoyed unqualified economic and military power. What generated concern was the fact that these changed circumstances could lead the United States to abandon a security partner that five administrations had pledged to protect. Tokyo, Manila, Singapore, or Bangkok could sever relations with Taipei to attempt to gain real or fancied economic or security benefits, but the severance of those relations by Washington meant that it was terminating a security treaty with a friendly nation that, for a quarter of a century, had honored that treaty to the letter.[23] In 1978, in an amendment to the International Security Assistance Act, Congress affirmed that "the United States and the Republic of China have for a period of twenty-four years been linked together by the Mutual Defense Treaty of 1954 [and] the Republic of China has during that twenty-four-year period faithfully and continually carried out its duties and obligations under that treaty."[24] The termination of that security arrangement in order to comply with the demands of Peking, to purchase what were taken to be bargaining advantages vis-à-vis the Soviet Union, could only tarnish the image and impair the credibility of the United States as a defense partner.

The Taiwan Relations Act, hastily put together by the Senate and passed by Congress after the Carter administration announced the termination of the security treaty with the Republic of China on Taiwan, was an attempt to deflect at least some of the criticism that was anticipated. The act clearly identified Taiwan as being essential to U.S. economic and security interests.[25] It also defined and strengthened the future U.S. commitment to the defense of Taiwan; by affirming the U.S. intention to "resist any resort to force" employed against the island, it communicated to Peking that any use of violence or coercion to achieve reunification would be a matter of "grave concern" to the United States.[26]

By providing some assurance of security to the ROC, the act restored some of the lost credibility suffered by the United States as a defense partner. The act was an innovative and skillful piece of domestic legislation that bore similarities to the "informal" arrangement contrived by the Japanese to maintain their economic and cultural contacts with the ROC after the severance of diplomatic relations. It was also a domestic effort to provide a surrogate for an international mutual defense treaty.[27] Congress had acted out of due concern for the safety and well-being of the people on Taiwan as well as a regard for the strategic interests of the United States. Control of Taiwan by any current or future adversary would seriously threaten the survival of both South Korea and Japan as allies of the United States and render U.S. defense of the West Pacific very difficult.

The evident fact is that both the Soviet Union and the People's Republic of China have a strategic interest in the island of Taiwan and the surrounding waters. Should Moscow be committed to a strategy of "encircling" mainland China, Taiwan would occupy an essential link in the chain of bases that would stretch from the Kuril Islands and Vladivostok to Danang and the Camranh Bay in Vietnam. Taiwan is the only place along the archipelagic chain separating continental Asia from the Pacific that would allow the mainland Chinese direct and secure access to open waters. A Soviet presence on Taiwan would restrict that access and thus would pose a serious threat to the maritime trade of the People's Republic of China. Moreover, such a presence would afford the USSR access to fueling and repair facilities, staging areas for aircraft, and submarine servicing capabilities available on Taiwan and would significantly enhance Soviet naval and air power projections over the western reaches of the Pacific.

The Bashi Channel between Taiwan and the Philippines (where the Soviet Union deployed a major naval force during its Okean II exercises in 1975) is the principal passageway for ships transiting between the Malacca Strait and the major ports in mainland China, South Korea, and Japan. The channel, 1,000 fathoms deep on either side, is a critical choke point well situated for submarine warfare. Subsea raiders, running at depth, could conceal themselves below the thermal gradients in order to escape easy detection. Obversely, naval forces on Taiwan would be well circumstanced for patrolling the channel, detecting submarine transits, and posing a deterrent to interdiction. The island of Taiwan would thus play a major role in a limited or general conventional conflict in the West Pacific.

In such a conflict, the most serious disability suffered by the Soviet navy would be its dearth of adequate basing facilities in East Asia. Some of those disabilities have been offset by the acquisition of use-as-needed rights to naval bases in Vietnam and the limited utilization of Najin in North Korea. What the Soviet Pacific Fleet really needs is a major basing facility along the rim of continental Asia. Naval bases on Taiwan would serve that end eminently well.

There is a major naval shipyard at Tsoying in the First Naval District of the Republic of China, located off the Bashi Channel. The Soviet navy could utilize the massive shipfitting and repair facilities of Kaohsiung, where some of the world's largest ships have been constructed and refitted in the recent past.

Peking has protested not only the "provocative" presence of Soviet naval combatants in the Taiwan region, but the evident Soviet interest in the island itself. Although it may be desirable in terms of Soviet security planning, Soviet access to Taiwanese facilities, under any set of foreseeable circumstances, is extremely unlikely.[28] The government of the Republic of China on Taiwan has made it quite clear that it is averse to any contact with the Soviet Union, despite its flawed relationship with the United States. That the Soviet Union could pose a direct threat to Taiwan except in a general conflict is so unlikely as to be dismissed as a serious strategic and defense concern.

The threat to Taiwan posed by the People's Republic of China is manifestly different. The enmity between these two nations is of long standing. The conflict in the Taiwan Strait is, in fact, one phase of the Chinese civil war that has been continuing for over half a century; mainland China has insisted that Taiwan is a part of sovereign China since the retreat of the Kuomintang forces to their "island redoubt" in 1949. There has been intermittent violence in the Taiwan Strait since the early 1950s. Since 1958, when the Communist Chinese attempted to blockade the Nationalist-held offshore islands of Quemoy and Matsu, naval and air battles have involved major elements of both armed forces; two ROC minesweepers were lost to the Communist Chinese navy in 1965.

Throughout this period, Peking has insisted that Taiwan must be "liberated." In 1975, after the process of normalization of diplomatic relations with the United States had begun, officials of the People's Republic of China insisted that they could not "preclude the use of armed forces in the liberation of Taiwan." They argued that the liberation of the island required that the PLA forces obtain "absolute sea and air superiority" in order to ensure that the island could be occupied. Given such superiority, an assault would be undertaken when the Soviet Union was preoccupied elsewhere and the United States had "pulled out of the area."[29] Since that time, Peking has neither officially renounced the use of military force in "reunifying" Taiwan with the mainland nor explicitly modified its overall strategy.

The People's Republic of China deploys military forces that outnumber those of the Republic of China on Taiwan by a ratio of about 10:1. The PLA is the largest general-purpose land army in the world. The PLA air force (PLAAF) is the third largest air force in the world, operating about 5,300 combat machines. The PLA navy (PLAN) has the world's third largest number of combat naval vessels; the total number of combatants available is estimated to range from 1,680 to 2,510.[30] Across the Taiwan Strait, the

Republic of China on Taiwan operates a relatively small military establish-ment by comparison. Its general-purpose ground forces are one-tenth the size of the PLA. Its air force has about 386 combat aircraft in inventory, and its navy operates about 100 combatants.

It is clear that should the armed forces of mainland China make a deter-mined amphibious assault against Taiwan, the Republic of China on Taiwan would be overwhelmed. Irrespective of their serious disabilities, the armed forces of the People's Republic of China have such overwhelming numerical advantage that any protracted defense of Taiwan that did not involve the support of a major military power would be all but impossible to sustain. That the PRC has not embarked upon such a course of action is attributable to two main considerations. Since the early 1960s, Peking has been preoccupied with the Soviet threat along its northern and western borders. Moreover, since early 1979, Peking has had to contend with the threat of U.S. involvement should the PLA undertake to "liberate" Taiwan by force of arms.

Both the Nixon and Ford administrations hesitated to enter into formal diplomatic relations with Peking—at least in part because such relations would have necessitated termination of the mutual security treaty with the Republic of China on Taiwan that had, until that time, insulated Taiwan from armed attack from the mainland. The Carter administration dealt with this particular issue in a curious fashion. In essence, its officials were prepared to argue, on the one hand, that the People's Republic of China was capable of serving Western interests as a military counterweight to the Soviet Union and, on the other, that it was incapable of or unwilling to undertake attack against its non-Soviet neighbors.[31] Some of them argued that all mainland China needed was a "flow of Western technology" to render its military capabilities so imposing that the Soviet Union would be "forced to pursue a conservative, defensive, and détente-oriented strategy."[32] Others argued that Communist China provided enough of a land army "to assure. . . sustained pressure upon, and attrition of, Soviet forces to make. . . strikes against vital Soviet interests meaningful."[33] During the Senate hearings that preceded passage of the Taiwan Relations Act, a spokesman for the Carter administration insisted that "the People's Republic of China does not have the military capability to invade Taiwan."[34] The contention was that the PRC would soon have the military capability to force the Soviet Union to become increasingly compliant, but it somehow would not have the ability to overwhelm Taiwan.

Other administration officials argued, perhaps more plausibly, that the PRC would act "responsibly" if it were afforded the security of rapprochement with the West, for it would then not risk alienating its newfound allies by embarking on a military adventure against any nation, including its non-Soviet neighbors. Therefore, Peking would attack neither Taiwan nor Vietnam.[35]

Finally, the argument was proffered that no matter what the capabilities of the Communist Chinese military, Peking's increasing dependency on Western capital and technology, in its drive to spur economic development, would preclude the possibility that it would act irresponsibly. In effect, by entering into formal diplomatic relations with Peking, the United States would acquire a credible military counterweight to the Soviet military threat and would not impair the security and stability of East Asia.

Since these arguments[36] were made public in the mid-1970s, it has become reasonably apparent that the People's Republic of China cannot serve as a military counterweight to the Soviet Union. The military capabilities of the PLA are so marginal vis-à-vis those of the Soviet Union as to make their influence negligible in any contest of force between the major military powers. As we have seen, most military analysts today recognize the serious disabilities that afflict the armed forces of Communist China when confronted by the Soviet Union. So many options are open to the Soviet military that any hope that the mainland Chinese forces might serve as a deterrent to Soviet aggression is unrealistic.[37] The People's Republic of China, by its own assessment, remains an "unarmed giant" in the contest between the contending superpowers. It is incapable of either undertaking initiatives against the forces of the Soviet Union or adequately defending itself against their initiatives.[38]

Mainland China's armed forces deploy sufficient military power to present a sustained threat against its littoral and insular neighbors, however. As a case in point, in 1979, almost immediately after the beginning of normalization of relations with the United States, Peking launched a "punitive war" against Vietnam—much to the public embarrassment of Washington. In that campaign the PRC employed a total of about 21 infantry divisions from 8 army corps. They were supported by an undetermined, but large, number of drawn artillery pieces and T-34/85 and Type 62 tanks. About 1,000 combat aircraft were marshaled for action in the region, including the most modern craft of the PLAAF. A total of about 500,000 troops were employed before the PLA broke off the attack.

Neither fear of the presence of Soviet military power along its northern borders nor sensitivity to Western fears that the conflict might expand deterred mainland China from launching its attack. Although the performance of the Communist Chinese forces left a great deal to be desired, the invasion did indicate that the People's Republic of China was fully prepared to use a considerable portion of its armed capabilities against its non-Soviet neighbors. Clearly, the Communist Chinese chose not to provoke the Soviet Union or the Western powers excessively. But equally evident was their disposition to pursue what they regarded as their own national interests by any means necessary, with little thought as to international reaction. Communist Chinese officials have reminded the West that mainland China was prepared to alienate the Soviet Union in the late 1950s and early 1960s when the PRC was almost totally dependent upon Moscow for economic and military assistance. There is little reason to believe that it would not do so with regard to the West should it feel that its interests so required.[39]

The People's Republic of China has used armed force in its relations with its neighbors throughout its history—often at the expense of alienating its allies. It used armed force in its efforts to resolve the Taiwan issue in 1958 over the opposition of the leadership in Moscow, which feared a confrontation with the United States. It used armed force in its border disputes with India between 1958 and 1962, when India was being courted by the Soviet Union; that adventure served increasingly to alienate Moscow. Peking also used armed force in securing the Paracel Islands in 1974 against the objections of its allies in Hanoi, who viewed the Paracels as inalienable "sovereign territory."[40] There is, as a consequence, little to support the argument that mainland China will not use armed force against any of its neighbors should it perceive its national interests as being jeopardized. The authorities in Taipei found little solace in the assessments of Carter administration spokesmen that the U.S. rapprochement with Communist China would reduce the threat of conflict in the Taiwan Strait. If Peking were prepared to embark on an adventure in Vietnam—irrespective of Soviet threats, risking alienation of the West, and for very little profit—what confidence could the leaders of the ROC have in U.S. assurances?

The fact is that the Republic of China on Taiwan remains threatened by military attack emanating from the mainland. The military forces at the disposal of Peking are sufficient to overwhelm the Republic of China on Taiwan. While amphibious invasion over 100 miles of blue water constitutes an obstacle of substantial magnitude, Communist China need not make recourse to that desperate option to subdue Taiwan.

By the time the U.S. normalized its relations with Peking, mainland China had sufficient naval capability in inventory to effectively blockade the island of Taiwan.[41] With the 100 diesel-powered attack submarines in inventory, the PLAN is capable of emplacing a naval blockade around Taiwan's major ports of entry. The Republic of China on Taiwan is almost entirely dependent upon ship traffic to sustain its economic viability. The simple announcement of an intended blockade would cause maritime insurance rates for vessels contemplating trade with Taiwan to escalate, and the loss of incoming cartage would be a predictable consequence even before a shot was fired.

That the United States would act decisively in the event of a conflict in the Taiwan Strait is at least doubtful, because the prospect of an armed confrontation with the People's Republic of China in order to preserve the sovereign existence of Taiwan would be politically disabling for any administration. Peking is of the opinion that former Secretary of State Alexander Haig was expressing Washington's judgment when he insisted that relations between the

United States and the People's Republic of China were "a fundamental strategic reality and a strategic imperative." As a consequence, Peking is convinced that the United States needs Communist China more than Communist China needs the United States.[42]

Peking has many political, strategic, and economic reasons for seeking an early resolution of the Taiwan issue in its favor. Taiwan has always been an inflammatory domestic political issue for Peking; "reunification" of Taiwan with the mainland would defuse domestic criticism of the policies of the current leadership. Moreover, acquisition of the island would preclude the possibility of Soviet "encirclement"; it would also allow Peking to control maritime traffic to and from the Northeast and thus to directly influence the foreign policies of both South Korea and Japan. In acquiring Taiwan, Peking would augment its long-standing claims over the disputed waters of the East China and South China seas.

Taiwan's land surface constitutes but 0.4 percent of that of mainland China, and Taiwan has but 1.9 percent of the population of the PRC. In 1977 the ROC conducted 54.6 percent of all Chinese international trade, floated 45 percent of all Chinese merchant ships, serviced 84 percent of all Chinese international traffic, and produced 17.5 percent of all the Chinese electrical power generated. Almost 47 percent of all Chinese students attending institutions of higher learning are enrolled on the island of Taiwan, and the citizens of the ROC enjoy a per capita income at least eight times that of the citizens of the PRC.[43] Bringing Taiwan "back to the bosom of the motherland" would thus bring substantial gains to the People's Republic of China. Those gains would be not only political and strategic but would include advanced industry, technology, and training institutions so lacking on the mainland.

Perhaps more fundamental is the fact that the suppression of the Republic of China on Taiwan would remove an eminently successful competitor for the allegiance of Chinese wherever they are to be found. This success is a direct result of Taiwan's economic accomplishments. Since the 1950s the authorities in Taipei have supervised an increasingly successful experiment in economic modernization; by 1980 the Republic of China on Taiwan had one of the most efficient economic systems in Asia. Taiwan's population enjoys Asia's second highest per capita income, and its rapidly growing social welfare system distributes economic benefits more equitably than that of any other developing country.[44]

Whatever its diplomatic successes in the recent past, Peking has not been able to resolve its very serious economic problems. Between 1952 and 1980, its agricultural labor productivity in terms of value output per man-day declined at a rate of between 15 and 36 percent. Even though grain and rice yields have almost doubled since then as a result of double-cropping and the addition of almost 100 million laborers, the rapid increase in population has left the per capita availability of both grain and rice at about the same level that it was in 1937.[45]

There is little doubt that in the industrial sector, total factor productivity rose sharply during the first decade of Communist Chinese rule; however, the fragmentary evidence suggests that further increases after 1965 were far less substantial. Labor productivity, which rose rapidly immediately after the accession of the Communists to power, has declined since 1965; from 1965 to 1980, it increased at an average rate of only 0.7 percent a year. Mainland Chinese officials complain of high material and energy utilization rates tying up working capital, affording poor returns on investment and reducing the average profit margin of industries.[46]

In effect, mainland China shows marked deficiencies in precisely those areas where Taiwan has displayed equally marked proficiency. The differences (however one chooses to explain them) have generated considerable political embarrassment for the authorities in Peking. Not merely a few of its citizens have raised the question of comparative performance.

For at least these reasons, Peking has remained absolutely adamant that reunification of Taiwan with the motherland is a project to be accomplished in the 1980s. To do so requires, perhaps above all else, that any military moves on the part of the PLA not be met by an effective military response.

Virtually the sole consideration preventing Communist Chinese adventure in the Taiwan Strait is the possibility of sizable losses of military equipment. Manpower losses, of course, can be sustained without serious consequence, for manpower is abundantly available to the PLA. The loss of equipment is an entirely different matter.

The PLA has never undertaken to put any substantial part of its equipment inventory at risk. During the "punitive" invasion of Vietnam in 1979, for example, the military authorities in Peking did not permit the PLAAF to engage the Vietnamese air force in combat. Although the combat aircraft of the PLAAF enjoyed at least a 2:1 superiority over those of the Vietnamese, the Communist Chinese chose to allow their foot-mobile infantry to attack enemy strongpoints without air support. As a consequence, manpower losses in contests with the Vietnamese irregulars were heavy (almost all the Vietnamese soldiers who engaged the invading Communist Chinese were members of the militia), but the PLAAF lost no aircraft to enemy action.

The authorities in Peking may have had other reasons for not committing the PLAAF to battle, but it seems evident that one overriding consideration was that the attrition rate of Communist Chinese air units would be unacceptable. Many of the combat aircraft in service with the Vietnamese air force (such as the re-engined and upgraded MiG-21bis and MiG-21F/PF fighter aircraft) were superior to the obsolescent interceptor fighters of the PLAAF. The Vietnamese aircraft had some all-weather capabilities, advanced fire control and search radar, and superior air-to-air missile systems, all of which gave them a qualitative advantage.

Given past Communist Chinese combat experience with technologically superior aircraft, the refusal of the PLAAF to engage the enemy in the punitive war against Vietnam is perfectly comprehensible. When the PLAAF engaged the superior aircraft of the United Nations during the Korean conflict, the loss ratio was about 8:1. When the PLAAF engaged the Nationalist Chinese air force during the Taiwan Strait conflict in 1958, it lost fifteen aircraft for every enemy machine destroyed. Certainly the PLAAF would ultimately prevail in any conflict that involved a numerically inferior air force, but if that air force had qualitative advantages, the PLAAF would lose a significant part of its available inventory and reveal its grave shortcomings.

The same conclusion can be reached concerning naval combatants. During the punitive invasion of Vietnam, the Soviet Union moved a detachment of Soviet vessels off the Vietnamese coast. The navy of the PRC made no similar move and presented no opposition to the Soviet resupply and transport effort that was essential to the maintenance of the Vietnamese elements engaged in frontal conflict with the PLA.

What all this makes clear is that Peking has been, and remains, very reluctant to undertake a military venture that does not promise success with minimal equipment loss. A cardinal proposition of Communist Chinese military doctrine, in fact, is that direct engagements with the enemy should be undertaken only when the enemy is weak and demoralized and when the PLA is possessed of overwhelming superiority. "In every battle, concentrate an absolutely superior force.... Strive to avoid battles of attrition in which we lose more than we gain or only break even.... Fight no battle you are not sure of winning."[47] These admonitions are particularly applicable when conflict involves the possible loss of expensive inventory and valuable personnel that are difficult to replace, such as technologically advanced combat aircraft, trained pilots, and the larger naval combatants. It so happens that in any use of force against Taiwan, unlike an armed attack against Vietnam, India, Burma, Laos, or Tibet, such aircraft and naval combatants would have to be the principal instruments. Amphibious invasion and naval blockade would necessarily involve both. For this reason, Peking has been particularly sensitive about the state of the armed forces of the ROC. As long as the ROC can mount a credible defense against invasion or naval blockade, Peking will hesitate to opt for a military solution to the issue of reunification, however alluring the political, strategic, and economic profit. In such a context, "credible defense" implies no more than the probability that defensive forces will be capable of exacting a heavy toll of aircraft, surface combatants, or attack submarines in any armed exchange.

Until the mid-1970s, the armed forces of the ROC were configured for joint action with those of the United States. Because of their limited air defense capabilities, the Second World War destroyers in service with the navy of the Republic of China could undertake wartime missions only if they were provided air cover by the defensive aircraft of the U.S. Seventh Fleet. The air command of the ROC was equipped only to contest tactical air superiority in the Taiwan Strait until U.S. forces could position themselves for combat. Since the mid-1970s, with the increasing evidence that Washington might choose to terminate its security arrangements with Taipei to meet the requirements for normalization of diplomatic relations laid down by Peking, the leadership of the ROC has attempted to put together a deterrent military force adequate to counter any threat mounted from the mainland. Accomplishing that goal is a monumental task.

Under the provisions of the Nixon Doctrine, Asian nations were to be allowed to purchase U.S. arms in order to assure their own security. Once Taipei decided to attempt to increase its defense capabilities in the early 1970s, it began a program of weapons procurement. At about the same time, the increasing rapprochement with Peking made Washington increasingly hesitant to undertake substantial arms sales to Taipei. Requests tendered by the ROC to purchase surface-to-surface missiles that would afford its naval vessels some measure of qualitative superiority over the hundreds of missile-armed fast attack craft of the PLAN—as well as requests for advanced early warning aircraft, enhanced detection systems, fire control devices, antisubmarine AN/ASQ-14 sonar equipment, and surface-to-air antiaircraft missiles —were denied by both the Carter and Reagan administrations. The request for an advanced fighter aircraft, with the capabilities of the F-16 or the F-5G, was similarly rejected.

The Taiwan Relations Act commits the United States to the sale of military equipment to the ROC that will allow for its "adequate defense," but Washington has failed to honor its commitment. In fact, many of the provisions of the act have been effectively gutted by executive department decisions.[48] Despite the public avowals of presidential hopeful Ronald Reagan during the 1980 election campaign, and contrary to every reasonable expectation,[49] the Reagan administration not only denied the ROC the opportunity to purchase advanced fighter aircraft necessary to the defense of the island, it also appears to have committed itself to an eventual cessation of all arms sales to its (former) security partner.[50]

However qualified and ambiguous the latter commitment might be, it probably precludes the possibility that the Republic of China on Taiwan will be able to mount an effective defense against any Communist Chinese attack in the foreseeable future. Without launching an amphibious invasion, the armed forces of the People's Republic of China can mount a blockade against Taiwan, supported by sufficient aircraft to win tactical air control over the

Taiwan Strait. They would be opposed only by the 250 F-5Es that the Nationalist Chinese have in inventory.

The PLAAF has about 2,000 combat aircraft on station within a radius of 500 nautical miles from Taiwan. These aircraft, if redeployed to airfields along the mainland China coast, would be only 7 to 10 minutes' flight time from the coast of Taiwan. They could be used to ensure air superiority over the Taiwan Strait and would thus preclude the use of ROC naval vessels in the area. As a consequence, the major ports of the Republic of China at Tainan and Kaohsiung could be sealed off by naval combatants of the PLAN.

In any conflict in the strait, defending aircraft from Taiwan would have only a 5-minute warning before PLAAF aircraft would be in the combat zone. The ROC aircraft, if in special alert facilities, could scramble in 3 to 5 minutes. This would allow only 1 or 2 minutes of intercept time over the strait before PLAAF aircraft attacked their open-water targets, or moved on to attack shore positions or harbor facilities. In effect, with the F-5Es presently available in inventory, it is unlikely that the air force of the ROC could exact the toll from aggressor aircraft that would be necessary to deter attack by the mainland Chinese. Only an aircraft that had better acceleration time, a more rapid rate of climb, and more endurance and that was capable of carrying more ordnance could provide Taiwan with the qualitative margin that might deter such an attack. The F-5G (a relatively lightweight fighter designed specifically for export) and the F-16 offer all these advantages, as well as respective increases in acceleration time of 30 percent and 50 percent over that of the F-5E.[51] Either would improve the ROC's defensive capabilities and consequently would counter any disposition Peking might have to resolve the Taiwan issue through the use of force.

To mount an effective defense against Communist Chinese attack, the ROC military would have to possess more extensive early warning capabilities, including intelligence monitoring of movements on the Chinese mainland. The air defense ground environment radar system operative on Taiwan is reasonably effective in signaling high-altitude incoming attack, but it could be easily overloaded by incoming targets. Given the proximity of the launch sites for air attack against both the island and the shipping lanes critical to its survival, the defensive properties of the radar and early warning systems on Taiwan leave a great deal to be desired.

The F-5Es that are the backbone of the ROC air command are only marginally superior to the MiG-19, which is now standard in the PLAAF. In certain flight envelopes, in fact (notably climb in critical altitudes above 10,000 feet), the MiG-19 has shown itself to be superior to the F-5E. Once the F-5E had fired its two Sidewinder air-to-air missiles, it would find itself in a classic gun duel with large numbers of MiG-19s, and any superior performance on the part of its adversaries would exact a predictably high toll.

Moreover, the PLAAF has about 150 MiG-21s in service that have formidable flight characteristics. The MiG-21 is probably equipped with advanced air-to-air missiles and is heavily armed with 23-mm cannons; it would sorely try the Nationalist Chinese F-5Es.

Against such opponents, it would be very difficult for the small numbers of ROC aircraft to maintain even tactical air superiority over the Taiwan Strait. Failure to accomplish that would make the use of antisubmarine warfare efforts by the ROC navy an almost hopeless task in the confined waters of the strait. Without air cover, the ROC navy's destroyers, of Second World War vintage, would be exposed to surface-to-surface missile attacks from the dozens of missile-armed fast attack craft in service with the PLAN. With only limited electronic countermeasures to protect against missile attack, the surface combatants of the ROC navy would be at grave risk beyond the anti-aircraft defenses of the shore.

Even in the less confined waters outside the strait, the 27 Grumman S-2A/E antisubmarine warfare trackers and the 12 Hughes 500MD helicopters of the ROC air command could operate only with some assurance of protection from air attack. Searching out submarines in the deep water on either side of the Bashi Channel would require intensive air-to-surface cooperation that would imply an adequate air defense of airborne and shipborne platforms. Only then could the limited variable-depth sonar and antisubmarine rockets and torpedoes available to the ROC military be put to some service. Without that protection, the antisubmarine warfare efforts of the ROC command would have to contend with air strikes on its air and ship assets and antiship attacks launched by missile- and torpedo-armed fast attack craft.

Given the restrictions that the United States government has imposed upon its own arms sales to the Republic of China on Taiwan, the authorities in Taipei have few immediate options other than to develop Taiwan's armament industry. Already capable of producing a wide range of military equipment, Taiwan's industry will probably be forced to attempt the manufacture of advanced fighter aircraft and defensive missilery. That such a task can be accomplished is unlikely. Taiwan's aircraft industry has produced, at great expense, a twin-engine jet trainer/light attack aircraft (the XAT-3). Although this is a significant achievement in design and technology for a small industry, an advanced fighter aircraft of the type required probably would entail prohibitive costs and necessitate the acquisition of metallurgical skills and electronic technology far beyond anything currently possessed by Taiwan.

In all probability, the U.S. decision that arms sold to the Republic of China on Taiwan since normalization of relations with the People's Republic of China should not increase in quantity or improve in quality will condemn the military capabilities of the ROC to increasing inferiority vis-à-vis the PLA. Given the predictable increase in the rate of inflation, as well as the accelerating real cost of armaments, the imposed dollar ceiling on any arms sold to Taiwan might ultimately lead to circumstances in which Taipei might not be able to purchase from the United States anything more than replacement supplies for its increasingly obsolescent equipment.

In effect, in direct violation of its commitments in the Taiwan Relations Act, the United States appears prepared to allow the defense capabilities of the ROC to decline. The refusal to allow the ROC to purchase any weapon systems superior to those already in inventory means that the defensive inadequacies of the ROC military will be successively compounded. Ultimately, the defenders of Taiwan will be both outnumbered and outgunned. At that point the option to use force to compel Taiwan to submit to unification with the mainland can be invoked at Peking's discretion. Should Peking for whatever reason, choose this option, there would be very little that the United States could, or would, do, having mortgaged itself to the goodwill of the authorities in Peking. The most plausible prognosis, however, is that at some point in time the authorities in Taipei will necessarily come to realize they no longer can mount a credible defense against the armed forces of the mainland. At that juncture the incorporation of Taiwan with the People's Republic of China might take place as a result of the threat, rather than the application, of violence.

As has been suggested, once in control of Taiwan, the PRC could influence developments in Northeast Asia in a number of ways. Command over some of the major waterways to South Korea and Japan would give the mainland Chinese leverage over the policies of both nations—an eventuality clearly not in the best interests of the United States. Any incident in the ongoing dispute between Communist China and the Republic of Korea over the East China Sea might easily precipitate a general conflict. Peking could use such an incident to force South Korea to submit to any number of concessions—concessions that might encourage action by the North Koreans.

That the United States could effectively intervene at any point in the developing confrontation is doubtful at best. A slow escalation of violence, once control of Taiwan was secured, could probably purchase the People's Republic of China significant political, strategic, and economic gains throughout Northeast Asia. The net result might very well be the collapse of the entire security structure of Northeast Asia. Peking would attempt to further cement its relations with an increasingly aggressive North Korea. Japan would find itself effectively isolated; it would have the choice of entering into some kind of security arrangement with Peking or Moscow, or opting for complete neutrality. In either case the U.S. position would become increasingly untenable.

A U.S. withdrawal from the basing facilities in Northeast Asia would seriously impair both the crisis management, and war-fighting, capabilities of the anti-Soviet alliance. Every strategist who must deal with the possibility of conflict with the Soviet Union in the Pacific recognizes that sealing the bulk of the Soviet Far East Fleet behind the island chain that borders the Asian continent would be essential to the conduct of the struggle. The Japanese bases are critical to such a strategy.

Without an aircraft and naval vessel presence in the immediate region, the United States would have to attempt to project its capabilities from alternative bases. Finding a reasonable substitute for the Yokosuka facilities in the region would be impossible. Facilities on Guam are as far away from Japanese waters as Subic Bay in the Philippines and do not provide dry-docking facilities for attack carriers. In fact, Guam's Apra Harbor has only a 37-foot draft and a radius so small that aircraft carriers cannot maneuver within its confines. Basing U.S. naval units at Pearl Harbor in the Hawaiian Islands would remove the Western military presence still further from Northeast Asia. Any attempt to increase the Seventh Fleet's logistical capacity to provide support in Northeast Asia at a level commensurate with that now provided by the replenishment ships operating out of Japanese ports would be extremely expensive and, given the long steaming time from Hawaii to Japanese waters, would expose the U.S. fleet to interdiction in times of conflict.

Having secured Taiwan, ingratiated itself with North Korea, and either neutralized or strengthened bilateral relations with Japan, Peking would then probably seek some kind of accommodation with Moscow, for it would be able to bargain from a position of relative strength. Although it is very unlikely that any accommodation that would result would be anything other than a suspicious tolerance, the relaxation of hostility would have multiple mutual benefits. Why this should be so is more conveniently considered in the next chapter.

The important consideration here is that the entire sequence could only commence with mainland China's acquisition of control over the island of Taiwan. Taiwan's loss of its freedom of action would destroy the security triangle that now sustains the integrity of Northeast Asia. The fates of Japan, South Korea, and the Republic of China on Taiwan are indissolubly linked by interests and geography. As the Japanese have suggested, South Korea and Taiwan are inextricably tied to Japan, by both economic and security interests. A disability suffered by one impairs the interests and survival of the others.

Japan, ensconced in a security arrangement with the United States, is presently under little threat of military attack. Only a general conflict in the Pacific could threaten Japan's security. Its territorial disputes with the Soviet Union and its offshore conflicts with the People's Republic of China are not likely to generate the level of hostility that could provoke military confrontation.

The threats to the Republic of Korea are manageable as long as the United States maintains a ground presence on the Korean peninsula. By 1990, the Republic of Korea will probably have developed the capacity to defend itself against any aggression originating in the North. All things remaining equal, the security threats to the survival of the ROK will probably diminish.

In Northeast Asia only the Republic of China on Taiwan remains perilously exposed. The island of Taiwan is an alluring target for the leadership in Peking. The support hitherto provided by the United States has dwindled to the point where the defensive capabilities of the armed forces of the ROC must gradually degrade—until they can offer only negligible resistance to any attack launched by the PRC. Unless there are substantive changes in Taiwan's circumstances, the threats to its integrity will increase in the 1990s.

In the past, the leadership in Peking has undertaken military adventure precisely at times when every major strategist in the United States discounted such a possibility. The present "pragmatic" leadership undertook just such an enterprise in the "punitive" war against Vietnam—and chanced frontal conflict with the Soviet Union. A similar attack against Taiwan could hardly entail greater costs to the PRC, and the promises of reward would be measurably more attractive. Such an attack would not only fatally weaken the Western security posture in Northest Asia, it would irremediably impair the credibility of the United States as a defense partner. The consequences in terms of U.S. and Western interests in East Asia might very well be incalculable.

The only alternative, other than to gamble on Peking's "sense of responsibility," would be to reinterpret the vague language of the arms sales limitation communiqué of August 17, 1982, in a manner that would permit Taiwan to procure, by purchase or transfer, sufficient military equipment to ensure a credible defensive capability. That might be accomplished by allowing third-party arms sales, or by not interfering in the coproduction of special weapon systems by a number of arms producers (such as the Republic of South Africa and Israel, together with the Republic of China on Taiwan).

Without U.S. counterpressures, it is possible that some sophisticated arms producers might be prepared to sell technologically advanced weaponry to the Republic of China—as did the Netherlands (which, in the early 1980s, sold two submarines to Taiwan over the strenuous objections of the PRC). Similarly, without U.S. obstruction, arms suppliers like the Republic of South Africa and Israel, which have only small domestic armaments markets, might find it advantageous to collaborate with the Republic of China on Taiwan to produce longer range missiles, large fast attack craft, and even sophisticated fighter aircraft.

Accomplishment of such changes will require considerable diplomatic skill on the part of the United States. Once it was convinced that these efforts would serve the ultimate best interests of all parties, the United States would also have to make a careful appraisal of its own interests in the region. It would finally have to recognize that the People's Republic of China offers very little in terms of security benefits and probably little more in terms of economic and investment opportunities. Realism would have to prevail over the romanticism that has often colored the U.S. perception of "China" as an abstract object of fascination.

The reality is that the Soviet Union constitutes the single most compelling threat to the security interest of the United States in Asia, and Communist China offers little that might offset that threat—certainly far too little to warrant mortgaging the future of the millions in Northeast Asia who depend on the United States to guarantee their future well-being and security. The People's Republic of China can act as a spoiler in any credible defense strategy in Northeast Asia—and Taiwan is the place where its actions can work the greatest mischief.

7 | The Security of Northeast Asia and the "China Connection"

China is not yet a stable and predictable factor in the affairs of East Asia.

Guy Pauker,
"The Security Implications of Regional Energy
and Natural Resource Exploitation,"
in Richard H. Solomon, ed.,
Asian Security in the 1980s.

Although the armed forces of the Soviet Union constitute the major security threat in Northeast Asia, it is the People's Republic of China that has introduced a full measure of unpredictability into the complex interactions that will determine the prospects for short- and long-term peace and stability in the region. There is very little credible evidence that Peking will allow its relationship with the capitalist West to unduly influence its international behaviors when those behaviors, in its judgment, are dictated by its national interests. In the late 1950s and early 1960s, it did not permit its substantial dependence on Moscow to influence its behaviors when its national security interest or its ideological conviction so recommended. At considerable economic cost and at the price of international isolation, Peking pursued its own policies. By the early 1980s, Peking's substantial involvement with the West and the identification of "parallel interests" notwithstanding, it had become evident that there were many areas of potential conflict where Peking, pursuing its own policies, could seriously threaten the security of the entire West Pacific.

There is relatively little likelihood that the Soviet Union could undertake initiatives in Northeast Asia that would produce similar results. The Soviet presence in the region is essentially military, and military capabilities suggest only a restricted repertoire of alternative peacetime behaviors. The Soviet Union has established an impressive war-fighting capability in Northeast Asia, but there seems to be little immediate danger that those forces are preparing for aggressive war. The entire infrastructural development, weapon systems deployment, and air and naval capabilities of the Soviet armed forces in Northeast Asia are marshaled for a general conflict with the United States and its allies; they are certainly not structured primarily or exclusively for regional war with mainland China.

What this means is that there is not likely to be any significant change in the Soviet Union's capabilities in Northeast Asia, no matter what its relations with Communist China. Soviet forces are in Asia to secure and defend the water passages leading from the Sea of Okhotsk and the Sea of Japan and to interdict the Western sea-lanes in the Pacific. As a consequence, Soviet forces will continue to remain in place in the Maritime Province and on Sakhalin Island. There will be no surrender of the disputed Kuril Islands to Japan. In effect, the Soviet military threat will remain a predictable constant in the constellation of factors that influence events in Northeast Asia.

Soviet relations with its neighbors will probably remain fairly stable for the immediate future. The Soviet Union probably will negotiate with the PRC and Japan, and probably will use political and diplomatic pressures to effect its purposes, but there is little reason to believe that Moscow will use military force to further its ends.

Of course Moscow will continue to compete with Peking for the favor of Pyongyang, to foreclose the possibility of a Communist Chinese monopoly of influence over North Korea. But it is most unlikely that Moscow will incite the North Koreans to military adventure as long as the configuration of forces on the Korean peninsula remains unchanged. Only a major shift in the military balance in the region could precipitate some initiatives from the Kremlin—in much the same fashion that the overthrow of the shah of Iran and the possibility of a U.S. response to the seizure of embassy hostages in Teheran influenced the Soviet decision to invade Afghanistan.

Because Moscow's nonmilitary options in Northeast Asia are relatively few, it is unlikely that, barring major alterations in the present balance, the Soviet Union will attempt to destabilize the region. The situation with regard to the People's Republic of China, however, is far different.

Although the PRC does not possess the military capabilities that might prompt pre-emptive Soviet moves, the Communist Chinese have it within their power to precipitate far-reaching destabilization elsewhere in Northeast Asia. It is very unlikely that Peking or Moscow will allow their border conflicts, which have diminished in frequency and intensity over the years, to escalate to the point of serious armed confrontation. Neither Moscow nor Peking would gain substantially from such a conflict, given the risks involved. Destabilization in Northeast Asia will not be caused by a Sino-Soviet conflict but by any of a number of possible moves directed by Peking against its noncommunist littoral and insular neighbors.

However impaired its capabilities when confronted by Soviet power, Peking does have the wherewithal to undertake initiatives in the Northeast that could very well destabilize the entire region. There are several issues that might trigger just such an eventuality. Peking, like Moscow, has a considerable investment in North Korea in terms of diplomatic and security interests, and those interests might involve Communist China, as they might the Soviet Union, in some kind of military activity should Pyongyang commence a "liberation" of the South on its own.

Peking has identified the "liberation" of South Korea with the "liberation" of Taiwan and has acceded to Pyongyang's self-identification as the "sole legal government" of the entire peninsula. It has thus become inextricably involved in the maneuvers of Pyongyang. Should the regime in the North, under one pretext or another, decide to undertake an adventure against the South, Peking would be compelled to take Pyongyang's side, in contravention of U.S. and Japanese interests, if only to preclude Moscow from making further inroads into the peninsula. Any informal assurances Peking has given Washington would have to be weighed against the possible loss of influence in a region that is critical to the security of China's energy-rich and heavily industrialized northeastern provinces.

More important than these generally acknowledged problem areas that Peking shares with Moscow is the issue of the contested claims to the seabed resources of the continental shelf off the mainland China coast. Since the early 1970s it has become increasingly apparent that a dispute might arise over these offshore resources that could easily undo the stability in Northeast Asia. And it would be Communist China, not the Soviet Union, that would be involved in any such dispute.

Since the conflict in the Falkland Islands, Americans are no longer so prepared to readily dismiss the importance of territorial conflict over remote offshore islands. The seriousness of that conflict and its far-reaching repercussions, as well as the increasing preoccupation of the international community with the exploitation of offshore mineral and fish resources along adjacent continental shelves, make the issue of contested maritime claims a matter of considerable significance for the security of Northeast Asia.

Ever since the Geneva Convention on the Continental Shelf was promulgated in 1958, more and more nations have shown an active interest in advancing sovereign claims to offshore resources. With the widely publicized findings of oceanographer K. O. Emery in 1968 and 1970,[1] the governments of Japan, the Republic of Korea, the Republic of China on Taiwan, and the People's Republic of China began to evince more than episodic interest in the resources of their respective offshore reaches. Emery's suggestion that the East China Sea and the Yellow Sea might constitute "another Persian Gulf" provoked not only speculation, but a flurry of seismic and oceanographic studies of the subsea region. As early as 1969, a Japanese government survey suggested that a portion of the East China Sea shelf surrounding the Senkaku Islands (Tiao-yü T'ai) might hold an offshore oil reserve of as much as 15 billion tons.

Since the issuance of these early reports, several offshore sedimentary basins have been identified that offer a high probability of substantial recoverable oil deposits. Of these, only the Po Hai Basin falls clearly within the territorial confines of the People's Republic of China. The Yellow Sea Basin, the Taiwan Basin, and the Liuchow Basin, on the other hand, occupy maritime regions variously claimed by the People's Republic of China, Japan, the Republic of Korea, and the Republic of China on Taiwan.[2]

In July 1970, almost immediately following the more detailed reports of the Emery study, a consortium of Japanese and Taiwanese business and political leaders announced a plan for tripartite oil development of the subjacent continental shelf to be undertaken by Japan, the Republic of China on Taiwan, and the Republic of Korea. The areas initially to be surveyed and exploited were an exploration zone off the western coast of Taiwan and an area surrounding the Senkaku Islands to the northeast of Taiwan. Both areas were identified as having large- to medium-sized geologic structures that had long been associated with oil and natural gas deposits.

The exploitation of those areas would not only provide energy resources for economies almost entirely devoid of fossil fuels, but it would cement relations between the three countries at a time when the United States was beginning to give evidence of a significant change in its Asian policies. The economic consequences of the joint development were as obvious as the political implications. The mainland Chinese response was portentous.

On December 4, 1970, *People's Daily* published an article entitled "U.S. and Japanese Reactionaries Out to Plunder Chinese and Korean Seabed Resources," in which the proposed "plundering" of "the sea floor of China's vast shallow water areas" was denounced. At approximately this time the United States had been observing Taipei beginning to engage U.S. seismic survey vessels in preliminary exploration of the subsea areas off the Taiwan coast. By the end of December, the United States was compelled to make a decision concerning what support was to be provided U.S. vessels in the disputed areas should the mainland Chinese attempt to interfere in the enterprise.

In fact, Peking had ordered a missile-armed fast attack craft to shadow two Gulf Oil Company seismic survey ships operating in the Taiwan Strait under a concession granted by the government of the Republic of China on Taiwan. Peking signaled that any effort to develop the continental shelf off the mainland Chinese coast might precipitate a major diplomatic and military confrontation. The United States, still deeply embroiled in the war in Vietnam, had begun attempting to extricate itself from its commitment to defend the integrity of the Taiwan Strait. A tentative decision had already been made to cease patrolling of the strait by elements of the Seventh Fleet in anticipation of a reformulation of U.S. China policy, and by the end of December 1970 it had become obvious that Washington did not wish to become involved in any offshore territorial dispute with the People's Republic of China. By April 1971 it had become clear why Washington deemed it "ill-advised" to support oil exploration in any disputed zones of the continental shelf of East Asia. At about the same time that a formal announcement of the reduction of U.S. naval patrols in the Taiwan Strait was being made, Secretary of State Henry Kissinger was preparing for his secret visit to Peking.

The United States had forestalled any cooperative development of the continental shelf by Japan, the Republic of Korea, and the Republic of China on Taiwan in anticipation of fostering a rapprochement with Peking. Peking proceeded to take advantage of the opening provided by Washington's reluctance to become involved in the offshore territorial dispute. Less than a year later, the PRC delegation to the United Nations Committee on the Peaceful Uses of the Sea-bed and the Ocean Floor Beyond the Limits of National Jurisdiction insisted: "We maintain that all coastal countries have the right of disposal of their natural resources in their coastal areas, seabed and the subsoil thereof so as to promote the well-being of their people and the development of their national economic interests."

That pronouncement was the first clear indication that Peking was prepared to claim exclusive exploitation rights over an undetermined extent of its coastal seabed area. In 1970 Peking had already broadcast its objections to any development of the subsea resources by any other nation in the region; it was only three years later that the mainland Chinese provided some indication of the geographic reach of their claims to the waters adjacent to their coast.

Before the same U.N. committee where they entered their first claims, the representatives of the Peking regime indicated that the "exclusive economic zone" over which the People's Republic of China laid claim would measure 200 nautical miles from a given baseline along the shore. These representatives repeated that a coastal state "may reasonably define an exclusive economic zone beyond and adjacent to its territorial sea in accordance with its geographical and geological conditions, the state of its natural resources and its needs of national economic development."[3] The "exclusive economic zone" thus characterized was understood to include that portion of the subsea continental shelf that could be geologically identified as a "natural prolongation of the continental territory." Within that zone all the living and nonliving resources of the "whole water column, seabed and its subsoil" would become the exclusive concern of the respective coastal state. Beyond that Peking was prepared to argue that a coastal state had the right to "reasonably define...the limits of the continental shelf under its exclusive jurisdiction" that went beyond its "exclusive economic zone." Since the "exclusive economic zone" was understood to extend 200 nautical miles from the coastal waters baseline, a coastal state presumably could "reasonably define" an extent of the continental shelf beyond that limit as being under its "exclusive jurisdiction" should it feel that geologic conditions so warranted.[4]

What all this has produced is a claim by the PRC to exclusive access to vast reaches of the Asian continental shelf that it has declared "inalienable sovereign territory" of the People's Republic of China.[5] This vast area stretches from the coast of mainland China to the southwest coast of the Republic of Korea to the Okinawa Trough, along the eastern coast of Taiwan, down along the island of Luzon and the Philippine island of Palawan, along the coasts of Brunei and Malaysia, then northward along the coast of Vietnam to the Gulf of Tonkin.[6]

Although Peking has insisted that it is prepared to "jointly determine the delimitation of the limits of jurisdiction of the continental shelves through consultations on an equal footing," its record leaves a great deal to be desired. As we have seen, when the first survey vessels attempted seismic studies of the waters off Taiwan, Peking's immediate response was to dispatch missile-armed fast attack craft to harass the effort. Since then Peking has given little evidence of a serious disposition to negotiate any of its offshore claims with any of the countries having competing claims.

As early as 1952, South Korea announced its intention to define an area off its coast, extending from 60 to 200 nautical miles, as falling within its claim to exploitation rights. Originally calculated to insulate fishing rights, that claim was subsequently invoked to allow for the development of undersea mineral resources. When the Emery survey gave rise to the expectation of substantial offshore oil recovery among the nations of East Asia, Seoul proceeded to plan for the exploration and drilling of its subjacent seabed. The government-sponsored Korea Oil Corporation planned exploratory drilling west of Kunsan and southwest of Cheju Island off the Korean coast that was expected to lead to commercial production by the year 1972.

Seoul quickly leased concessions to U.S. oil companies, including Gulf, Shell, and Texaco, and between 1969 and 1972 survey ships collected subsea topographic data from the most promising sites in the seabed of the Yellow Sea. Soon Communist Chinese naval craft began to harass the survey vessels. On several occasions in 1971, Communist Chinese fishing boats, lightly armed with machine guns, proceeded to cut the floating tracer cables used by the U.S. seismic studies vessels. By 1973 the mainland Chinese had escalated their harassment to the point of dispatching missile-armed fast attack craft to the concession areas being worked by Gulf Oil Company drilling rigs. In March of that year several *Komar*-class missile boats circled the rig *Glomar IV* until it ceased its operations.

Since 1970, Washington has consistently sought to dissuade U.S. oil companies from aiding in the subsea exploration of any of the disputed areas. In fact, the State Department has been so accommodating with respect to Peking's claims that U.S. companies have displayed considerable irritation. Some made their irritation known by addressing a query to Washington as to whether "the Republic of Korea has any territorial waters at all."[7]

The regime on the mainland of China has made its position eminently clear. Although the PRC has argued that "the question of how to divide the continental shelf in the East China Sea should be decided by China and the other countries concerned through consultation,"[8] it refuses to countenance consultations with governments it will not recognize. Since it recognizes the governments in neither Taipei nor Seoul, Peking has asserted a non-negotiable claim to an "inviolable sovereignty over the East China sea continental shelf" that "forms an integral part of the mainland."[9] Peking's putative jurisdiction thus extends almost to the coast of South Korea and completely encompasses the island of Taiwan.

More ominous still has been Peking's response to Japan's interest in exploring the subsea mineral potential in its surrounding waters. Peking recognizes the legitimacy of the government in Tokyo, and since 1972 the PRC and Japan have enjoyed normal diplomatic relations. But for all that, there has not been a resolution of the conflicting claims to the offshore waters advanced by both.

Japan is, of course, heavily dependent upon fossil fuel imports. About 90 percent of the oil used in the Japanese economy is imported, so that when the Emery report suggested the possibility of vast recoverable oil deposits in the Taiwan Basin off the southwestern coast of Japan, Tokyo made immediate plans to begin seismic survey and exploratory drilling in the area. Using the recognized principle of "equidistance" embodied in the prevailing law of the sea that provides that two nations sharing a continental shelf draw a median line from fixed base points to divide the sea that connects them, the Japanese earmarked a projected area for economic development. The concession zone that resulted includes waters surrounding the Ryukyus and the Senkaku Islands.

Peking has refused to countenance the Japanese claims and consistently adheres to the principle that the continental shelf be considered a natural geological prolongation of its continental territory. This would make all of the seabed west of the Ryukyu Trench "sovereign" mainland Chinese territory. The Okinawa Trough would remain disputed, but the entirety of the Taiwan Basin, including the waters around the Senkaku Islands, would fall under Peking's exclusive jurisdiction.

Between 1971 and 1975 several Japanese oil companies and foreign concessionaires explored the projected Japanese exploitation zones. In 1975 and 1976 the Japanese government allocated funds for the development of these zones, attempting to restrict development to areas immediately offshore in order not to provoke the mainland Chinese. But since it remains unclear whether the claims of the PRC include not only the continental shelf, but the slope of the shelf and the rise at the bottom of the slope, it is uncertain whether the Japanese could even explore the potential of the Okinawa Trough without engaging Peking in dispute.

The degree of Peking's hostility was revealed by the dispute that arose over the Senkaku Islands in 1978. Even while Tokyo and Peking were negotiating the peace and friendship treaty that was to cement their growing rapprochement, the Japanese suggestion that the dispute about the ownership of the uninhabited Senkaku Islands be resolved in the course of the treaty negotiations precipitated an armed response from the PRC: Peking dispatched a flotilla of fishing boats, half of them armed with machine guns, to circle the islands.[10]

There is little doubt that the vessels dispatched were under formal PLA naval command. At one point there were as many as 140 Communist Chinese vessels within 30 nautical miles of the Senkaku Islands; they could have collected there only with the approval of the highest echelons of the Communist Chinese government. Equally certain is the reason behind what has been termed the PRC's "overreaction." Given the location of the Senkaku Islands on the continental shelf, Japanese sovereignty over them would establish Japan as a shelf power entitled to invoke the equidistance rule in establishing a median line between the mainland and the islands. That would correspondingly restrict Peking's jurisdiction over a substantial part of the shelf.[11]

In order to obtain the peace and friendship treaty with Tokyo, Peking was prepared to shelve the issue until some indeterminate time in the future. How it might be resolved has been left exceedingly vague. Peking has been loath to commit itself to any arrangement that would entail compulsory adjudication. Although it has spoken of negotiating a settlement with regard to such issues and has committed itself, in principle, to such negotiation with the Philippines concerning the disputed claims over the Spratly Islands in the South China Sea, the recent history of such disputes indicates that Peking favors the use of force, rather than negotiation, in their resolution. This has been the case in its dealings not only with governments that Peking has refused to recognize, but also with allied nations.[12]

In 1974 the Communist Chinese launched an amphibious assault against the Paracel Islands in the South China Sea to resolve a dispute concerning sovereignty. The immediate object of attack was the "enemy" in Saigon, but it was equally directed against the allied government in Hanoi. Both North and South Vietnam had long insisted that the Paracel Islands were part of the sovereign territory of Vietnam.

The issue in the Paracel Islands dispute involved a variety of interests. Vietnam (both North and South) has long held that ownership of the Paracel

Islands was established by the frequent assertion of ownership by the historic governments of Vietnam. On the basis of these claims the government of South Vietnam, in 1973, opened 30 offshore tracts to competitive bidding. Four Western oil companies entered into negotiation with Saigon for rights to exploit the subsea resources involved. The opening of tracts to bidding was calculated to further confirm the Vietnamese claim, which was predicated on the presupposition that the Paracel Islands constituted part of the geologic extension of continental Vietnam.

The People's Republic of China responded to these efforts in January 1974. Peking was not prepared to allow Vietnam to establish its sovereignty over the territory in question—simply because jurisdiction over the Paracels would afford exploitation rights over the adjacent waters and over whatever seabed resources might be uncovered as underwater technology evolved.[13]

Peking had maintained a military presence on two of the Paracel Islands since at least 1958. In mid-1971, several Communist Chinese patrol boats and supply ships were sighted in the vicinity, and there was evidence of the construction of radar and ship-servicing facilities on Yung-hsing and Tung islands. In September 1973, the Saigon government put the Spratly Islands under the jurisdiction of the Phuoc Tuy Province of South Vietnam. This pre-empted any claim by any other power to the waters between the Spratlys and the continental baseline—effectively including the Paracels under South Vietnam's jurisdiction.

On January 11, 1974, Peking announced that the government of mainland China would "never tolerate any infringement on China's territorial integrity and sovereignty."[14] About a week later seven PRC naval vessels, supported by air cover provided by the PLAAF flying out of Hainan, launched an amphibious invasion of the Paracels. Six hundred marine infantry were offlanded against outnumbered Vietnamese defenders, and in two days the forces of Peking had secured the Paracel Islands.

Had the range of the MiG air cover extended to the Spratly Islands, there is little doubt that the armed forces of Communist China would have attempted to secure them as well.[15] Since that time the naval vessels of the PRC have conducted exercises in the area that evidence Peking's serious concern with its claims to sovereignty over the entire maritime territory of the South China Sea.

In sum, Communist China has displayed impressive determination in pursuing its territorial claims to the continental shelf of the Yellow Sea and East China Sea and the maritime reaches of the South China Sea. Irrespective of its proclaimed policy of negotiating with the various nations involved, Peking has shown remarkable reluctance to arbitrate its offshore claims. Not only has it refused to enter into discussions with Seoul and Taipei—authorities it refuses to recognize—but it has failed to negotiate with Tokyo or Hanoi. Its announced readiness to negotiate with Manila has yet to produce any results. In every instance of challenge, Peking has responded with the threat or the employment of military force.

Peking has used the threat of force against South Korea, the Republic of China on Taiwan, and Japan. It has used military force against South Vietnam and subsequently has refused to negotiate with the Socialist Republic of Vietnam over maritime disputes in the South China Sea. It has supported the legitimacy of North Korean challenges against South Korean efforts to exploit potential offshore resources—together, Pyongyang and Peking have undertaken to discredit South Korea's efforts to develop the seabed that is immediately adjacent to the coast. Finally, Peking has refused to consider the legitimacy of median line negotiations with Tokyo for resolving the East China Sea dispute.

In the Northeast Asian context it appears that Peking is not only asserting its own interests in seeking to preclude any development of the continental shelf by any power other than itself—it is also advancing the cause of Pyongyang as the only legitimate government of the Korean peninsula. Peking has insisted that any resolution of the territorial dispute in the waters around Korea can be undertaken only with the participation of North Korea and, moreover, that any such resolution will be contingent upon a formula that will acknowledge Taiwan's subordination to Peking.[16]

In all this the United States has admonished all its allies in the region (Japan, South Korea, and Taiwan) to avoid any effort at development in the disputed waters. As a consequence, it has given credence to mainland China's maximal claims. Communist China has never relinquished its most extreme claims in the South China Sea, East China Sea, and Yellow Sea—and those claims bring it into potential conflict not only with Japan, South Korea, and the Republic of China on Taiwan, but with the Socialist Republic of Vietnam, the Philippines, Malaysia, Brunei, and perhaps Singapore. Any of these disputes could erupt into armed conflict, depending on the prevailing circumstances.

One of the circumstances that could contribute to increased hostility over offshore resources would be any failure of mainland China's onshore oil exploration, exploitation, and production. In that regard, there is some reason for pessimism. In 1978, after almost three decades of steady growth, mainland Chinese onshore energy production suddenly reached an output plateau. From 1973 through 1975 oil production had increased at a rate of about 20 percent per annum. In 1976 that rate declined to 15 percent, and fell to 8 percent in 1977.[17] In 1978 the annual production rate fell to 2 percent; it declined to −5 percent in 1980. In fact, mainland China's total energy production (raw coal, crude oil, natural gas, and hydroelectric power) showed a negative rate of growth of −3.8 percent in 1981.[18]

Because energy production has become one of the major constraints on the economic development of mainland China, the search for recoverable oil may become one of the principal preoccupations of Peking in the immediate future. If Communist China fails to discover and recover more oil or finds it impossible to increase the efficiency of its industrial use of energy, it will be compelled to import an estimated equivalent of 1.7 million barrels of oil per day by 1990.[19] Mainland China appears to have entered a period of protracted energy crisis. What this implies is that its growing export trade, built in part on exports of crude oil and petroleum-based products, must necessarily falter. In 1979 exports of both to Japan reached a peak of 17 million tons, only to decline to less than half that amount by early 1980. With the decline in total petroleum product exports—exports that earned enough to offset roughly 25 percent of mainland China's total import bill—Peking's entire program of technology acquisitions has been seriously jeopardized.

As early as 1978, Vice-Premier Yu Ch'ui-li announced that mainland China was limiting its production of steel in "order to reduce the pressure on fuel and power supplies,"[20] suggesting that energy shortfalls were then already impacting on the program of development. More extensive retrenchments were reported in 1981.[21]

Estimates of mainland China's future energy needs vary as a function of some critical initial assumptions—but by the early 1980s the PRC's energy production had fallen far short of even the most conservative projected requirements. In the late 1970s, Tatsu Kambara of the Japan Petroleum Development Corporation estimated that mainland China's total energy needs in 1982 would be 422.7 million tons, assuming an average annual economic growth rate of only 5 percent. Analysts believe that about half of all of Communist China's energy needs are met with petroleum. This means that in order to meet its domestic requirements, mainland China's oil production in 1982 should have been about 200 million tons. In fact, crude oil production on the mainland has averaged about 100 million tons per year since 1980, and every piece of evidence suggests that the resulting shortfall in production has generated serious problems for the nation's entire economy.[22]

It is not difficult to derive some of the implications for mainland China's domestic and international behaviors. Robert North has argued that the more Communist China feels itself "deprived of resources relative to population and the requirements of a growing technology, the more we might expect a Chinese disposition toward expansionism of one kind or another. . . . Peking may . . . reassert control over areas that are viewed as integral parts of China provided the task can be accomplished without undue risk or threat."[23] One fairly obvious direction this expansion could take would be to assert control over the disputed offshore reaches of the Yellow Sea, East China Sea, and South China Sea.

Communist China's growing difficulties in meeting its energy needs have put "an extraordinarily high premium . . . on rapid development of [its] off-shore theaters. It could accurately be said that the development of the energy sector as a whole, and ultimately the success of the modernization program, hinges on an effective program of offshore exploration and development."[24]

As mainland China develops the technology to exploit the seabed at greater depths, it can be expected to make more aggressive moves throughout the entire contested offshore area. Since the United States has shown no disposition to scrutinize mainland China's claims, and has actively supported those oil companies that are collaborating with Peking in the exploration and exploitation of offshore resources, it is most unlikely that Washington will be in a position to intercede to protect the offshore interests of South Korea, the Republic of China, or Japan. If one considers the possibilities in Southeast Asia, the consequences of U.S. indifference concerning the offshore disputes in East Asia become even more ominous.

There is a potential for conflict between the People's Republic of China and almost all its neighbors—and almost all those disputes turn on offshore claims to regions that may become of critical economic significance in the near future. Already the United States has placed itself in a position that does not allow it effectively to defend the interests of South Korea in the Yellow Sea and East China Sea. Washington makes no pretense of attempting to defend the offshore waters of Taiwan. And it is more than doubtful that the United States would choose to become involved in any conflict between Japan and the PRC over offshore jurisdiction.

For their part the Japanese, like the Americans, have chosen not to test Peking's determination concerning these issues. Since the mid-1970s Tokyo has convinced itself that the safer course to follow is to negotiate crude oil sales with the Communist Chinese rather than to develop offshore reserves on its own. The problem is that Peking has not been able to meet its petroleum export commitments to the Japanese—and much of the crude oil that has been supplied to Japan has been of high specific gravity, heavy with paraffin, and consequently of reduced utility to Japanese industry.

For many Japanese the euphoria with which normalization of diplomatic relations with the People's Republic of China was greeted has largely dissipated. An atmosphere of mutual suspicion affects the trade and investment relations between Tokyo and Peking. Peking's traumatic cancellation of major contracts with Japan in 1981 and the rapidity with which mainland Chinese orders for plant and equipment have dried up have left the Japanese business community sorely disappointed.

When the Japanese negotiated oil import agreements with Peking, they expected a minimum petroleum import of 40 million tons per annum. In 1980 mainland China exported a trifle more than 8.3 million tons to Japan with little prospect that larger quantities would be forthcoming in the immediate future.

Kenichiro Maiya, one of Japan's foremost oil analysts, has suggested that if 20 million tons of crude oil per annum is the best that Japan can expect from Communist Chinese sources, then Japanese interest in the Senkaku Islands exploration zone will necessarily increase.[25]

Japan's subsea oil exploitation capabilities are superior to those of mainland China. Its jack-up, and semisubmersible deep-water, oil drilling rigs are capable of exploiting the relatively shallow waters to the east of the hypothetical Sino-Japanese median line based on Tokyo's claim to the Senkaku Islands. Clearly the major shift in U.S. policy after 1971 made it necessary for Tokyo to suspend operations in the disputed zones and to withdraw from its joint exploration agreements with South Korea and the Republic of China on Taiwan. Tokyo would clearly prefer to enter into some kind of joint venture with Peking to develop the shelf, but Peking has shown firm reluctance to allow Japan even nominal exploration and coproduction access to what mainland China insists is "sacred Chinese territory."

Japan retains very valid and long-standing claims to a share in the potential riches of the continental shelf. It is thus difficult to determine how long Japan will remain content to be excluded from any efforts at exploitation. Japan has become fully aware that Peking, in frustrating any non-PRC development of the resources of the continental shelf, is pursuing not only its own economic interests, but its political and security interests as well. It has made itself the champion of Pyongyang's cause. Peking has sought to satisfy some of North Korea's major petroleum energy requirements while foreclosing South Korea's development of any energy independence.

Japan, the Republic of Korea, and the Republic of China on Taiwan all have important interests in the development of the resources of the continental shelf, but pursuit of those interests has been frustrated by direct U.S. intervention. How long the noncommunist nations of Northeast Asia will remain content with the prevailing circumstances is difficult to predict. What is clear is that there is a potential for conflict. By contrivance or accident, military units of the People's Republic of China and those of Japan, South Korea, or Taiwan could easily engage in a firefight in the offshore reaches of the Yellow Sea, East China Sea, or South China Sea. The United States would then find itself in a situation in which it would have to choose between its long-established allies in the region and a mainland China with whom it shares only some increasingly ephemeral "parallel interests."

It has become more and more evident that the enthusiasm that sustained the long negotiations that led to the normalization of diplomatic relations between the United States and the People's Republic of China has worn thin. The "parallel interests" shared by Washington and Peking do not extend to a commitment by Peking to support pluralistic political systems or market-oriented economies. As a consequence, Washington's distress concerning the suppression of the free labor union movement in Poland was not shared by Peking. Washington's efforts to improve relations with New Delhi have not prompted much enthusiasm in Peking. The long-standing territorial dispute between India and the People's Republic of China has precipitated armed conflict between them on more than one occasion. The U.S. interest in the stability in East Asia did little to constrain mainland China's "punitive war" against Vietnam. Nor did it inhibit Peking's use of military force to bring Japan's tentative efforts at exploration of the continental shelf to a halt. Washington's attempt to defend the integrity of South Korea has been impeded by Peking's insistent support of the communist regime in Pyongyang—and Washington's expression of "grave concern" with the "well-being of the people of Taiwan" has been met with open hostility in Peking.

Mainland China's far-reaching claims to the continental shelf off the coast of Asia, its exploitation of those claims to serve its own political and security interests, and its failure to share some of the most critical Western commitments all become important when considered in the context of Peking's vision of the future. The declared foreign policy of mainland China has long been sustained by a collection of propositions, among which is the judgment that the United States, irrespective of the relative harmony of Sino-U.S. relations, remains second only to the Soviet Union in malevolence.

In the late 1960s, Chou En-lai put together the rationale that still shapes Peking's behavior. It was an international strategy calculated to defeat both "imperialist" superpowers—the United States and the Soviet Union—and predicated on the conviction that the contemporary world was composed of two major classes of actors: the two superpowers (the United States and the Soviet Union) and the Third World. Between the two were the "medium-sized and small countries struggling together against the U.S. and the USSR."[26] In a world so constituted, the United States—a nation in evident decline—found itself embroiled in manifest "contradictions" in its relations not only with the other "hegemonist" power, the Soviet Union, and with the second-rank powers of Asia and Europe, but with the nations of the Third World as well. Chou anticipated increasing tensions for the United States in the "intermediate zones" between the superpowers and the Third World. Under such circumstances, he considered Peking's position to be particularly auspicious: "The U.S. imperialists have no choice but to improve their relations with China in order to counter the Soviet revisionists." Thus although Peking would not, under any circumstances, "give up [its] principles and sell out . . . revolution," he deemed it in Communist China's best interests to enter into tactical negotiations with the U.S. imperialists in order to "take full advantage of the contradiction between the U.S. and the USSR."[27]

In 1977, when Washington was making frenzied efforts to accomplish the normalization of diplomatic relations with Peking, Teng Hsiao-p'ing reiterated essentially the same contentions. "We belong to the Marxist camp," he insisted at that time, "and can never be so thoughtless that we cannot distinguish friends from enemies. Nixon, Ford, Carter and future American imperialistic leaders all fall into this [latter] category. They want to use the split between us and the USSR to destroy the world socialist system in order to manipulate and lessen the Soviet threat toward themselves. Why can't we take advantage of the contradiction and grudge that exists between them and initiate actions that would be favorable to our national policy?"[28]

Teng had already given expression to these convictions in his speech at the Sixth Special Session of the United Nations General Assembly in April 1974. In that rendering, he did not speak, as Chou had done, of "intermediate zones" between the superpowers and the Third World, but only of "Three Worlds": the imperialists, the developing nations, and a "Second World" composed of the already industrialized countries that occupy the intermediate space between the First and Third Worlds. Mainland China's express policy toward the United States, one of the "biggest international exploiters and oppressors of today," should be to undertake artful diplomacy and collaborate with all three "worlds" when and where it was in Peking's interests to do so, and to exploit "contradictions" in U.S. policy whenever possible and profitable.[29]

When Ch'iao Kuan-hua, Communist China's foreign minister at the time, elaborated on these themes in 1975, he argued that the two superpowers "should be dealt with separately; otherwise, if we push too hard, they might be forced to unite and make the problem more thorny. We must divide our objectives into primary and secondary ones. This is called defeating the enemy piecemeal."[30] Because the industrialized nations of the intermediate zones— or the Second World—often found themselves at odds with the United States and fearful of the Soviet Union, Ch'iao anticipated that they could be utilized in Communist China's "dual revolutionary policy." He insisted, however, that whatever the relationship between mainland China and the noncommunist industrialized nations, it should be clear that such relations were, at best, tactical, and that "we will overthrow their system in the future."[31]

Peking has not officially modified its position to the present day—for all the increased "pragmatism" of its present leadership. "While [Peking's] leaders are quick to assert that their current policy of cooperation with the West is based on long-term interests, their manipulative...styles tend to undermine such arguments."[32] Mainland China, at every appropriate opportunity, will continue to seek enhancement of its own interests, as it interprets those interests in terms of its "dual revolutionary policy." Ultimately, that can only be accomplished at the expense of the nonsocialist nations of the Pacific, and those of Northeast Asia in particular.

One expects that each nation will pursue its national interests as it defines those interests. All that is required of a rational foreign policy in such circumstances is that each nation recognize the vision of the world order held by each of the players in the international game. That Peking conceives itself, in some profound sense, in an adversarial relationship with the United States is a fact of international life that Washington can neglect only at considerable economic, political, and strategic cost.

The communist leadership in Peking has not abandoned its revolutionary program for Asia. It insists on its inalienable right to continue to arm insurrectionary forces even in those nations with which it has established diplomatic relations.[33] It anticipates the ultimate collapse of the "capitalist world system" and the creation of a new "socialist order." The "exploitative" relations of the United States vis-à-vis Asia thus will finally be overcome. All the "bourgeois democracies" in the region will perish with the final withdrawal of the economic, political, and military forces of the United States.

It is evident that in the interim, Peking will seek to exploit every real or fancied weakness of the United States to strengthen its own position. Convinced that Washington conceives of the PRC as a significant strategic asset, Peking has insisted upon U.S. abandonment of the Republic of China on Taiwan as the price of collaboration. Exploiting its position, it has won U.S. compliance with its demand that no nation embark on any program of developing the continental shelf without its approval.

Washington has behaved as though it cannot, or will not, see what is transpiring. Seemingly convinced that mainland China's strategic significance and promise of market and investment opportunities warrant the cost, Washington has been remarkably cooperative. The threat that renders officials in Washington so tractable is that if the United States does not satisfy Peking, the Communist Chinese authorities will undertake rapprochement with the Soviet Union—to the irreversible detriment of the U.S. and Japanese defense posture in the West Pacific. Washington appears loath to risk "losing China" once again.

The U.S. rapprochement with the People's Republic of China has undermined, rather than enhanced, its position in the West Pacific, however. It was Washington's initiatives with regard to Peking that prompted India to conclude the peace and friendship agreement with Moscow. New Delhi had previously been reluctant to commit itself to so close a relationship with the Soviet Union; only Washington's "tilt" toward Peking made such a move advisable.

Beyond that, it was Washington's normalization of relations with Peking that provided the last bit of confidence to support mainland China's "punitive" invasion of Vietnam—from which only the Soviet Union profited. And it was apparently Moscow's concern with the Washington-Peking connection that ultimately influenced the Soviet Union's decision to invade Afghanistan.

It is very difficult to identify the security benefits that Washington has purchased as a result of its rapprochement with Peking. The People's Republic of China is essentially a poor and militarily weak nation of almost 1 billion inhabitants, 80 percent of whom earned a per capita income of about $91 in 1980. Workers in the state industries of mainland China earned a per capita income of about $459 in 1980. In that same year the Communist Chinese per capita net material product was $217.

According to one observer,

> China is extremely backward militarily. Nothing that either China or the U.S. can do will bring about any time soon the technological modernization of the People's Liberation Army.... Foreign experts who were given unprecedented opportunities to inspect the most sensitive installations in the PRC have come home shaking their heads at the primitiveness of China's defense industries and weaponry.... The consensus of Western experts is that China's military-industrial base is ten to twenty years behind that of the USSR. Even if China could afford massive amounts of American or Western European armaments—which it definitely cannot —the infusion would not do much good in redressing the Sino-Soviet balance in modern weaponry and firepower.[34]

What all this suggests is that the United States, at some point in time, will realize that it can concede only so much to Peking and its "dual revolutionary" policies. Washington ultimately will require more substantive returns than it has received from the rapprochement that has cost it so much in terms of credibility in East Asia.

But without an increased measure of hardheaded, realistic assessment in Washington, and without any effort on the part of the United States to strike a more equitable balance in its relations with all the nations in Northeast Asia, it seems reasonably clear that Peking, in the foreseeable future, will opt to reduce the level of hostility that afflicts its relations with Moscow. Harbingers of a reconciliation of some kind are already abundant.

In the final analysis, Communist China still considers itself a "socialist" nation sharing more affinities (in terms of political and economic institutions) with the Soviet Union than it does with the capitalist nations. Very few of the ideological differences that precipitated the Sino-Soviet conflict still remain. The "revisionism" that provoked so much Communist Chinese ire during the 1960s and 1970s has now been accepted by Peking's "pragmatic" leadership. Communist China has entered into sustained contact with the Western industrial powers; it has acknowledged the functional utility of differential wages in stimulating economic growth; it has reduced its emphasis on domestic "class struggle"; and it has allowed more regional entrepreneurial independence and increased use of cost accounting.[35] Mainland China is today neither more nor less "revisionist" than the Soviet Union.[36]

However much it may have been revised, the economic and political system of Communist China remains fundamentally different from that of any Western nation. Because its economy is highly bureaucratized, there are few market mechanisms that allow rational resource and investment allocation or wage and price determination. Widespread use of effective cost accounting procedures would require wide-ranging information inputs from regional productive units, more freedom of expression than Peking is likely to permit, and more independence in decision-making than the system can allow. To introduce the market mechanisms that would render the system rational and efficient would require more extensive institutional reform than could be attempted without threatening an entire class of bureaucrats that has long been a part of the mainland system.

That system remains essentially unresponsive and centralized, dominated by the Communist party and its self-selected leadership. Whatever revisions are introduced into the economic and political structures of the PRC will have to be compatible with the centralized, bureaucratized, and party-dominated system that prevails. For at least that reason, Communist Chinese economists and political leaders tend to be, and will remain, more responsive to Soviet than to Western developmental and political policies.[37] Any changes made will be marginal at best.

Moreover, if (as seems more than likely) mainland China undergoes modernization incrementally—utilizing existing plant and technological capabilities rather than leapfrogging to the sophisticated technologies proffered in great abundance by the West but too expensive for Peking to purchase—it will probably call upon the Soviet Union. Most of mainland China's existing productive facilities are of Soviet origin. It is estimated, for example, that 70 percent of Communist China's machine tools are of Soviet or Eastern European origin. Their repair and resupply would most naturally come from those quarters—at far lower cost than any suitable replacements from the West. Although the Soviet Union is not a good supplier, should Communist China find itself burdened by investment and exchange constraints, it might appeal to Moscow for economic trade and capital goods transfers.[38]

The Soviet Union has continued to make overtures to Peking in an effort to reduce the prevailing level of hostility. Since the fall of 1981, the Soviet Union has been making regular allusion to its readiness to begin talks with the Communist Chinese to resolve the territorial disputes along their mutual border. It has affirmed the principle of noninterference in Peking's internal affairs and has denied having any aggressive intentions against its neighbor, which it now recognizes as "socialist," rather than "feudal fascist." Similarly, Peking no longer refers to the USSR as a "social fascist" polity but recognizes its "socialist" credentials.

Mainland China has given some indications that it is prepared to export some foodstuffs to the Soviet Union when Soviet harvests are poor. Peking has also announced its willingness to allow the shipment of Soviet goods through its territory to third parties, including Vietnam. The Soviet Union, in turn, has agreed to allow the shipment of Communist Chinese goods to Eastern Europe and Iran by means of the trans-Siberian Railway.[39]

The tenor of the security debates in Peking in the early 1980s suggested that the Communist Chinese leadership no longer felt particularly threatened by the Soviet forces on its borders. The Soviet Union was being perceived more and more as a nation beset with a number of disabling problems that render it less disposed to such military initiatives.[40]

All of this probably augurs a reduction in friction between Peking and Moscow in the foreseeable future. Relations will not ever be as cordial as they were during the early 1950s, but it is clear that both the PRC and the USSR would profit from a reduction of enmity. If Peking were to mitigate some of its most strident criticisms, Moscow might lose its somewhat tarnished image among Third World countries.

The savings for either Moscow or Peking in terms of military expenditure, of course, would be only marginal. Moscow's principal expenditures in the Soviet Far East have been for construction of the vast infrastructure that enhances weapon system survivability, sustains transport, and ensures armed forces mobility. Most of the Soviet divisions on the Communist Chinese borders have always been and will remain understrength, so that any savings that might result from a greater degree of Sino-Soviet rapprochement would not be substantial.

A Sino-Soviet rapprochement would not be particularly damaging to the defense posture of the United States or its allies. With or without the People's Republic of China as a "strategic partner," the United States is compelled by the prevailing circumstances to develop something approximating strategic and conventional military parity with the USSR in Northeast Asia and the West Pacific.

8 | Conclusions

With the advent of the Reagan administration, it has become increasingly obvious that the United States is enduring another painful reassessment of its international security policy. The steadily improving Soviet nuclear capability has prompted a change from the "massive retaliation" and the "assured mutual destruction" policies of the past to the strategic doctrine of "flexible response," with its increased emphasis on the reconstruction of conventional forces capable of engaging in conflict below the nuclear threshold. The evident improvement of Soviet strategic capabilities has reached a level where a deterrent defense, based primarily on nuclear retaliation by the United States, has lost much of its credibility. Nuclear stalemate has become accepted as a fact of life.

Even when the United States and its allies enjoyed an unqualified superiority in nuclear capabilities, it was obvious to many that a certain level of conventional military strength was essential to contain Soviet initiatives. The fear of U.S. nuclear superiority did little (with some qualification) to deter the Soviet Union from exploiting targets of opportunity throughout Africa, the Caribbean, and Asia. Moreover, even when the United States enjoyed a massive nuclear advantage, it was compelled to fight two major conflicts in Asia (the Korean and Vietnam wars) without recourse to that advantage—that is, with conventional arms.[1]

The United States now finds itself in a security environment in which its obligations seem to far outstrip its capabilities. Given the prevailing nuclear parity, it is difficult to see how the United States might ensure adequate conventional deterrence against Soviet initiatives in at least three areas in which Washington has significant security interests: NATO, the Persian Gulf, and Northeast Asia. The NATO defense capabilities have fallen below the level of prudence, and a credible protection of the oil fields of the Persian Gulf necessitates far more military resources than are currently available. No less an important body than the Joint Chiefs of Staff has referred to the grievous "mismatch between our strategy and our resources." Finally, there is every indication that the military buildup advocated by the Reagan administration will not be fully funded and that the gap between our assumed obligations and our military resources will continue for some time in the future.

One of the available options in the effort to reduce the Soviet advantage is "horizontal escalation," that is, Washington may choose to expand a conflict initiated by the Soviet Union to other geographic areas more favorable to the United States and its allies.[2] What this implies is the ability to transfer forces rapidly from one theater to another in times of crisis, which, in turn, means that U.S. allies must plan for a contingency requiring autonomous defense, at least in the short term, should major U.S. forces be employed elsewhere.

This option necessitates the availability of a surface fleet and attendant replenishment and supply vessels capable of supporting U.S. transregional mobility. The ability to maintain maritime superiority and control of the sea would also be essential to the requisite rapid force transfer. If the United States must be prepared to extend any conventional conflict "horizontally," its navy must be equipped to carry the war to the enemy in all relevant theaters simultaneously or in rapid serial order. As a consequence, there is talk of expanding the United States naval order of battle from approximtely 450 combatants to a projected total of 610 vessels by 1990, to include at least 15 large-carrier battle groups and their escort antimissile *Aegis* cruisers.

The fact that a fully equipped large-carrier battle group costs approximately $17 billion has generated the kind of congressional discussion that signals serious political difficulties in securing funds for all of them. The U.S. Navy probably will have to discharge its obligations throughout the world with forces in inventory substantially below optimum levels.

What remains of the United States Seventh and Third fleets in the Pacific consists of only 6 aircraft carriers, 39 submarines, and a total of 87 surface combatants. In the event of a general conflict, those forces will be obliged, in the short term, to seal the Soviet navy in the Sea of Okhotsk, maintain the sea-lanes of communication along the entire exposed coast of East Asia and across the Pacific, and secure the critical choke points in Southeast Asia, as well as undertake contingency deployment in the Indian Ocean. Although U.S. naval forces in the Pacific enjoy certain advantages over their Soviet counterparts in terms of antisubmarine warfare capabilities, seaborne replenishment capabilities, basing facilities, on-board gear, communications, air power, and training, such multiple missions might overwhelm them. It is in this context that the stability and security of Northeast Asia could prove critical to the outcome of any military crisis in East Asia.

If some of the tasks of the U.S. Navy could be responsibly assumed by secure allies in the region, the limited forces availble to the navy could be deployed to contain other challenges. What this implies is that the United States, for the foreseeable future, must be capable of steering a traditional confederation so that it will prove a deterrent to local and more general conflict and also so that associated members will be able to carry out reasonably well-defined responsibilities on the occasion of conflict.

It is more than doubtful that mainland China could, or would, choose to play a role in such an alliance system. Nor does either Washington or Peking seem to be pursuing such an arrangement; there seems to be little profit for either in doing so. The People's Republic of China, for example, could not assist in sealing the choke points that allow Soviet egress from the Sea of Okhotsk. Only the Republic of Korea and Japan are positioned to aid in that mission. The People's Republic of China does not have the blue-water naval capabilities or the long-range air power that would allow it to protect the extended sea-lanes of communication essential to the viability of Northeast Asia. Finally, the People's Republic of China is not bound by mutual security arrangements that would involve it in conflict with the Soviet Union. It has, in fact, every reason to avoid such a conflict given its vulnerabilities.

Any unlikely effort to include Peking in a security treaty with the United States would confuse U.S. relations with the Republic of Korea (the legiti-macy of which Peking refuses to recognize) and Japan (with whom Peking still disputes maritime territorial claims). Moreover, any such effort would further expose the Republic of China to the threats and importunings of Peking—to the general disservice of the interests of both the noncommunist nations of Northeast Asia and the United States.

Both Seoul and Tokyo have continued to evince concern about the security of the Republic of China on Taiwan[3]—for reasons that have already been considered. Moreover, all the nations of East Asia would be threatened by any further enhancement of mainland China's military capabilities that might follow from more intimate security relations with the United States. Peking's foreign policy has always been supremely independent, and Peking will continue to deploy whatever capacity it develops on behalf of its own national interests.[4] Its interests have not always been consonant with those of its neighbors.[5] For at least these reasons, Admiral Noel Gayler has insisted that it would be a "grave mistake" for the United States to proceed "too far" in its military association with the People's Republic of China.[6]

It is in Peking's national interest to maintain its foreign policy indepen-dence. For Peking's purposes a U.S. military presence in East Asia is sufficient to deny the Soviet Union the overwhelming conventional firepower advantage that might tempt it to embark on an adventure.[7] It is not in Peking's interest, however, to permanently alienate Moscow by joining an anti-Soviet entente. In all probability, Peking will attempt to maintain Sino-Soviet hostility below the level of overt conflict and will pursue some moderate abatement of tensions.

Although the Soviet Union can now project its military power into Asia to a degree that would have been impossible in the early 1960s, it has not been able to translate that power into commensurate political influence.[8] North Korea is no longer simply a client state, and although Vietnam is a dependency, it is not at all clear that Hanoi is content with the arrangement. Whatever strategic advantage has accrued to Moscow as a result of the Vietnamese connection has been purchased at the cost of increasing enmity from ASEAN. Finally, nowhere in Asia is the Soviet Union perceived as a credible political and economic model to emulate. The Soviet Union's influence in Asia arises solely out of the influence that attends its military power.[9]

In Northeast Asia the Soviet Union has not been able to take advantage of the powerful appeal that its exploitation of Siberia's energy resources and raw materials would have on the Japanese because of the strategic necessity of maintaining a firm grip on the northern islands of Iturup, Kunashir, Shikotan, and Habomai that Tokyo still considers national territory. Continued Soviet concern over free passage out of the inland Sea of Okhotsk largely precludes an accommodation with Japan that might influence its strategic ties with the United States. The USSR's equally demanding preoccupation with the possibility that the Communist Chinese might gain pre-emptive influence over North Korea renders any accommodation with Seoul unlikely, and the continued presence of U.S. ground forces along the major invasion routes into the Republic of Korea will probably forestall any change in the strategic balance in the region in the near future.

In these circumstances the United States would seem to enjoy considerable political advantage. Its policy in the West Pacific in general, and Northeast Asia in particular, is clearly designed to further economic growth and foster peace and stability by deterring revolutionary change and military misadventure. Ultimately, it is a policy based on the conviction that Western economic strategies and political institutions will prevail in an environment of peace and evolutionary change—if for no other reasons than that they have shown themselves to be of greater utility and effectiveness and that they satisfy more of the most urgent human needs at appreciably less human cost than any revolutionary alternative.

The gradual enhancement of the military capabilities of both Japan and the Republic of Korea serves that ultimate purpose. The development of Japanese capabilities has been painfully slow in the past largely because of Tokyo's singular lack of concern for priorities and mission planning. By the early 1980s, the missions assigned to the Japanese Self-Defense Forces were being more clearly defined, and resources were increasingly being allocated to the tasks of minelaying and air interception. In February 1983, Prime Minister Nakasone clearly identified Japan's security mission as including a first-line defense against Soviet bombers and a blockade of the critical Sōya, Tsushima, and Tsugaru straits. In fact, he declared that Japan would permit U.S. forces to seal those straits even if Japan itself were not under direct Soviet attack.

Aside from that, between 1978 and 1979 Japan began to intensify cooperation with South Korea on mutual defense issues. In 1979, the annual Korean-Japanese Parliamentary Conference on Security Affairs was established, and in July of the same year the director general of the Japanese Defense Agency made his first official visit to Seoul.

The United States military in the region has the available facilities to maintain continuous intelligence contacts between the armed forces of both nations as well as the potential for establishing regional early warning and surveillance capabilities. The United States has arranged to have units of the Twenty-fifth Infantry Division stationed in Hawaii flown to South Korea for joint exercises with South Korean troops, and the entire division remains on alert for service on the peninsula. As defense planning for the region progresses, the resources of the Ninth Infantry Division stationed at Fort Lewis, Washington, and of the Seventh Division stationed at Fort Ord, California, could be enhanced by the transfer of the marine division now stationed in Southern California to the Aleutians or to Alaska. These forces, together with the marine division stationed in Okinawa, would provide substantial assets in any defense of Northeast Asia and would complicate any risk assessments undertaken by the Soviet regional military command there.

It is clear that Japan will not be a dominant military power in the region in the foreseeable future—nor would the nations of East Asia welcome such an eventuality. The United States and the Soviet Union will remain the principal military actors in the area. The Japanese should be required to provide the United States with collateral support by putting together a credible deterrent defense of the northern home islands in the event of a general conflict, and by preparing to impose an initial blockade of the waterways leading from the Sea of Okhotsk, where the major elements of the Soviet fleet are berthed. In accomplishing this, a great deal will depend on the ability of Prime Minister Nakasone to influence the Finance Ministry, an agency that has, in the past, regularly reduced Defense Agency procurement requests to a disabling minimum. Although Japanese procurement plans for the first half of the 1980s exceed for the first time the $10 billion limit imposed on all previous plans, they do not adequately provide for the minelaying and escort vessels necessary for a fully credible blockade capability.[10] Nor are the air defense assets of the

Japanese Self-Defense Forces adequate to their projected tasks. All the Japanese military forces, moreover, require sustained increases in stockpiled reserves, ammunition, spare parts, and fuel; such increases would probably require defense expenditure increases of 7 or 8 percent per annum in real terms in the second half of the 1980s.

Japan, in effect, has moved closer to the position adopted by U.S. strategists. The problem, of course, will be to make such defense postures acceptable to the Japanese public and the broad-based opposition in the Diet. Washington must remain sensitive to the constraints generated by Japanese public opinion; every knowledgeable U.S. analyst has recommended close and continuous consultation between the leaders in the two countries to avoid unnecessary misunderstanding and ill feelings. Joint policies that involve mutual responsibilities necessitate confidence-building efforts. There is little, if any, justification for a failure to communicate and exchange counsel.

During his visit to the United States in 1983, Prime Minister Nakasone first alluded to his conviction that Japan must develop effective air defenses against Soviet attack, a capacity to seal the critical straits allowing Soviet passage to the open Pacific, and the ability to help defend the major sea-lanes to Guam and as far south as the Taiwan area. The same themes had been mentioned earlier in the influential publication of Tokyo's Research Institute for Peace and Security, *Asian Security*.[11] In fact, the defense debate in Japan in the early 1980s focused on these responsibilities, and it is evident that national security, and the specific missions of the Japanese Self-Defense Forces, have become increasingly important issues in Japanese domestic politics.[12] Nakasone's persuasiveness, given the constraints of divided public opinion and bureaucratic bargaining, will determine how quickly Japan can responsibly discharge its security obligations in the region.

The United States can, and should, judiciously urge Japan to accelerate its defense buildup. To meet all Japan's defense needs, the 6.5 percent increase in the 1983–84 military budget should probably have been a minimum of 10 or 11 percent, but the Reagan administration perhaps wisely shifted the dialogue between the two countries' representatives away from percentages to potential security roles and military missions. Once those are firmly defined, given a suitable domestic environment, procurement funds may be forthcoming. It seems evident that those Japanese who are responsible for security policy are prepared to accept the conclusions of the U.S.-Japan Security Conference of 1981 that priority should be given to local strait and air control in Japanese defense planning.[13] The first full effect of these decisions should reveal itself in the Japanese defense budgets of 1984–85 and 1985–86.

The United States, to facilitate these developments, must restore its credibility as a secure defense partner. In this regard, the Japanese have been quite candid. The policies of the Carter administration seriously impaired the image of the United States as a guarantor of security in the eyes of Asians in general, and the Japanese in particular.[14] The decision to withdraw United States ground forces from South Korea was perhaps the most disastrous mistake of Carter's undistinguished presidency. It emboldened the North Koreans and thoroughly unsettled the Japanese.[15] With the termination of the Mutual Defense Treaty with the Republic of China on Taiwan, both flanks of the Japanese security perimeter were threatened. The situation was remedied only by the decision to halt the withdrawal from South Korea and by congressional passage of the Taiwan Relations Act—which was conceived as a surrogate, in domestic law, for the faulted U.S.-ROC defense treaty.

In re-establishing its credibility, the United States will have to both assist the South Koreans in their development of a credible deterrent capacity and significantly alter its policy of allowing the defense capabilities of the Republic of China on Taiwan to gradually erode. This latter course will be the more difficult to pursue, but the entire logic of the circumstances in Northeast Asia recommends it.

Taiwan provides potential basing and servicing facilities for high-performance jet aircraft in any serious contingency. During the Vietnam War many of the F-4 Phantom jets of the U.S. armed forces were repaired and overhauled in facilities on Taiwan, and Taiwan still maintains many of the critical capabilities to serve in just such a capacity. The availability of a reservoir of trained personnel, active in the ROC's electronics and high-technology industries, would be important in the event of a conflict; prudence suggests that their skills not be allowed to diminish.

Air interceptor assets based on Taiwan could offset a shortfall in U.S. aircraft carriers in the region and would allow greater flexibility in protecting the sea-lanes that are proximate to the island. Moreover, a suitably enhanced ROC air force could conceivably obstruct the free passage of Soviet aircraft through gaps that remain, and will remain for the foreseeable future, in the archipelagic defense line to the southwest of the Japanese home islands.

This would mean the continued provision of the military assets and training necessary for the self-defense of the ROC in accordance with the clear language of the Taiwan Relations Act.[16] The acquisition by Taiwan of modern high-performance interceptors, for example, with longer range and greater ordnance-carrying capabilities, manned by suitably trained crews, would allow its military forces to ensure the integrity of the island; they might also serve as the first line of defense against high-altitude, high-speed Soviet bombers making their way to the shipping lanes of the West Pacific.

If such assets were under the control of the military command in Taipei, their commitment in an anti-Soviet defense of Northeast Asia would be assured. Peking has little reason to commit its armed forces against the USSR unless subject to direct attack, but Taipei has every economic, ideological, and strategic reason for doing just that. The strategic commitment of the ROC to the West was unequivocally expressed by General Chiang Wei-kuo (the half brother of ROC President Chiang Ching-kuo) in his *Strategic Significance of Taiwan*—a 1974 policy statement that was reissued in 1977[17] and reaffirmed by President Chiang in June 1982.[18]

Although there would be immediate and strategic advantages, the sale and transfer of such high-performance aircraft to the ROC would produce serious strains in the existing relationship between Washington and Peking. At some point in time Washington will have to decide just how intimate its relations with Peking are to be. If the United States expects to foster more intensive military collaboration with Communist China, or to develop more complex economic and political ties, then it will probably have to sacrifice Taiwan. It would seem that policymakers in Washington are very close to that juncture when they will be obliged to undertake a hardheaded cost-benefit analysis of U.S. relations with the People's Republic of China.

A great deal has changed in the ongoing relationship between the United States and the PRC since the late 1970s; the PRC has proven to be "smaller in life than in our imagination."[19] The anticipated export market supplement of one billion customers that would have relieved the United States of its burden of a deficit trade balance, for instance, has failed to materialize. There are few windfall export profits to be made in trade with mainland China. There is profit potential in offshore joint ventures in oil and gas recovery—but the garnering of those profits would involve the United States in underwriting risky capital-intensive operations that would tend to lend credibility to mainland China's destabilizing and provocative claims all along the East Asian continental shelf. Bilateral trade will probably increase, but under the best of circumstances it will be a long time before such trade exceeds the levels of trade and investment the United States now enjoys with the Republic of China on Taiwan.[20]

As far as strategic advantages, the United States probably has already received whatever benefits it has any reason to expect from the People's Republic of China. In fact, those benefits were arguably already enjoyed before the normalization of relations between Washington and Peking. As has been indicated, the Soviet Union will in all probability maintain its forces in the Far East, at least at the levels existing in the early 1980s, under almost any conceivable circumstances.[21] There is very little that Peking can do that would alter the present situation—nor is there any reason to believe that Communist Chinese hostility toward Moscow will increase, however accommodating Washington might choose to be. Cordial relations with the PRC cannot serve as a substitute for an effective unilateral U.S. security program in Northeast Asia, and if a suitably armed ROC is part of that program, Washington is counseled to prudently pursue that end.[22] Although there are many reasons for the United States to maintain normal diplomatic and economic relations with the People's Republic of China, Washington has little, if any, reason to further mortgage its defense, and the defense of the nations of Northeast Asia, to appease Peking.

Whatever the relations between Peking and Washington, too much has transpired along the Sino-Soviet border to imagine that Communist China will not complicate Soviet risk assessments and strategic planning in Northeast Asia. No matter how amicable future relations between the Soviet Union and the People's Republic of China might become, the mere existence of Communist China will require Moscow to retain a significant portion of its available forces along the border to deter the leadership in Peking from making any policy shifts and to ensure the neutrality of the PRC in any confrontation with the United States.[23] The Soviet Far East theater command structure, and its attendant costs in terms of maintaining troop strength and force projection capabilities sufficient to oppose the United States and Japan, would certainly remain. The Soviet Sea of Okhotsk bastion would remain; so, too, would the support forces necessary to sustain Soviet ambitions in Southeast Asia and the Indian Ocean.

The fact is that the People's Republic of China does not have it within its power to significantly influence the military balance, or the security of the United States and the members of the anti-Soviet alliance, in Northeast Asia. On the other hand, as long as the United States maintains balanced relations with Communist China, the inability of Moscow to anticipate how the United States might react to any actions taken against the PRC provides Peking with some assurance that any Soviet actions will be constrained by the necessity of operating in an unpredictable military environment. In substance, Communist China has more reason to concern itself about its "U.S. connection" than the United States has reason to court a "Chinese connection."

This allows the United States the freedom to act with considerable discretion to protect its own security interests without paying disabling costs in the effort to forestall a Sino-Soviet rapprochement. Any conceivable Sino-Soviet rapproachement would not materially alter the security circumstances in Northeast Asia. As a consequence, the United States is free to provide, or contrive to have others provide, the military assets necessary for the secure defense of the Republic of China on Taiwan without anticipating prohibitive costs. Not only would a secure Taiwan help stabilize the entire Northeast, but its upgraded military assets might be incorporated into an integrated anti-Soviet defense of the region. This would serve to close one of the major gaps in the forward defense line that stretches along the perimeter of East Asia.

Soviet behavior since the early 1970s does not appear to have been significantly influenced by any preoccupation with Sino-U.S. collaboration. Soviet restraint seems to have been governed rather by calculations of military risk.

That risk cannot be increased by any Western attempt to upgrade the armed forces of mainland China. For the remainder of this century the armed forces of the PRC cannot be made to serve as a counterweight to Soviet military power. By increasing the response capabilities of the noncommunist littoral and island states of Northeast Asia, on the other hand, the United States would significantly complicate Soviet risk assessments.

Arms sales by the West to the People's Republic of China would only increase Peking's ability to threaten the Republic of China on Taiwan and the Republic of Korea as well. Any enhancement of the military capabilities of Communist China would increase the danger of armed confrontations between Peking and all the nations of Southeast Asia—none of which would serve the economic, political, or security interests of the United States.[24]

Despite mainland China's evident vulnerabilities, it has the potential for creating more problems in East Asia in the immediate future than does the Soviet Union. This has been made manifest by Peking's quarrel with Vietnam, its "special relationship" with the Korea of Kim Il-sung, its continued involvement with the indigenous communist guerrilla movements in Southeast Asia, and its inflexible commitment to its offshore territorial claims. Peking can use armed force when it perceives such use to be in its own interests—as it has done in Burma, Laos, Tibet, India, Vietnam, the Taiwan Strait, the Paracel Islands, and along the Sino-Soviet border. During the Great Proletarian Cultural Revolution, it was even involved in local firefights with the troops of North Korea. Its missile boats have stalked unarmed U.S. seismic exploration vessels, and it sent armed fishing boats to harass the Japanese at the time of the dispute over the Senkaku Islands.

Peking retains the capacity to either increase or diminish assistance to communist guerrilla movements in such hard-pressed states as Burma and Thailand and perhaps the Philippines as well. It can insist on maximum territorial claims along the continental shelf—and it has the capability to undertake a military solution to the problem of Taiwan.

The initial intuition of the Reagan administration, that the United States should place primary emphasis on the strengthening of its own defense capabilities and avoid unnecessary reliance on ties to countries that do not share its political values, social goals, and economic interests, had much to recommend it. Former Secretary of State Alexander Haig's insistence that Communist China constituted a "security asset" for the United States, and the confusion that it generated, are only to be lamented. The importance of the PRC lies in the fact that it ties down about a half million Soviet troops along its borders. But it would do that in any case—whether well- or ill-disposed toward the United States and the noncommunist nations of East Asia.

The Soviet Union has always been cautious in exposing itself to military risks. It has acted with determination only in those areas where the military risks were small—as in Angola and Afghanistan. Where enemy response capabilities have been robust, the Soviet Union has displayed commendable caution. A credible U.S. and noncommunist defense capability in Northeast Asia would foreclose Soviet military initiatives. It would thus provide the mainland Chinese the opportunity to pursue their plans for modernization— the effort to force the PRC into the twentieth century. Such a defense capability would have the added benefit of reducing any disposition Peking might have to incite local quarrels, increase its support to local insurgent groups, or press its territorial claims to the continental shelf.

The PRC has been one of the principal beneficiaries of the security environment created by the U.S. presence in East Asia, which has allowed mainland China to gradually reduce its defense expenditures. (They grew only very slowly between 1972 and 1977 and thereafter actually declined in real terms.)[25] Peking gives every evidence, by its public assessments and its overt behavior, of being convinced that the Soviet forces in East Asia are there to counter the military capabilities of the United States and its security partners.[26] As a consequence, the leadership in Peking is prepared to allow the United States and its security partners to shoulder the burdens of deterrent defense. In Northeast Asia the U.S. security partners are Japan, the Republic of Korea, and the Republic of China on Taiwan—the noncommunist states that together constitute the "iron triangle." However much the People's Republic of China may be discomfited by the reality of the present circumstances, it is upon the defense capabilities of those nations that its ultimate security depends.

The present China policy of the United States does little to mitigate the security threat presented by the strengthening of Soviet forces in East Asia. In fact, such a policy might well undermine the integrity and the security of all the nations of Northeast Asia—Japan among them—to the ultimate disservice of U.S. economic, strategic, and moral interests. The future of East Asia will be significantly influenced, if not determined, by what the United States chooses to do, or not to do, in the West Pacific in the 1990s. What it cannot do, if it intends to contribute to the stability and economic development of the region, is to allow the collapse of the iron triangle upon which so much of the future depends.

Notes

Chapter 1

1. For an interesting treatment of this situation, see James C. Thomson, Jr., Peter W. Stanley, and John Curtis Perry, *Sentimental Imperialists: The American Experience in East Asia* (New York: Harper & Row, 1981).

2. See William V. Kennedy, "The Perceived Threat to China's Future," in Ray Bonds, ed., *The Chinese War Machine* (New York: Crescent Books, 1979), pp. 179–81.

3. See Thomson, Stanley, and Perry, *Sentimental Imperialists*, p. 301; John C. H. Fei, Gustav Ranis, and Shirley W. Y. Kuo, *Growth with Equity: The Taiwan Case* (New York: Oxford University Press, 1979).

4. See A. James Gregor and Maria Hsia Chang, *The Republic of China and U.S. Policy* (Washington, D.C.: Ethics and Public Policy Center, 1983).

5. See "Kim's Build-up to Blitzkrieg," *Far Eastern Economic Review*, March 5, 1982, pp. 26–30; Edwin K. Snyder, A. James Gregor, and Maria Hsia Chang, *The Taiwan Relations Act and the Defense of the Republic of China* (Berkeley: University of California, Institute of International Studies, 1980).

6. See Armin Rappaport, "Determinants of United States Policy in the Western Pacific: Past and Future," in *Emerging Western Pacific Community: Problems and Prospects, Proceedings of the Seminar on Western Pacific Community* (Taipei: Freedom Council, 1980), pp. 240–41.

7. See *World Development Report, 1980* (New York: Oxford University Press, 1980), p. 157, table 24.

8. Montek Ahluwalia, "Income Inequality: Some Dimensions of the Problem," in Hollis Chenery et al., eds., *Redistribution with Growth* (Oxford: Oxford University Press,

1974), p. 809; see also Irma Adelman and Cynthia T. Morris, *Economic Growth and Social Equity in Developing Countries* (Stanford: Stanford University Press, 1973).

9. See the discussion in A. James Gregor and Maria Hsia Chang, *Republic of China*, chaps. 1 and 5.

10. For the "classic" expression of this theory, see James D. Cockroft, André Gunder Frank, and Dale L. Johnson, *Dependence and Underdevelopment* (New York: Anchor Books, 1972). For a general discussion of dependency theory, see Tony Smith, "The Underdevelopment of Development Literature," *World Politics* 31, no. 2 (January 1979): 247–88.

11. James E. Dornan, Jr., "The Changing Security Environment in Northeast Asia," in Richard B. Foster, James E. Dornan, Jr., and William M. Carpenter, eds., *Strategy and Security in Northeast Asia* (New York: Crane, Russak, 1979), p. 3.

12. See R. J. Rummel, "Soviet Strategy and Northeast Asia," *Korea and World Affairs* 2 (Spring 1978): 23–25.

13. William V. Kennedy, "China's Role in a New U.S. Deterrence Strategy," in Douglas T. Stuart and William T. Tow, eds., *China, the Soviet Union, and the West: Strategic and Political Dimensions in the 1980s* (Boulder, Colo.: Westview, 1982), pp. 259–60. See also Richard G. Stilwell, "Challenge and Response in the Northeast Asia of the 1980s: The Military Balance," in Foster, Dornan, and Carpenter, *Strategy and Security*, p. 95.

14. Richard B. Foster and William M. Carpenter, "Great-Power Interactions in Northeast Asia," in Foster, Dornan, and Carpenter, *Strategy and Security*, p. 44; and Hideoki Kase, "Northeast Asian Security: A View from Japan," in ibid., p. 107.

15. See Wolf Mendl, *Issues in Japan's China Policy* (New York: Oxford University Press, 1978), p. 113.

16. See Richard H. Solomon, "American Defense Planning and Asian Security: Policy Choices for a Time of Transition," in Richard H. Solomon, ed., *Asian Security in the 1980s: Problems and Policies for a Time of Transition* (Cambridge, Mass.: Oelgeschlager, Gunn & Hain, 1980), p. 16.

Chapter 2

1. See John M. Collins, *American and Soviet Military Trends Since the Cuban Missile Crisis* (Washington, D.C.: Georgetown University, 1978).

2. Central Intelligence Agency, *Estimating Soviet Defense Spending in Rubles* (Washington, D.C.: Central Intelligence Agency, May 1976), p. 16; Andrew W. Marshall, *Comparisons of U.S. and S.U. Defense Expenditures* (Washington, D.C.: Department of Defense, September 16, 1975), p. 164; Daniel O. Graham, "The Soviet Military Budget Controversy," *Air Force Magazine*, May 1976, pp. 36–37.

3. See W. T. Lee, "Soviet Defense Expenditures," *Osteuropa Wirtschaft*, December 1977, pp. 273–92, and Karl Kaiser et al., *Western Security: What Has Changed? What Should Be Done?* (London: Royal Institute of Foreign Affairs, 1981), p. 27.

4. Osamu Miyoshi, "The Growth of Soviet Military Power and the Security of Japan,"

in Richard B. Foster, James E. Dornan, Jr., and William M. Carpenter, eds., *Strategy and Security in Northeast Asia* (New York: Crane, Russak, 1979), p. 59.

5. V. D. Sokolovskii, ed., *Soviet Military Strategy*, trans. Herbert S. Dinerstein, Leon Goure, and Thomas W. Wolf (Englewood Cliffs, N.J.: Prentice-Hall, 1963), pp. 314, 349.

6. Harold Brown, *Annual Report of the Department of Defense, FY 1979* (Washington, D.C.: Department of Defense, 1978), p. 21.

7. See the discussion in Edward N. Luttwak, "Against the China Card," *Commentary* 66, no. 4 (October 1978): 37–43.

8. For a discussion of Soviet force deployments in the East, see Kenneth Hunt, "Sino-Soviet Theater Force Comparisons," in Douglas T. Stuart and William T. Tow, eds., *China, the Soviet Union, and the West: Strategic and Political Dimensions in the 1980s* (Boulder, Colo.: Westview, 1982), pp. 103–14; Stuart E. Johnson and Joseph A. Yager, *The Military Equation in Northeast Asia* (Washington, D.C.: Brookings Institution, 1979), pp. 10–20; *The Military Balance, 1980–1981* (London: International Institute for Strategic Studies, 1980).

9. See Nico Sgarlato, *Soviet Aircraft of Today* (Carrollton, Texas: Squadron, 1979).

10. For a discussion of these considerations, see Drew Middleton, *The Duel of the Giants: China and Russia in Asia* (New York: Scribner's, 1978), chap. 6.

11. See Harrison E. Salisbury, *War Between Russia and China* (New York: Norton, 1969), pp. 146–48.

12. See Lawrence Freedman, "Economic and Technological Factors in the Sino-Soviet Dispute," and Thomas W. Robinson, "Sino-Soviet Competition in Asia," in Stuart and Tow, *China, the Soviet Union, and the West*, pp. 82, 180.

13. Harold C. Hinton, *The Sino-Soviet Confrontation: Implications for the Future* (New York: Crane, Russak, 1976), p. 43.

14. As quoted, Middleton, *Duel of the Giants*, p. 152.

15. Karl Kaiser et al., *Western Security*, p. 26; see also *Is America Becoming Number 2?* (Washington, D.C.: Committee on the Present Danger, 1978), p. 26.

16. See *Japanese Defense White Paper* (Tokyo: Japanese Self-Defense Agency, 1976), pp. 17, 148.

17. See Tan Su-cheng, *The Expansion of Soviet Seapower and the Security of Asia* (Taipei: Asia and the World Forum, 1977), pp. 4–5.

18. For estimates of Soviet naval capabilities in East Asia, see Defense Intelligence Agency, *Unclassified Communist Naval Orders of Battle* (Washington, D.C.: Defense Intelligence Agency, November 1979), pp. 1–6, 10–16.

19. "Ivan Rogov: Extending the Soviet Sphere," *All Hands*, December 1978, p. 27; Tan Su-cheng, *Soviet Naval Implications in the 1980s: An Analysis of the Security Factor*, mimeographed (Taipei: Asia and the World Forum, June 1979), pp. 12–13.

20. N. N. Baransky, *Economic Geography of the U.S.S.R.* (Moscow: Foreign Languages Press, 1956), p. 280.

21. Tan, *Expansion of Soviet Seapower*, p. 38.

22. See Jacquelyn K. Davis and Robert L. Pfaltzgraff, Jr., *Soviet Theater Strategy: Implications for NATO* (Washington, D.C.: United States Strategic Institute, 1978).

23. See William V. Kennedy, "The Perceived Threat to China's Future," in Ray Bonds, ed., *The Chinese War Machine* (New York: Crescent Books, 1979).

24. See Edward N. Luttwak, "Why We Need More 'Waste, Fraud, and Mismanagement' in the Pentagon," *Commentary* 73, no. 2 (February 1982): 17.

25. Paul H. Nitz and Leonard Sullivan, Jr., *Securing the Seas: The Soviet Naval Challenge and Western Alliance Options* (Boulder, Colo.: Westview, 1979), pp. 380–82, 402–3.

26. William D. O'Neil, "Backfire: Long Shadow on the Sea-Lanes," *United States Naval Institute Proceedings*, March 1977, pp. 26–35; Georg Panyalev, "Backfire—Soviet Counter to the American B-1," *International Defense Review*, October 1975, p. 639.

Chapter 3

1. Justin Galen (the pen name of a former senior Department of Defense civilian specialist), "U.S.' Toughest Message to the USSR," *Armed Forces Journal International*, February 1979, p. 30.

2. Ibid.

3. See Edwin K. Snyder, A. James Gregor, and Maria Hsia Chang, *The Taiwan Relations Act and the Defense of the Republic of China* (Berkeley: University of California, Institute of International Studies, 1980), chap. 1.

4. Galen, "U.S.' Toughest Message," p. 32.

5. Ibid., pp. 35–36.

6. Estimates of the military capabilities of the PRC are found in *The Military Balance, 1981–1982* (London: International Institute for Strategic Studies, 1981); Ray Bonds, ed., *The Chinese War Machine* (New York: Crescent Books, 1979); Harlan W. Jencks, *From Muskets to Missiles: Politics and Professionalism in the Chinese Army, 1945–1981* (Boulder, Colo.: Westview, 1982); Jonathan D. Pollack, "China as a Military Power," in Onkar Marwah and Jonathan Pollack, eds., *Military Power and Policy in Asian States: China, India, Japan* (Boulder, Colo.: Westview, 1979); Harry G. Gelber, *Technology, Defense, and External Relations in China, 1975–1978* (Boulder, Colo.: Westview, 1979), chap. 2; John Franklin Copper, *China's Global Role* (Stanford: Hoover Institution Press, 1980), chap. 5; Stuart E. Johnson and Joseph A. Yager, *The Military Equation in Northeast Asia* (Washington, D.C.: Brookings Institution, 1979); Kenneth Hunt, "Sino-Soviet Theater Force Comparisons," in Douglas T. Stuart and William T. Tow, eds., *China, the Soviet Union, and the West: Strategic and Political Dimensions in the 1980s* (Boulder, Colo.: Westview, 1982), chap 7.

7. Donald C. Daniel, "Sino-Soviet Relations in Naval Perspective," in Stuart and Tow, *China, the Soviet Union, and the West*, p. 117.

8. See William V. Kennedy, "The Perceived Threat to China's Future," in Bonds, *Chinese War Machine*, pp. 174–75.

9. For a more extensive discussion, see Jonathan Pollack, "China as a Nuclear

Power," in William H. Overholt, ed., *Asia's Nuclear Future* (Boulder, Colo.: Westview, 1977).

10. See Gelber, *Technology, Defense, and External Relations*, pp. 76–77.

11. For a discussion of PLAAF pilot training, see Fan Yuan-yen, *Question and Answer: A Testimony of a Chinese Communist Pilot* (Taipei: China Press, 1978), pp. 45–48; Jencks, *From Muskets to Missiles*, pp. 155–56.

12. Drew Middleton, *The Duel of the Giants: China and Russia in Asia* (New York: Scribner's, 1978), pp. 199–200.

13. Bill Sweetman, "The Modernization of China's Air Force," in Bonds, *Chinese War Machine*, p. 142.

14. Harvey W. Nelson, "The Organization of China's Ground Forces," in ibid., p. 91.

15. Kennedy, "The Perceived Threat to China's Future," ibid., p. 178.

16. Gelber, *Technology, Defense, and External Relations*, pp. 50–51.

17. Jencks, *From Muskets to Missiles*, p. 148.

18. Victor Louis, *The Coming Decline of the Chinese Empire* (New York: Times Books, 1979), p. 187; see pp. 15, 16, 64–65, 92.

19. Noel Gaylor, "Security Implications of the Soviet Military Presence in Asia," in Richard H. Solomon, ed., *Asian Security in the 1980s: Problems and Policies for a Time of Transition* (Cambridge, Mass.: Oelgeschlager, Gunn & Hain, 1980), p. 59.

20. William C. Green and David C. Yost, "Soviet Military Options Regarding China," in Stuart and Tow, *China, the Soviet Union, and the West*, p. 143.

21. "Su Yu Reveals the Probability of War with Russia," *Inside China Mainland* 1 (March 1979): 1.

22. See Middleton, *Duel of the Giants*, chap. 9.

Chapter 4

1. For a discussion of the evolution of Japan's defense policy, see Masataka Kosaka, ed., *Asian Security* (Tokyo: Research Institute for Peace and Security, 1981), pp. 145–59.

2. See Sadao Seno and James E. Auer, "The Navy of Japan," in Barry M. Blechman and Robert P. Berman, eds., *Guide to Far Eastern Navies* (Annapolis, Md.: U.S. Naval Institute, 1978), pp. 199–203.

3. See Robert Shymant, "Officially Japan Doesn't Have an Army, but This Is What It Has for Self-Defense," *The Times* (London), February 5, 1978, p. 5; Yasuhisa Nakada, "Japan's Security Perceptions and Military Needs," in Onkar Marwah and Jonathan D. Pollack, eds., *Military Power and Policy in Asian States: China, India, Japan* (Boulder, Colo: Westview, 1979), pp. 171–75.

4. See Ikutaro Shiizu, "The Nuclear Option: Japan, Be a State," *Japan Echo* 7, no. 3 (1980): 34–37.

5. See Edwin O. Reischauer, *The Japanese* (Cambridge, Mass.: Harvard University Press, 1981), chap. 34; Robert E. Bedeski, "The Sino-Japan Treaty of Peace and Friendship, and Japan's Defense Debate," *Issues and Studies* 18, no. 4 (April 1982): 54–70;

Donald C. Hellman, "Japanese Security and Postwar Japanese Foreign Policy," in Robert A. Scalapino, ed., *The Foreign Policy of Modern Japan* (Berkeley and Los Angeles: University of California Press, 1977), p. 332.

6. See *Mainichi Shimbun*, Tokyo, November 21, 1979.

7. See Morton H. Halperin, "The U.S. Nuclear Umbrella and Japanese Security," in Franklin B. Weinstein, ed., *U.S.-Japan Relations and the Security of East Asia: The Next Decade* (Boulder, Colo.: Westview, 1978), pp. 93–105.

8. See the discussion in John R. Dewenter, "The East China and Yellow Seas," *U.S. Naval Institute Proceedings* 101, no. 867 (May 1975): 190–311; Tan Su-cheng, *The Expansion of Soviet Seapower and the Security of Asia* (Taipei: Asia and the World Forum, 1977), chaps 1–3; James William Morely, "A Time for Realism in the Military Defense of Japan," in Weinstein, *U.S.-Japan Relations*, pp. 61–62.

9. See Paul H. Nitz and Leonard Sullivan, Jr., *Securing the Seas: The Soviet Naval Challenge and Western Alliance Options* (Boulder, Colo.: Westview, 1979), p. 114.

10. Chu Shao-hsien, "The Impact of Washington's Relations with Taipei, Seoul, and Tokyo on the Security of Northeast Asia," in *Asian Regional Security and the Free World, Proceedings of the 1977 Conference of Sino-Korean-Japanese Professors* (Taipei: Pacific Cultural Foundation, 1978), p. 116.

11. A. Doak Barnett, *China and the Major Powers in East Asia* (Washington, D.C.: Brookings Institution, 1977), p. 143.

12. Yung H. Park, "Japan's Korean Policy, and Her Perceptions and Expectations Regarding America's Role in Korea," in Yung-hwan Jo, ed., *U.S. Foreign Policy in Asia: An Appraisal* (Santa Barbara, Calif.: ABC-Clio, 1978), pp. 357, 360.

13. See the *Defense of Japan: Defense White Paper* (Summary) (Tokyo: Japan Defense Agency, June 1976); A. Doak Barnett, *China and the Major Powers*, p. 146.

14. Peter W. Soverel, "Problems of Sea Power in the Western Pacific as We Approach the Twenty-First Century," in James L. George, ed., *Problems of Sea Power as We Approach the Twenty-First Century* (Washington, D.C.: American Enterprise Institute, 1978), p. 169.

15. Morimachi Kuramae, "The Strategy for the Pacific Basin and the Role of Japan," in *The Pacific Era: Issues for the 1980s and Beyond, Proceedings of the Eighth International Conference on World Peace* (Tokyo: Professors' World Peace Academy of Japan, 1979), p. 305.

16. Kenichi Kitamura, "The Pacific Region and Its Maritime Security," in ibid., pp. 343, 347.

17. Hisahiko Okazaki, "Japan's Taiwan Relations After Normalization with Peking," in Yung-hwan Jo, ed., *Taiwan's Future* (Hong Kong: Union Research Institute for Arizona State University, 1974), p. 112. See also Douglas H. Mendel, Jr., "Japanese Public Views on Taiwan's Future," *Asian Survey* 15, no. 3 (March 1975): 215–33.

18. Cf. A. Doak Barnett, *China and the Major Powers*, p. 141.

19. David Nelson Rowe, *Informal "Diplomatic Relations": The Case of Japan and the Republic of China, 1972–1974* (Hamden, Conn.: Foreign Area Studies Publications, 1975), pp. 7–8.

20. Wolf Mendl, *Issues in Japan's China Policy* (New York: Oxford University Press, 1978), p. 109.

21. See Stephen P. Gilbert, "The U.S. Concept of National Security," in James E. Dornan, Jr., ed., *The U.S. War Machine* (New York: Crown, 1978), p. 24.

22. See William V. Kennedy, "China's Role in a New U.S. Deterrence Strategy," in Douglas T. Stuart and William T. Tow, eds., *China, the Soviet Union, and the West: Strategic and Political Dimensions in the 1980s* (Boulder, Colo.: Westview, 1982), pp. 255–56.

23. See David Shilling, "A Reassessment of Japan's Naval Needs," *Asian Survey* 16, no. 3 (March 1976): 227–28.

24. See John J. Stephen, "The Kurile Islands: Japan Versus Russia," *Pacific Community* 7, no. 3 (April 1976): 311–30.

25. Stuart E. Johnson and Joseph A. Yager, *The Military Equation in Northeast Asia* (Washington, D.C.: Brookings Institution, 1979), pp. 75–76.

26. See the recommendations of Tan Su-cheng, *Expansion of Soviet Seapower*, p. 41.

27. See Ko Tun-hwa, "The Strategic Importance of Taiwan," in Chang King-yuh, ed., *Western Pacific Security in a Changing Context: Problems and Prospects* (Taipei: Freedom Council, 1982), pp. 79–87.

28. Franklin B. Weinstein, "Conclusions and Policy Recommendations," in Weinstein, *U.S.-Japan Relations*, p. 276.

29. *Report on Comprehensive National Security* (English translation) (Tokyo: n.p., 1980), pp. 7, 52.

Chapter 5

1. Duk-joo Kim, "The U.S. and Japan's Policy on Peace and Security in Korea," *East Asian Review* 3, no. 4 (Winter 1976): 534–35; Claude A. Buss, *The United States and the Republic of Korea: Background for Policy* (Stanford: Hoover Institution Press, 1982), p. 109.

2. See Alexander L. George, *The Chinese Communist Army in Action: The Korean War and Its Aftermath* (New York: Columbia University Press, 1967), pp. viii, 1.

3. Buss, *United States and the Republic of Korea*, p. 116.

4. See Nathan N. White, *U.S. Policy Toward Korea: Analysis, Alternatives, and Recommendations* (Boulder, Colo.: Westview, 1979), p. 53.

5. See Sang-chul Suh, "Trade and Investment in Northeast Asia: A South Korean Perspective," in Richard B. Foster, James F. Dornan, Jr., and William M. Carpenter, eds., *Strategy and Security in Northeast Asia* (New York: Crane, Russak, 1979), pp. 290–93.

6. See Pyong-gil Chay, "The Policy Directions of the North Korean Regime: The Content Analysis of the Party Reports and Kim Il-sung's Annual Addresses," *East Asian Review* 3, no. 4 (Winter 1976): 465–95.

7. See *Puk Han Chongch'iron* [On North Korean politics] (Seoul: Far East Problems Research Institute, 1976), p. 318.

8. Bong-shik Park, "North Korea in Sino-Soviet Dispute," *East Asian Review* 3, no. 4 (Winter 1976): 504–05.

9. Deok Kim, "Sino-Soviet Dispute and North Korea," *Korea Observer* 10, no. 1 (Spring 1979): 29.

10. Buss, *United States and the Republic of Korea*, p. 103.

11. In this regard see Samuel S. Kim, "Korea: The Last Frontline Domino," in James C. Hsiung and Winberg Chai, eds., *Asia and U.S. Foreign Policy* (New York: Praeger, 1981), p. 55.

12. Sang-woo Rhee, "North Korean Politics: Present and Future," in Foster, Dornan, and Carpenter, *Strategy and Security*, p. 263.

13. For a discussion of the military balance in Korea, see *The Military Balance, 1981–82* (London: International Institute for Strategic Studies, 1982), pp. 82–84.

14. Dale Van Atta and Richard Nations, "Kim's Build-up to Blitzkrieg," *Far Eastern Economic Review*, March 5, 1982, pp. 26–32.

15. Stuart E. Johnson and Joseph A. Yager, *The Military Equation in Northeast Asia* (Washington, D.C.: Brookings Institution, 1979), pp. 58–59.

16. Van Atta and Nations, "Kim's Build-up," pp. 27–28.

17. Robert A. Scalapino, "China and Northeast Asia," in Richard H. Solomon, ed., *The China Factor: Sino-American Relations and the Global Scene* (Englewood Cliffs, N.J.: Prentice-Hall, 1981), pp. 190–91.

18. Robert R. Simmons, *The Strained Alliance: Peking, Pyongyang, Moscow, and Politics* (New York: Free Press, 1975), p. 103.

19. John Despres et al., *Timely Lessons of History: The Manchurian Model for Soviet Strategy* (Santa Monica, Calif.: Rand Corporation, July 1976).

20. Lilita Dzirkals, *Soviet Policy Statements and Military Deployments in Northeast Asia* (Santa Monica, Calif.: Rand Corporation, October 1978), p. 17.

21. Kyung-won Kim, "Korea and Security in Northeast Asia," in Foster, Dornan, and Carpenter, *Strategy and Security*, pp. 247–48; Hogan Yoon, "The Tensions on the Korean Peninsula," in Joyce E. Larson, ed., *New Foundations for Asian and Pacific Security* (New Brunswick, N.J.: Transaction Books, 1980), p. 127.

22. In this regard, see Frederick L. Shiels, *Tokyo and Washington* (Lexington, Mass.: D. C. Heath, 1980), p. 104; and Paul C. Warnke, "We Don't Need a Devil (To Make or Keep Our Friends)," *Foreign Policy* 25 (1977): 80.

23. See the discussion in Kim Woodard, "China and Offshore Energy," *Problems of Communism* 30 (November–December 1981): 32–45.

24. Robert A. Scalapino, "Current Dynamics of the Korean Peninsula," in ibid., p. 31.

25. Anthony Kahng, "Will South Korea Be Another Vietnam?" in Yung-hwan Jo, ed., *U.S. Foreign Policy in Asia: An Appraisal* (Santa Barbara, Calif.: ABC-Clio, 1978).

26. William Watts, *The United States and Asia: Changing Attitudes and Policies* (Lexington, Mass.: D. C. Heath, 1982), p. 69.

Chapter 6

1. See Ralph N. Clough, *Island China* (Cambridge, Mass.: Harvard University Press, 1978), chap. 1; William M. Bueler, *U.S. China Policy and the Problem of Taiwan* (Boulder: Colorado Associated University Press, 1971), chap. 1.

2. *Mutual Defense Treaty Between the Republic of China and the United States of America*, Preamble and Art. VII, in *Treaties Between the Republic of China and Foreign States (1927–1957)* (Taipei: Ministry of Foreign Affairs, 1958), pp. 824–26.

3. See Chiang Wei-kuo, *The Strategic Significance of Taiwan in the Global Strategic Picture* (Taipei: Armed Forces University, 1977), pp. 89–102.

4. Nicholas Katzenbach, *Communist China: A Realistic View* (Washington, D.C.: Department of State, Bureau of Public Affairs, June 1968), p. 4.

5. Joseph Lelyveld, "A 1½-China Policy," *New York Times Magazine*, April 6, 1975.

6. John Fairbank, "Ticklish Taiwan," *New Republic*, March 1975, p. 7.

7. William Watts et al., *Japan, Korea, and China: American Perceptions and Policies* (Lexington, Mass.: Lexington Books, 1979), pp. 134–35. See also Michael Y. M. Kau et al., "Public Opinion and U.S. China Policy," in Hungdah Chiu, ed., *Normalizing Relations with the People's Republic of China* (Baltimore: University of Maryland, School of Law, 1978), pp. 85–99.

8. See Tsai Wei-ping, "Thoughts on an Historic Event: Carter's Decision to Sever Diplomatic Ties with ROC and to Abrogate the Mutual Defense Treaty," *Issues and Studies*, January 1979, pp. 5–6.

9. See Robert L. Downen, *The Taiwan Pawn in the China Game: Congress to the Rescue* (Washington, D.C.: Georgetown University, 1979).

10. U.S., Congress, Senate, *Taiwan: Hearings Before the Committee on Foreign Relations*, 96th Cong., 1st sess., February 5–8, 21–22, 1979, p. 1.

11. For a discussion of the deliberations that preceded passage of the Taiwan Relations Act, see Edwin K. Snyder, A. James Gregor, and Maria Hsia Chang, *The Taiwan Relations Act and the Defense of the Republic of China* (Berkeley: University of California, Institute of International Studies, 1980); and Jeffrey T. Bergner, "America and Taiwan: Implementing the Taiwan Relations Act in the 1980s," in King-yuh Chang, ed., *Emerging Western Pacific Community: Problems and Prospects* (Taipei: Freedom Council, 1979), pp. 229–33.

12. Lyushun Shen, "The Taiwan Issue in Peking's Foreign Relations in the 1970s: A Systematic Review," *Chinese Yearbook of International Law and Affairs* 1 (1981): 75.

13. David Nelson Rowe, *Informal "Diplomatic Relations": The Case of Japan and the Republic of China, 1972–1974* (Hamden, Conn.: Foreign Area Studies Publications, 1975), pp. 7–8.

14. Wolf Mendl, *Issues in Japan's China Policy* (New York: Oxford University Press, 1978), p. 61.

15. Ibid., p. 97.

16. *International Herald Tribune*, July 21, 1976; *Financial Times*, July 23, 1976.

17. A. Doak Barnett, *China and the Major Powers in East Asia* (Washington, D.C.: Brookings Institution, 1977), p. 143.

18. Mendl, *Japan's China Policy*, p. 86.

19. *Asian Security, 1980* (Tokyo: Research Institute for Peace and Security, 1980), pp. 107–8.

20. *Asian Security, 1979* (Tokyo: Research Institute for Peace and Security, 1979), pp. 93–94.

21. UPI-Manila, January 2, 1979, as cited by Hungdah Chiu, "The Question of Taiwan in Sino-American Relations," in Hungdah Chiu, ed., *China and the Taiwan Issue* (New York: Praeger, 1979), p. 197.

22. See Paul F. Langer, "Changing Japanese Security Perspectives," in Richard H. Solomon, ed., *Asian Security in the 1980s: Problems and Politics for a Time of Transition* (Cambridge, Mass.: Oelgeschlager, Gunn & Hain, 1980), p. 83; Takuya Kubo, "Security in Northeast Asia," in ibid., p. 96; Frank N. Trager, "Perspectives on War and Peace: The United States and Asia at the Beginning of the 1980s," in Joyce E. Larson, ed., *New Foundations for Asian and Pacific Security* (New Brunswick, N.J.: Transaction Books, 1980), p. xviii.

23. Gaston J. Sigur, "Normalization and Pacific and Triangular Diplomacy," in Hungdah Chiu and Karen Murphy, eds., *The Chinese Connection and Normalization* (Baltimore: University of Maryland, School of Law, 1980), p. 10; Richard Walker, "The Taiwan Issue," ibid., p. 22.

24. Robert A. Scalapino, "Sino-American Relations in an International Context," in Hungdah Chiu, ed., *Normalizing Relations with the People's Republic of China* (Baltimore: University of Maryland, School of Law, 1978), p. 14.

25. U.S., Congress, Senate, *Congressional Record*, 95th Cong., 2d sess., no. 138 (September 7, 1978), p. H9229, sec. 26 (a), paras. 2 and 3.

26. Downen, *Taiwan Pawn in the China Game*, p. 49.

27. Robert L. Downen, *Of Grave Concern: U.S.-Taiwan Relations on the Threshold of the 1980s* (Washington, D.C.: Georgetown University, 1981), p. 1.

28. See A. James Gregor and Maria Hsia Chang, "Taiwan: The 'Wild Card' in U.S. Defense Policy in the Far Pacific," in James C. Hsiung and Winberg Chai, eds., *Asia and U.S. Foreign Policy* (New York: Praeger, 1981), pp. 136–38. For an assessment of Moscow's intentions with regard to Taiwan as perceived by Peking, see "Red China's Taiwan Policy," a translation of Pi Ting-chun's speech to Fukien Provincial Communist Party Committee cadres on April 8, 1975, in *Inside China Mainland* 1 (February 1979): 22–23.

29. Pi Ting-chun, "Red China's Taiwan Policy," p. 24.

30. The military balance between the PRC and the ROC is discussed in Snyder, Gregor, and Chang, *Taiwan Relations Act*, chap. 3.

31. See James C. Hsiung, "China, Part II: The Conceptual Foundations of U.S.-China Policy," in Hsiung and Chai, *Asia and U.S. Foreign Policy*, pp. 121–22.

32. Justin Galen, "U.S.' Toughest Message to the USSR," *Armed Forces Journal International*, February 1979, p. 30.

33. Kenneth R. McGruther, "Two Anchors in the Pacific: Strategy Proposal for the U.S. Pacific Fleet," *United States Naval Institute Proceedings*, May 1979, p. 128.

34. Statement of Warren Christopher, in *Taiwan: Hearings*, pp. 16, 20.

35. Galen, "U.S.' Toughest Message," p. 36.

36. For the entire collection of arguments favoring the rapprochement between the West and the People's Republic of China, see Roger Glenn Brown, "Chinese Politics and American Policy: A New Look at the Triangle," *Foreign Policy*, July 1976; Jerome Cohen, "A China Policy for the Next Administration," *Foreign Policy*, October 1976; Ross Terrill, "China and the World: Self-Reliance or Interdependence?" *Foreign Affairs*, January 1977; Michael Pillsbury, "U.S.-Chinese Military Ties?" *Foreign Affairs*, October 1975; A. Doak Barnett, "Military-Security Relations Between China and the United States," *Foreign Affairs*, April 1977.

37. William C. Green and David C. Yost, "Soviet Military Options Regarding China," in Douglas T. Stuart and William T. Tow, eds., *China, the Soviet Union, and the West: Strategic and Political Dimensions in the 1980s* (Boulder, Colo.: Westview, 1982), p. 143.

38. See Drew Middleton, *The Duel of the Giants: China and Russia in Asia* (New York: Scribner's, 1978), chap. 9.

39. See "On the U.S. 'Taiwan Relations Act,'" in *China and the World* 1 (1982): 90–91.

40. See Alexander Woodwide, "Nationalism and Poverty in the Breakdown of Sino-Vietnamese Relations," *Pacific Affairs*, Fall 1979, p. 382.

41. In this regard see Edwin K. Snyder and A. James Gregor, "The Military Balance in the Taiwan Strait," *Journal of Strategic Studies*, October 1981, pp. 306–17; James B. Linder and A. James Gregor, "Taiwan's Troubled Security Outlook," *Strategic Review*, Fall 1980, pp. 48–55.

42. "On the U.S. 'Taiwan Relations Act,'" p. 90.

43. See Jürgen Domes, "Aspekte des politischen Systems der Republic China auf T'aiwan," *Zeitschrift für Politik*, September 1978, pp. 255–56.

44. See Jan S. Prybyla, *The Societal Objective of Wealth, Growth, Stability, and Equity in Taiwan* (Baltimore: University of Maryland, School of Law, 1978); A. James Gregor, Maria Hsia Chang, and Andrew Zimmerman, *Ideology and Development: Sun Yat-sen and the Economic History of Taiwan* (Berkeley: University of California, Center for Chinese Studies, 1981), chap. 5; John C. H. Fei, Gustav Ranis, and Shirley W. Y. Kuo, *Growth with Equity: The Taiwan Case* (New York: Oxford University Press, 1979).

45. See Anthony Tang, "Input-Output Relations in the Agriculture of Communist China, 1952–1965," in W. A. Douglas Jackson, ed., *Agrarian Policies and Problems in Communist and Non-Communist Countries* (Seattle, Wash.: University of Seattle Press, 1971), pp. 289, 295; Thomas G. Rawski, *Economic Growth and Employment in China* (New York: Oxford University Press, 1979), pp. 119–22.

46. See Chu-yuan Cheng, *China's Economic Development: Growth and Structural Change* (Boulder, Colo.: Westview, 1982), pp. 355–56.

47. Mao Tse-tung, "The Present Situation and Our Tasks," *Selected Works of Mao Tse-tung* (Peking: Foreign Languages Press, 1967), 4: 161.

48. See A. James Gregor, "The United States, the Republic of China, and the Taiwan Relations Act," *Orbis* 24, no. 3 (Fall 1980).

49. See A. James Gregor, "The Reagan Administration's China Policy Options," in John C. Kuan, ed., *Symposium on R.O.C.-U.S. Relations* (Taipei: Asia and World Institute, 1981), pp. 43–51.

50. See editorial, *Ming Pao* (Hong Kong), August 20, 1982, p. 1; *Time*, August 30, 1982, p. 21.

51. See Martin L. Lasater, *The Security of Taiwan: Unraveling the Dilemma* (Washington, D.C.: Georgetown University, 1982), pp. 62–64.

Chapter 7

1. See Monty Hoyt, "China Seas Oil Bonanza," *Christian Science Monitor*, October 15, 1971, p. 1; K. O. Emery et al., *Geological Structures and Some Water Characteristics of the East China Sea and the Yellow Sea, Technical Bulletin, Technical Advisory Group Report* (New York: United Nations Economic Commission for Asia and the Far East, 1969).

2. See figure 3 in Selig Harrison, *China, Oil, and Asia: Conflict Ahead?* (New York: Columbia University Press, 1977).

3. Hungdah Chiu, *Chinese Attitude Toward Continental Shelf and Its Implication on Delimiting Seabed in Southeast Asia* (Baltimore: University of Maryland, School of Law, 1977), pp. 19–21.

4. Hungdah Chiu, "South China Sea Islands: Implications for Delimiting the Seabed and Future Shipping Routes," *China Quarterly*, December 1977, pp. 752–53.

5. See Hungdah Chiu, *China and the Law of the Sea Conference* (Baltimore: University of Maryland, School of Law, 1981).

6. See figure 1 in Harrison, *China, Oil, and Asia*.

7. As quoted in Harrison, *China, Oil, and Asia*, p. 132.

8. *Peking Review*, February 8, 1974, p. 3.

9. *Peking Review*, June 17, 1977, p. 17.

10. Daniel Tretiak, "The Sino-Japanese Treaty of 1978: The Senkaku Incident Prelude," *Asian Survey* 18, no. 12 (December 1978): 1241–42.

11. Harrison, *China, Oil, and Asia*, p. 181.

12. Chiu, *China and the Law of the Sea Conference*, p. 17.

13. Hungdah Chiu and Choon-ho Park, "Legal Status of the Paracel and Spratly Islands," *Ocean Development and International Law* 3, no. 1 (1975): 1–28.

14. *Peking Review*, January 11, 1974, p. 3.

15. Harrison, *China, Oil, and Asia*, p. 198.

16. Ibid., p. 188.

17. John Franklin Copper, *China's Global Role* (Stanford: Hoover Institution Press, 1980), p. 46.

18. Kim Woodard, "China and Offshore Energy," *Problems of Communism*, November–December 1981, p. 38.

19. See Robert Delfs, "A New Kind of Planning," *Far Eastern Economic Review*, August 14, 1981, p. 49.

20. Yu Ch'iu-li, *Report on the Draft of the 1979 National Economic Plan, 21 June 1979*, Hsin-hua News Agency (Peking), news bulletin no. 11122, June 29, 1979, p. 13.

21. See Chao Chih-yang, *China's Economy and Development Principles* (Peking: Foreign Languages Press, 1982), p. 93.

22. In this regard, compare the discussion in Harrison, *China, Oil, and Asia*, chap. 2, with Woodard, "China and Offshore Energy."

23. Robert C. North, *The Foreign Relations of China* (North Scituate, Mass.: Duxbury, 1978), p. 213.

24. Woodard, "China and Offshore Energy," p. 37.

25. As cited in Harrison, *China, Oil, and Asia*, p. 168.

26. Chou En-lai, "Why Did Our Country Accede to Nixon's Request for a Visit?" in King C. Chen, ed., *China and the Three Worlds: A Foreign Policy Reader* (White Plains, N.Y.: M. E. Sharpe, 1979), pp. 133–34.

27. Ibid., p. 138.

28. "Teng Hsiao-p'ing Talks on 'U.S.-China Relations,'" *Inside China Mainland*, January 1979, p. 1.

29. Teng Hsiao-p'ing, "China and the Three Worlds," *Peking Review*, April 19, 1974, pp. 6–11.

30. Ch'iao Kuan-hua, "Speech on Foreign Policy," in Warren Kuo, ed., *Speeches by Chinese Communist Leaders, 1963–1975* (Taipei: Institute of International Relations, 1976), p. 12.

31. Ibid., pp. 17, 23.

32. Douglas T. Stuart, "Sino-Soviet Competition: The View from Western Europe," in Douglas T. Stuart and William T. Tow, eds., *China, the Soviet Union, and the West: Strategic and Political Dimensions in the 1980s* (Boulder, Colo.: Westview, 1982), p. 219.

33. See Justus M. van der Kroef, *Communism in Southeast Asia* (Berkeley and Los Angeles: University of California Press, 1981), pp. 232–33, 264–67.

34. Strobe Talbott, "The Strategic Dimension of the Sino-American Relationship: Enemy of Our Enemy or True Friend?" in Richard H. Solomon, ed., *The China Factor: Sino-American Relations and the Global Scene* (Englewood Cliffs, N.J.: Prentice-Hall, 1981), pp. 95–96.

35. See Derek Davies, "Putting People in the Picture," *Far Eastern Economic Review*, July 6, 1979, pp. 11–13; and Melinda Liu, "Painting a New Portrait," in ibid., pp. 36–37.

36. See Richard Lowenthal, "The Degeneration of an Ideological Dispute," in Stuart and Tow, *China, the Soviet Union, and the West*, pp. 59–71.

37. See Nayan Chanda, "Brezhnev Breaks the Ice," *Far Eastern Economic Review*, April 2, 1982, pp. 12–16.

38. Lawrence Freedman, "Economic and Technological Factors in the Sino-Soviet Dispute," in Stuart and Tow, *China, the Soviet Union, and the West*, p. 80.

39. *Far Eastern Economic Review*, March 19, 1982, p. 14.

40. Gerald Segal, "China's Security Debate," *Survival*, March–April 1982, pp. 60–69.

Chapter 8

1. For an extensive discussion, see Robert W. Komer, "Maritime Strategy vs. Coalition Defense," *Foreign Affairs*, Summer 1982, pp. 1124–44.

2. See Caspar W. Weinberger, *Annual Defense Department Report, FY 1983* (Washington, D.C.: Department of Defense, February 8, 1982), pp. 1, 14–17.

3. In this regard, see Steven I. Levine, "The Soviet Perspective," and Chong-sik Lee, "Normalization of Sino-American Relations and the Korean Peninsula," in John Bryan Starr, ed., *The Future of U.S.-China Relations* (New York: New York University Press, 1981), pp. 89, 98–99.

4. Donald C. Hellman, "U.S.-China Normalization: The Japanese Perspective," ibid., p. 146; U.S. Congress, House, Committee on Foreign Affairs, *The United States and the People's Republic of China: Issues for the 1980's* (Washington, D.C.: Government Printing Office, 1980), pp. 18–22.

5. Guy J. Pauker, "The Security Implications of Regional Energy and Natural Resource Exploitation," in Richard H. Solomon, ed., *Asian Security in the 1980s: Problems and Policies for a Time of Transition* (Cambridge, Mass.: Oelgeschlager, Gunn & Hain, 1980), p. 230; Robert A. Scalapino, "Strategic Issues in U.S. Policies Toward Asia," in Starr, *Future of U.S.-China Relations*, p. 153.

6. Noel Gayler, "Issues in U.S.–East Asian Policy," in *Future of U.S.-China Relations*, p. 172.

7. See the discussion on the Soviet disposition to exploit evident military weaknesses in Robert E. Osgood, *Containment, Soviet Behavior, and Grand Strategy* (Berkeley: University of California, Institute of International Studies, 1981), pp. 3, 8, 9, 13, 15.

8. With some qualification, Donald Zagoria's 1978 article, "The Soviet Quandary in Asia," *Foreign Affairs*, January 1978, pp. 306–23, still accurately describes some of Moscow's difficulties in Asia.

9. See Robert A. Scalapino, "The Case for Complexity," in Osgood, *Containment, Soviet Behavior, and Grand Strategy*, p. 64.

10. See Larry A. Niksch, "A Military Build-up," *Foreign Service Journal*, March 1983, pp. 26–29, 33.

11. See Masataka Kosaka, ed., *Asian Security* (Tokyo: Research Institute for Peace and Security, 1981), pp. 43, 78.

12. See Robert E. Bedeski, "The Sino-Japan Treaty of Peace and Friendship, and Japan's Defense Debate," *Issues and Studies* 18, no. 4 (April 1982): 54–70.

13. See Larry A. Niksch, "Why Japan's Defense Budget Won't Satisfy the U.S.," *Asian Wall Street Journal*, January 25, 1983.

14. Kosaka, *Asian Security*, pp. 45, 73.

15. Strobe Talbott, "The Strategic Dimension of the Sino-American Relationship," in Richard H. Solomon, ed., *The China Factor: Sino-American Relations and the Global Scene* (Englewood Cliffs, N.J.: Prentice-Hall, 1981), p. 103.

16. See Lester L. Wolff and David L. Simon, eds., *Legislative History of the Taiwan Relations Act: An Analytic Compilation with Documents on Subsequent Developments* (New York: American Association for Chinese Studies, 1982).

17. Chiang Wei-kuo, *The Strategic Significance of Taiwan in the Global Strategic Picture* (Taipei: Armed Forces University, 1977).

18. Chiang Ching-kuo, "To Stay United and Struggle Forward to Open up a Bright Prospect," Speech at the Central Committee Meeting of the Kuomintang, June 2, 1982.

19. Richard H. Solomon, "The China Factor in America's Foreign Relations," in Solomon, *China Factor*, p. 6.

20. Nai-ruenn Chen and Elaine M. De Federico, "U.S.-China Trade: A Decade of Development and Prospects for Growth," *Business America*, June 28, 1982, pp. 2–10.

21. See Harry Gelman, *The Soviet Far East Buildup and Soviet Risk-Taking Against China* (Santa Monica, Calif.: Rand Corporation, August 1982).

22. Solomon, in Solomon, *China Factor*, p. 25.

23. Gelman, *Soviet Far East Buildup*, p. 112; see also Banning N. Garrett, *Soviet Perceptions of China and Sino-American Military Ties* (Arlington, Va.: Harold Rosenblum Associates, June 1981), pp. 48, 60.

24. Scalapino, in Starr, *Future of U.S.-China Relations*, p. 158.

25. See Paul H. B. Godwin, "China's Defense Modernization," *Air University Review*, November–December 1981, pp. 2–19.

26. See Jonathan D. Pollack, *Security, Strategy, and the Logic of Chinese Foreign Policy* (Berkeley: University of California, Institute of East Asian Studies, 1981), pp. 41, 50.

Bibliography

Abramowitz, Morton. *Moving the Glacier: The Two Koreas and the Powers*. London: International Institute for Strategic Studies, 1971.

Adelman, Irma, and Cynthia T. Morris. *Economic Growth and Social Equity in Developing Countries*. Stanford: Stanford University Press, 1973.

Amer, James E. *The Postwar Rearmament of Japanese Maritime Forces, 1945–71*. New York: Praeger, 1973.

Asian Regional Security and the Free World. Proceedings of the 1977 Conference of Sino-Korean-Japanese Professors. Taipei: Pacific Cultural Foundation, 1978.

Asian Security, 1979. Tokyo: Research Institute for Peace and Security, 1979.

Asian Security, 1980. Tokyo: Research Institute for Peace and Security, 1980.

Baransky, N. N. *Economic Geography of the U.S.S.R.* Moscow: Foreign Languages Press, 1956.

Barnett, A. Doak. *China and the Major Powers in East Asia*. Washington, D.C.: Brookings Institution, 1977.

———. *China Policy: Old Problems and New Challenges*. Washington, D.C.: Brookings Institution, 1977.

Basov, N. I., et al. *The Philosophical Heritage of V. I. Lenin and Problems of Contemporary War*, translated by the U.S. Government. Washington, D.C.: Government Printing Office, n.d.

Bathurst, Robert B. *Understanding the Soviet Navy: A Handbook*. Newport, R.I.: Naval War College, 1979.

Blechman, Barry M., and Robert P. Berman, eds. *Guide to Far Eastern Navies*. Annapolis, Md.: U.S. Naval Institute, 1978.

Bonds, Ray, ed. *The Chinese War Machine*. New York: Crescent Books, 1979.

Breyer, Siegfried. *Guide to the Soviet Navy*. Annapolis, Md.: U.S. Naval Institute, 1970.

Brodie, Bernard. *A Guide to Naval Strategy*. Princeton: Princeton University Press, 1958.

Brown, Harold. *Annual Report of the Department of Defense, FY 1979*. Washington, D.C.: Department of Defense, 1978.

Buck, James H. *The Modern Japanese Military System*. Beverly Hills, Calif.: Sage, 1975.

Bucknell, Howard. *Energy Policy and Naval Strategy*. Beverly Hills, Calif.: Sage, 1975.

Bueler, William M. *U.S. China Policy and the Problem of Taiwan*. Boulder: Colorado Associated University Press, 1971.

Buss, Claude A. *The United States and the Republic of Korea: Background for Policy*. Stanford: Hoover Institution Press, 1982.

Butler, William E. *The Soviet Union and the Law of the Sea*. Baltimore: Johns Hopkins Press, 1971.

Byely, Boris, et al. *Marxism-Leninism on War and Army*. Moscow: Progress Publishers, 1972.

Central Intelligence Agency. *Estimating Soviet Defense Spending in Rubles*. Washington, D.C.: Central Intelligence Agency, May 1976.

Chai, Winberg, ed. *The Foreign Relations of the People's Republic of China*. New York: Capricorn Books, 1972.

Chan, F. Gilbert, and Ka-che Yip, eds. *China's Foreign Relations: Selected Studies*. Baltimore: University of Maryland School of Law, 1980.

Chang, King-yuh, ed. *Emerging Western Pacific Community: Problems and Prospects*. Taipei: Freedom Council, 1979.

————, ed. *Western Pacific Security in a Changing Context: Problems and Prospects*. Taipei: Freedom Council, 1982.

Chao, Chih-yang. *China's Economy and Development Principles*. Peking: Foreign Languages Press, 1982.

Chen, King C., ed. *China and the Three Worlds: A Foreign Policy Reader*. White Plains, N.Y.: M. E. Sharpe, 1979.

Chenery, Hollis, ed. *Redistribution with Growth*. New York: Oxford University Press, 1974.

Cheng, Chu-yuan. *Economic Relations Between Peking and Moscow*. New York: Praeger, 1964.

————. *China's Economic Development: Growth and Structural Change*. Boulder, Colo.: Westview, 1982.

Chiang, Wei-kuo. *The Strategic Significance of Taiwan in the Global Strategic Picture*. Taipei: Armed Forces University, 1977.

Chinese Communist Internal Politics and Foreign Policy. Taipei: Institute of International Relations, 1974.

Chiu, Hungdah. *China and the Law of the Sea Conference*. Baltimore: University of Maryland, School of Law, 1981.

———. *Chinese Attitude Toward Continental Shelf and Its Implication on Delimiting Seabed in Southeast Asia*. Baltimore: University of Maryland, School of Law, 1977.

———, ed. *China and the Taiwan Issue*. New York: Praeger, 1979.

———, ed. *Normalizing Relations with the People's Republic of China*. Baltimore: University of Maryland, School of Law, 1978.

———, and Robert L. Downen, eds. *Multi-System Nations and International Law: The International Status of Germany, Korea, and China*. Baltimore: University of Maryland, School of Law, 1981.

———, and Karen Murphy, eds. *The Chinese Connection and Normalization*. Baltimore: University of Maryland, School of Law, 1980.

Cline, Ray S. *World Power Assessment*. Washington, D.C.: Center for Strategic and International Studies, 1975.

Clough, Ralph N. *Island China*. Cambridge, Mass.: Harvard University Press, 1978.

Cockroft, James P.; André Gunder Frank; and Dale L. Johnson. *Dependence and Underdevelopment*. New York: Doubleday, Anchor Books, 1972.

Collins, John M. *American and Soviet Military Trends Since the Cuban Missile Crisis*. Washington, D.C.: Georgetown University, 1978.

Copper, John F. *China's Foreign Aid in 1979–80*. Baltimore: University of Maryland School of Law, 1981.

———. *China's Global Role*. Stanford: Hoover Institution Press, 1980.

Cottrell, Alvin, and Robert J. Hanks. *The Military Utility of U.S. Facilities in the Philippines*. Washington, D.C.: Georgetown University, 1980.

Crankshaw, Edward. *The New Cold War: Moscow v. Peking*. Baltimore: Penguin Books, 1963.

Davis, Jacquelyn K., and Robert L. Pfaltzgraff, Jr. *Soviet Theater Strategy: Implications for NATO*. Washington, D.C.: United States Strategic Institute, 1978.

Defense Intelligence Agency. *Unclassified Communist Naval Orders of Battle*. Washington, D.C.: Defense Intelligence Agency, November 1979.

Defense of Japan: Defense White Paper. Summary. Tokyo: Japan Defense Agency, June 1976.

Despres, John. *Timely Lessons of History: The Manchurian Model for Soviet Strategy*. Santa Monica, Calif.: Rand Corporation, July 1976.

Deutscher, Isaac. *Russia, China, and the West*. New York: Oxford University Press, 1970.

Digby, James. *The Emerging American Strategy: Application to Southwest Asia*. Santa Monica, Calif.: Rand Corporation, 1981.

Doolin, Dennis J. *Territorial Claims in the Sino-Soviet Conflict*. Stanford: Hoover Institution Press, 1977.

Dornan, James E., Jr., ed. *The U.S. War Machine*. New York: Crown, 1978.

Downen, Robert L. *Of Grave Concern: U.S.-Taiwan Relations on the Threshold of the 1980s*. Washington, D.C.: Georgetown University, 1981.

———. *The Taiwan Pawn in the China Game: Congress to the Rescue*. Washington, D.C.: Georgetown University, 1979.

Duignan, Peter, and Alvin Rabushka, eds. *The United States in the 1980s.* Stanford: Hoover Institution Press, 1980.

Dzirkals, Lilita. *Soviet Perceptions of Security in East Asia: A Survey of Soviet Media Comment.* Santa Monica, Calif.: Rand Corporation, 1977.

————. *Soviet Policy Statements and Military Deployments in Northeast Asia.* Santa Monica, Calif.: Rand Corporation, October 1978.

Eckstein, Alexander. *China's Economic Revolution.* New York: Cambridge University Press, 1977.

Emerging Western Pacific Community: Problems and Prospects. Proceedings of the Seminar on Western Pacific Community. Taipei: Freedom Council, 1980.

Fairbank, John. "Ticklish Taiwan." *New Republic*, March 1975.

Fairhall, David. *Russian Sea Power.* Boston: Gambit, 1971.

Fan, Yuan-yen. *Question and Answer: A Testimony of a Chinese Communist Pilot.* Taipei: China Press, 1978.

Fei, John C. H.; Gustav Ranis; and Shirley W. Y. Kuo. *Growth with Equity: The Taiwan Case.* New York: Oxford University Press, 1979.

Forum on ASEAN. Taipei: Asia and the World Forum, 1980.

Forum on the Security of the Western Pacific. Taipei: Asia and the World Forum, 1977.

Foster, Richard B.; James E. Dornan, Jr.; and William M. Carpenter, eds. *Strategy and Security in Northeast Asia.* New York: Crane, Russak, 1979.

Fraser, Angus M. *The People's Liberation Army: Communist China's Armed Forces.* New York: Crane, Russak, 1973.

Freedman, Lawrence. "Economic and Technological Factors in the Sino-Soviet Dispute." In *China, the Soviet Union, and the West*, edited by Douglas T. Stuart and William T. Tow. Boulder, Colo.: Westview, 1982.

Garrett, Banning N. *Soviet Perceptions of China and Sino-American Military Ties.* Arlington, Va.: Harold Rosenblum Associates, June 1981.

Gelber, Harry G. *Technology, Defense, and External Relations in China, 1975–1978.* Boulder, Colo.: Westview, 1979.

Gelman, Harry. *The Soviet Far East Buildup and Soviet Risk-Taking Against China.* Santa Monica, Calif.: Rand Corporation, August 1982.

George, Alexander L. *The Chinese Communist Army in Action: The Korean War and Its Aftermath.* New York: Columbia University Press, 1967.

George, James L., ed. *Problems of Sea Power as We Approach the Twenty-First Century.* Washington, D.C.: American Enterprise Institute, 1978.

Giannettini, Guido. *Pekino tra Washington e Mosca.* Rome: Volpe, 1972.

Goldman, Marshall. *Soviet Foreign Aid.* New York: Praeger, 1967.

Gordon, Bernard K. *The Dimensions of Conflict in Southeast Asia.* Englewood Cliffs, N.J.: Prentice-Hall, 1966.

Gorshkov, Sergei. *Red Star Rising at Sea.* Annapolis, Md.: U.S. Naval Institute, 1974.

————. *The Sea Power of the State.* Annapolis, Md.: U.S. Naval Institute, 1979.

Gottlieb, Thomas M. *Chinese Foreign Policy Factionalism and the Origins of the Strategic Triangle*. Santa Monica, Calif.: Rand Corporation, 1977.

Graham, Daniel O. "The Soviet Military Budget Controversy." *Air Force Magazine*, May 1976, pp. 36–37.

Gregor, A. James, and Maria Hsia Chang. *The Republic of China and U.S. Policy*. Washington, D.C.: Ethics and Public Policy Center, 1983.

————; Maria Hsia Chang; and Andrew Zimmerman. *Ideology and Development: Sun Yat-sen and the Economic History of Taiwan*. Berkeley: University of California, Center for Chinese Studies, 1981.

Grobe, Karl. *Chinas Weg nach Westen*. Frankfurt am Main: China Studien und Verlags-Gesellschaft, 1980.

Harrison, Selig S. *China, Oil, and Asia: Conflict Ahead?* New York: Columbia University Press, 1977.

Haselkorn, Adigdor. *The Evolution of Soviet Security Strategy, 1965–1975*. New York: Crane, Russak, 1978.

Hellman, Donald C. *Japanese-American Relations*. Washington, D.C.: American Enterprise Institute, 1975.

Herrick, Robert W. *Soviet Naval Strategy*. Annapolis, Md.: U.S. Naval Institute, 1968.

Hindley, Donald. *The Communist Party of Indonesia*. Berkeley and Los Angeles: University of California Press, 1964.

Hinton, Harold C. *The China Sea: The American Stake in Its Future*. New York: National Strategy Information Center, 1980.

————. *China's Turbulent Quest: An Analysis of China's Foreign Relations Since 1949*. Bloomington: Indiana University Press, 1972.

————. *Communist China in World Politics*. Boston: Houghton Mifflin, 1966.

————. *The Sino-Soviet Confrontation: Implications for the Future*. New York: Crane, Russak, 1976.

————. *Three and a Half Powers: The New Balance in Asia*. Bloomington: Indiana University Press, 1975.

Hollick, Ann L., and Robert E. Osgood. *New Era of Ocean Politics*. Baltimore, Md.: Johns Hopkins University Press, 1974.

Horelick, Arnold L. *The Soviet Union's "Asian Collective Security" Proposal: A Club in Search of Members*. Santa Monica, Calif.: Rand Corporation, March 1974.

Hsiung, James C. *The Conceptual Foundations of U.S. China Policy: A Critical Review*. Baltimore: University of Maryland, School of Law, 1980.

————, and Winberg Chai, eds. *Asia and U.S. Foreign Policy*. New York: Praeger, 1981.

Hudson, G. F.; Richard Lowenthal; and Roderick MacFarquhar. *The Sino-Soviet Dispute*. London: China Quarterly, 1962.

Hunt, Kenneth. "Sino-Soviet Theater Force Comparisons." In *China, the Soviet Union, and the West: Strategic and Political Dimensions in the 1980s*, edited by Douglas T. Stuart and William T. Tow. Boulder, Colo.: Westview, 1982.

Important Documents Concerning the Question of Taiwan. Peking: Foreign Languages Press, 1955.

Is America Becoming Number 2? Washington, D.C.: Committee on the Present Danger, 1978.

"Ivan Rogov: Extending the Soviet Sphere." *All Hands*, December 1978.

Jackson, W. A. Douglas, ed. *Agrarian Policies and Problems in Communist and Non-Communist Countries*. Seattle, Wash.: University of Seattle Press, 1971.

Japanese Defense White Paper. Tokyo: Japanese Self-Defense Agency, 1976.

Jencks, Harlan W. *From Muskets to Missiles: Politics and Professionalism in the Chinese Army, 1945–1981*. Boulder, Colo.: Westview, 1982.

———. *The Politics of Chinese Military Development, 1945–1977*. 2 vols. Ann Arbor, Mich.: University Microfilms, 1978.

Jo, Yung-hwan, ed. *Taiwan's Future*. Hong Kong: Union Research Institute for Arizona State University, 1974.

———, ed. *U.S. Foreign Policy in Asia: An Appraisal*. Santa Barbara, Calif.: ABC-Clio, 1978.

Johnson, Stuart E., and Joseph A. Yager. *The Military Equation in Northeast Asia*. Washington, D.C.: Brookings Institution, 1979.

Jukes, Geoffrey. *The Soviet Union in Asia*. Sydney, Australia: Angus and Robertson, 1973.

Kahn, Herman. *World Economic Development: Projections from 1978 to the Year 2000*. Boulder, Colo.: Westview, 1978.

Kaiser, Karl; Winston Lord; Thierry de Montbrial; and David Watt. *Western Security: What Has Changed? What Should Be Done?* London: Royal Institute of Foreign Affairs, 1981.

Kao, Ch'ung-yun. *Chung-kung yu tung-nan-ya* [Communist China and Southeast Asia]. Taipei: Li-ming wen-hua shih-yeh kung-szu, 1981.

Kao, Hsiang-kao. *Chung-kung tui-wai kuan-hsi chih fa-chan* [The Development of China's Foreign Relations]. Taipei: Cheng-chung shu-chü, 1978.

Katzenbach, Nicholas. *Communist China: A Realistic View*. Washington, D.C.: Department of State, Bureau of Public Affairs, June 1968.

Kintner, William. *Peace and Strategic Conflict*. New York: Praeger, 1967.

Kosaka, Masataka, ed. *Asian Security*. Tokyo: Research Institute for Peace and Security, 1981.

Kuan, John C., ed. *Symposium on R.O.C.-U.S. Relations*. Taipei: Asia and World Institute, 1981.

Kuo, Tung-hua. *A Brief Account of the Sino-Vietnamese War*. Mimeographed. Pattaya, Thailand: New Foundation for Asian and Pacific Security Conference, December 1979.

Kuo, Warren, ed. *Speeches by Chinese Communist Leaders, 1963–1975*. Taipei: Institute for International Relations, 1976.

Lall, Arthur. *How Communist China Negotiates*. New York: Columbia University Press, 1968.

Larson, Joyce E., ed. *New Foundations for Asian and Pacific Security.* New Brunswick, N.J.: Transaction Books, 1980.

Lasater, Martin L. *The Security of Taiwan: Unraveling the Dilemma.* Washington, D.C.: Georgetown University, 1982.

Lawrence, Alan. *China's Foreign Relations Since 1949.* London: Routledge & Kegan Paul, 1975.

Lee, Shih-feng. *Strategic Role for the Southeast Asian Nations.* Taipei: Broadcasting Corporation of China, 1980.

Lee, W. T. "Soviet Defense Expenditures." *Osteuropa Wirtschaft,* December 1977, pp. 273–92.

Lemay, Curtis. *America Is in Danger.* New York: Funk & Wagnalls, 1968.

Liu, Ta-chung, and Kung-chia Yeh. *The Economy of the Chinese Mainland: National Income and Economic Development, 1933–1959.* Princeton: Princeton University Press, 1965.

Lomov, N. A., ed. *Scientific-Technical Progress and the Revolution in Military Affairs,* translated by the U.S. Air Force. Washington, D.C.: Government Printing Office, n.d.

Louis, Victor. *The Coming Decline of the Chinese Empire.* New York: Times Books, 1979.

Luttwak, Edward N. "Against the China Card." *Commentary* 66, no. 4 (October 1978).

———. "Why We Need More 'Waste, Fraud, and Mismanagement' in the Pentagon." *Commentary* 73, no. 2 (February 1982).

MacGuire, Michael, ed. *Soviet Naval Developments: Context and Capability.* Halifax, N.S.: Dalhousie University, 1972.

———, ed. *Soviet Naval Influence: Domestic and Foreign Dimensions.* New York: Praeger, 1976.

———, ed. *Soviet Naval Policy: Objective and Constraints.* New York: Praeger, 1975.

McNamara, Robert S. *Statement Before the Senate Armed Services Committee and the Subcommittee on Department of Defense Appropriation on the FY 1965–1969 Defense Program and the 1965 Defense Budget.* Washington, D.C.: Government Printing Office, January 27, 1964.

———. *Statement on the FY 1969 Defense Budget.* Washington, D.C.: Government Printing Office, 1968.

Mao, Tse-tung. *Selected Works of Mao Tse-tung.* 5 vols. Peking: Foreign Languages Press, 1965–1977.

Marriott, John, ed. *Brassey's Fast Attack Craft.* New York: Crane, Russak, 1978.

Marshall, Andrew W. *Comparisons of U.S. and S.U. Defense Expenditures.* Washington, D.C.: Department of Defense, September 16, 1975.

Martin, Edwin W. *Southeast Asia and China: The End of Containment.* Boulder, Colo.: Westview, 1977.

Marwah, Onkar, and Jonathan D. Pollack, eds. *Military Power and Policy in Asian States: China, India, Japan.* Boulder, Colo.: Westview, 1979.

Mendl, Wolf. *Issues in Japan's China Policy.* New York: Oxford University Press, 1978.

Middleton, Drew. *The Duel of the Giants: China and Russia in Asia.* New York: Scribner's, 1978.

The Military Balance. London: International Institute for Strategic Studies, annual publication.

Mitchell, Donald W. *A History of Russian and Soviet Sea Power.* London: Macmillan, 1974.

Moore, John E. *The Soviet Navy Today.* New York: Stein and Day, 1976.

Mozingo, David. *Chinese Policy Toward Indonesia, 1949-1967.* Ithaca, N.Y.: Cornell University Press, 1976.

Myers, Ramon H. *The Chinese Economy: Past and Present.* Belmont, Calif.: Belmont, 1980.

———, ed. *A U.S. Foreign Policy for Asia.* Stanford: Hoover Institution Press, 1982.

Nelson, Harvey W. *The Chinese Military System: An Organizational Study of the Chinese People's Liberation Army.* Boulder, Colo.: Westview, 1977.

Nitz, Paul H., and Leonard Sullivan, Jr. *Securing the Seas: The Soviet Naval Challenge and Western Alliance Options.* Boulder, Colo.: Westview, 1979.

North, Robert C. *The Foreign Relations of China.* North Scituate, Mass.: Duxbury, 1978.

Oksenberg, Michel, ed. *China's Developmental Experience.* New York: Praeger, 1973.

——— and Robert B. Oxnam, eds. *Dragon and Eagle: United States-China Relations: Past and Future.* New York: Basic Books, 1978.

O'Neil, William D. "Backfire: Long Shadow on the Sea-Lanes." *United States Naval Institute Proceedings*, March 1977.

Oppose U.S. Occupation of Taiwan and "Two China" Plot. Peking: Foreign Languages Press, 1958.

Osamu, Miyoshi. "The Growth of Soviet Military Power and the Security of Japan." In *Strategy and Security in Northeast Asia*, edited by Richard B. Forester; James E. Dornan, Jr.; and William M. Carpenter. New York: Crane, Russak, 1979.

Osgood, Robert E. *Containment, Soviet Behavior, and Grand Strategy.* Berkeley: University of California, Institute of International Studies, 1981.

Overholt, William H., ed. *Asia's Nuclear Future.* Boulder, Colo.: Westview, 1977.

———. *The Rise of the Pacific Basin.* Croton-on-Hudson, N.Y.: Hudson Institute, 1973.

Oxnam, Robert B. *Japan, Korea, and China: American Perceptions and Policies.* Lexington, Mass.: Lexington Books, 1979.

The Pacific Era: Issues for the 1980s and Beyond. Proceedings of the Eighth International Conference on World Peace. Tokyo: Professors' World Peace Academy of Japan, 1979.

Panyalev, George. "Backfire—Soviet Counter to the American B-1." *International Defense Review*, October 1975.

Parakal, Pauly. *Peking's Betrayal of Asia.* New Delhi: Sterling, 1976.

Pollack, Jonathan D. *Defense Modernization in the People's Republic of China.* Santa Monica, Calif.: Rand Corporation, 1979.

————. *Security, Strategy, and the Logic of Chinese Foreign Policy*. Berkeley: University of California, Institute of East Asian Studies, 1981.

Polmar, P. *Soviet Naval Power: Challenge for the 1970s*. New York: Crane, Russak, 1974.

Powor, Thomas S. *Design for Survival*. New York: Coward, McCann, 1965.

Prospects for Regional Stability: Asia and the Pacific. Report Submitted by a Special Study Mission to Asia and the Pacific, January 2–22, 1978. Washington, D.C.: Government Printing Office, 1978.

Prybyla, Jan S. *The Societal Objective of Wealth, Growth, Stability, and Equity in Taiwan*. Baltimore: University of Maryland, School of Law, 1978.

Rawski, Thomas G. *Economic Growth and Employment in China*. New York: Oxford University Press, 1979.

Reischauer, Edwin O. *Beyond Vietnam: The United States and Asia*. New York: Random House, 1968.

————. *The Japanese*. Cambridge, Mass.: Harvard University Press, 1981.

Remer, C. F., ed. *Three Essays on the International Economics of Communist China*. Ann Arbor: University of Michigan Press, 1959.

Report on Comprehensive National Security. English Translation. Tokyo: n.p., 1980.

Rohwer, Juergen. *Superpower Confrontation on the Seas: Naval Development and Strategy Since 1945*. Beverly Hills, Calif.: Sage, 1975.

Rosen, Steven J., and James R. Kurth, eds. *Testing Theories of Economic Imperialism*. Lexington, Mass.: D. C. Heath, 1974.

Rowe, David Nelson. *Informal "Diplomatic Relations": The Case of Japan and the Republic of China, 1972–1974*. Hamden, Conn.: Foreign Area Studies Publications, 1975.

Russell, Maud. *The Sino-Soviet Ussuri River Border Clash: The Historical Background and the Current Implications*. New York: Far East Reporter, n.d.

Salisbury, Harrison E. *War Between Russia and China*. New York: Norton, 1969.

Scalapino, Robert A. *Asia and the Major Powers*. Washington, D.C.: American Enterprise Institute, 1972.

————. *Asia and the Road Ahead*. Berkeley and Los Angeles: University of California Press, 1975.

————. *China and the Balance of Power*. Berkeley: University of California, Institute of International Studies, 1974.

————, ed. *The Foreign Policy of Modern Japan*. Berkeley and Los Angeles: University of California Press, 1977.

Sgarlato, Nico. *Soviet Aircraft of Today*. Carrollton, Tex.: Squadron, 1979.

Shiels, Frederick L. *Tokyo and Washington*. Lexington, Mass.: D. C. Heath, 1980.

Sidowenko, A. A. *The Offensive*, translated by the U.S. Air Force. Washington, D.C.: U.S. Air Force, n.d.

Simmons, Robert R. *The Strained Alliance: Peking, Pyongyang, Moscow, and Politics.* New York: Free Press, 1975.

Sino-Korean Forum on Northeast Asia. Taipei: Asia and the World Forum, 1977.

Snyder, Edwin K.; A. James Gregor; and Maria Hsia Chang. *The Taiwan Relations Act and the Defense of the Republic of China.* Berkeley: University of California, Institute of International Studies, 1980.

Sokolovskii, V. D., ed. *Soviet Military Strategy,* translated by Herbert S. Dinerstein, Leon Goure, and Thomas W. Wolfe. Englewood Cliffs, N.J.: Prentice-Hall, 1963.

Solomon, Richard H. *The China Factor in America's Foreign Relations: Perceptions and Policy Choices.* Santa Monica, Calif.: Rand Corporation, 1981.

————, ed. *Asian Security in the 1980s: Problems and Policies for a Time of Transition.* Cambridge, Mass.: Oelgeschlager, Gunn & Hain, 1980.

————, ed. *The China Factor: Sino-American Relations and the Global Scene.* Englewood Cliffs, N.J.: Prentice-Hall, 1981.

Sonnenfeld, Helmut, and William G. Hyland. *Soviet Perspectives on Security.* London: International Institute for Strategic Studies, 1979.

Southeast Asian Affairs, 1978. Singapore: Heinemann, 1978.

Starr, John Bryan, ed. *The Future of U.S.-China Relations.* New York: New York University Press, 1981.

Stephan, Jon J. *The Kurile Islands: Russo-Japanese Frontiers in the Pacific.* New York: Oxford University Press, 1975.

Stuart, Douglas T., and William T. Tow, eds. *China, the Soviet Union, and the West: Strategic and Political Dimensions in the 1980s.* Boulder, Colo.: Westview, 1982.

Tan, Su-cheng. *The Expansion of Soviet Seapower and the Security of Asia.* Taipei: Asia and the World Forum, 1977.

————. *Soviet Naval Implications in the 1980s: An Analysis of the Security Factor.* Mimeographed. Taipei: Asia and the World Forum, June 1979.

The Third U.N. Law of the Sea Conference. Washington, D.C.: Government Printing Office, February 5, 1975.

Thompson, W. Scott, ed. *National Security in the Eighties: From Weakness to Strength.* San Francisco: Institute for Contemporary Studies, 1980.

Thomson, George G. *Problems of Strategy in the Pacific and Indian Oceans.* New York: Crane, Russak, 1970.

Thomson, James C.; Peter W. Stanley; and John Curtis Perry. *Sentimental Imperialists: The American Experience in East Asia.* New York: Harper & Row, 1981.

Treaties Between the Republic of China and Foreign States (1927–1957). Taipei: Ministry of Foreign Affairs, 1958.

U.S., Congress, House, Subcommittee on Appropriations. *Department of Defense Appropriations, 1966.* 89th Cong., 1st sess., 1965.

U.S., Congress, House, Committee on the Armed Services. *The Changing Strategic Balance.* 90th Cong., 1st sess., July 1967.

U.S., Congress, House, Subcommittee on Appropriations. *Department of Defense Appro-*

priations for 1979: Hearings Before a Subcommittee of the Committee on Appropriations. 95th Cong., 2d sess., 1978.

U.S., Congress, House, Committee on Foreign Affairs. *The United States and the People's Republic of China: Issues for the 1980's.* Washington, D.C.: Government Printing Office, 1980.

U.S., Congress, Senate. *Congressional Record.* 95th Cong., 2d sess., no. 138, September 7, 1978, p. H9229.

U.S., Congress, Senate, Committee on Foreign Relations. *Taiwan: Hearings before the Committee on Foreign Relations.* 96th Cong., 1st sess., 1979.

U.S. Defense Policy: Weapons, Strategy, and Commitments. Washington, D.C.: Congressional Quarterly, April 1978.

van der Kroef, Justus. *Communism in South East Asia.* Berkeley and Los Angeles: University of California Press, 1980.

Van Ness, Peter. *Revolution and Chinese Foreign Policy: Peking's Support for Wars of National Liberation.* Berkeley and Los Angeles: University of California Press, 1970.

Walt, Lewis W. *America Faces Defeat.* Woodbridge, Conn.: Apollo, 1972.

Watts, William. *The United States and Asia: Changing Attitudes and Policies.* Lexington, Mass.: D. C. Heath, 1982.

———; George R. Packard; Ralph N. Clough; and Robert B. Oxnam. *Japan, Korea, and China: American Perceptions and Policies.* Lexington, Mass.: Lexington Books, 1979.

Wegener, Edward. *The Soviet Naval Offensive.* Annapolis, Md.: U.S. Naval Institute, 1975.

Weinberger, Caspar W. *Annual Defense Department Report, FY 1983.* Washington, D.C.: Department of Defense, February 8, 1982.

Weinstein, Franklin B., ed. *U.S.-Japan Relations and the Security of East Asia: The Next Decade.* Boulder, Colo.: Westview, 1978.

Weinstein, Martin A. *Japan's Postwar Defense Policy, 1947-68.* New York: Columbia University Press, 1970.

White, Nathan N. *U.S. Policy Toward Korea: Analysis, Alternatives, and Recommendations.* Boulder, Colo.: Westview, 1979.

Whiting, Allen S. *Soviet Policies in China, 1917-1924.* New York: Columbia University Press, 1954.

Whitson, William W. *The Chinese High Command: A History of Communist Military Politics, 1927-71.* New York: Praeger, 1973.

———. *The Military and Political Power in China in the 1970s.* New York: Praeger, 1972.

Wilcox, Wayne. *Forecasting Asia Strategic Environments for National Security Decision-making: A Report and a Method.* Santa Monica, Calif.: Rand Corporation, 1970.

Wolff, Lester L., and David L. Simon, eds. *Legislative History of the Taiwan Relations Act: An Analytic Compilation with Documents on Subsequent Developments.* New York: American Association for Chinese Studies, 1982.

Woodward, David. *The Russians at Sea.* New York: Praeger, 1965.

World Development Report, 1980. New York: Oxford University Press, 1980.

Wu, Yuan-li. *The Strategic Land Ridge: Peking's Relations with Thailand, Malaysia, Singapore, and Indonesia.* Stanford: Hoover Institution Press, 1975.

Yanov, Alexander. *Détente After Brezhnev: The Domestic Roots of Soviet Foreign Policy.* Berkeley: University of California, Institute of International Studies, 1977.

Yeh, Hsiang-chih. *Chung-kung tui-wai kuan-hsi lun-ts'ung* [Essays on the foreign relations of Communist China]. Taipei: Cheng-chung shu-chü, 1977.

Yu, Ch'iu-li. *Report on the Draft of the 1979 National Economic Plan, 21 June 1979.* Hsiu-hua News Agency (Peking), news bulletin no. 11122, June 29, 1979.

Zagoria, Donald S. *The Sino-Soviet Conflict.* Princeton: Princeton University Press, 1962.

Zhou, Guo, ed. *China and the World.* Peking: Foreign Affairs Series, 1982.

Index

HOOVER INTERNATIONAL STUDIES